General Alonso de León's
Expeditions into Texas,
1686–1690

❧

General Alonso de León's Expeditions into Texas, 1686–1690

EDITED AND TRANSLATED BY

Lola Orellano Norris

Texas A&M University Press   College Station, Texas

This paper meets the requirements of ANSI/NISO Z39.48–1992
(Permanence of Paper).
Binding materials have been chosen for durability.
Manufactured in the United States of America

∞ ♻

LIBRARY OF CONGRESS CATALOGING-IN-PUBLICATION DATA

Names: León, Alonso de, approximately 1610–1661, author. | Norris, Lola
    Orellano, 1957– translator, editor.
Title: General Alonso de León's expeditions into Texas, 1686–1690 / edited
    and translated by Lola Orellano Norris.
Other titles: Elma Dill Russell Spencer series in the West and Southwest ;
    no. 41.
Description: First edition. | College Station, Texas : Texas A&M University
    Press, [2017] | Series: Elma Dill Russell Spencer series in the West and
    Southwest ; number forty-one | Includes bibliographical references and
    index. | Includes original Spanish texts and their translations into
    English.
Identifiers: LCCN 2016047173 | ISBN 9781623495404 (hardcover-printed case :
    alk. paper) | ISBN 9781623495411 (ebook)
Subjects: LCSH: Texas—Discovery and exploration—Sources. |
    Texas—History—17th century—Sources. | León, Alonso de, approximately
    1610–1661—Travel—Texas. | Explorers—Texas—Diaries. | León, Alonso de,
    approximately 1610–1661—Manuscripts. | Manuscripts, Mexican—17th
    century. | León, Alonso de, approximately 1610–1661—Translations into
    English.
Classification: LCC F389 .L45 2017 | DDC 976.4/01—dc23
LC record available at https://lccn.loc.gov/2016047173

(Cover Illustration)
Alonso de León portrait (painting by Erika Buentello)

A list of titles in this series is available at the end of the book.

Contents

Illustrations

Acknowledgments

Numerous individuals walked with me through the long process of writing this book and need to be recognized. Foremost, I owe a debt of gratitude to Brian Imhoff for introducing me to the riveting world of paleography and archival research. I still remember my ginger first steps in deciphering portions of the Domínguez de Mendoza expedition and the exhilaration I felt after completing the transcription of the text. Everything I know about Spanish colonial manuscripts I learned from Brian. Another person who was instrumental in my understanding of Spanish Texas and who deserves my deep gratitude is Jerry Thompson.

This book would not have been possible without his constant encouragement and wise counsel. I also greatly benefited from Nancy Joe Dyer's and José Pablo Villalobos's expert advice throughout the extensive research for this volume and from Stephen Duffy's keen insights and unwavering support during the revision process.

The Hispanic History of Texas Project at the University of Houston and the Department of Hispanic Studies at Texas A&M University provided financial support for my travels to the archives in Seville, Mexico City, Monterrey, Saltillo, Austin, and Tulsa. I received generous assistance from archivists and clerks in locating the manuscripts and processing reproductions. I would like to especially thank Michael Hironymous at the Benson Latin American Collection at the University of Texas at Austin, Ingrid Lennon-Pressey at the Beinecke Rare Book and Manuscript Library at Yale University, and Diana Cox at the Gilcrease Museum in Tulsa. My grateful thanks are also extended to Donald E. Chipman, the late William C. Foster, and the late Robert S. Weddle for their feedback and suggestions, and to Jesús F. de la Teja for his thorough response to the manuscript. *Un grand merci à* Julien Carriere for sharing his expertise in French.

The team at Texas A&M University Press deserves my very special thanks: to Mary Lenn Dixon for believing in the project from the beginning, to Jay Dew for his patience and understanding, and to Patricia Clabaugh and Laurel Anderton for taking care of all the details in bringing this manuscript to its published form.

To Jyotsna Mukherji, Deborah Blackwell, and Frances Gates Rhodes, thank you for your friendship. To my Spanish–Swiss–Native American family I give my thanks for their unconditional love across international boundaries: my mother, Vicenta Fernández Soriano; brothers José Orellano, Christian Orellano, and their families; my children Tinskua, Tekuani, Tsapki, Eraani, Quanah, and Ashuni, and my daughter-in-law Jackie. To my granddaughter Tsiriki, thank you for your sweet smiles and coos. Finally, my very special thanks are extended to my husband, Jim, whose steadfast support and most excellent cuisine were instrumental in bringing this book to conclusion.

Sigla and Archival Location
of the Manuscripts

1686 Expedition

86-A   Yale Collection of Western Americana, Beinecke Rare Book
        and Manuscript Library, MSS S-327, folios 46r–53r.

1687 Expedition

87-A   Yale Collection of Western Americana, Beinecke Rare Book
        and Manuscript Library, MSS S-327, folios 53r–53v.

1688 Expedition

88-A   Benson Latin American Collection, University of Texas–Austin,
        WBS 2053, folios 17r–22v.

88-B   Archivo General de Indias (AGI), Audiencia de México,
        legajo 616, expediente 62, folios 3v–12r.

88-C   Archivo General de Indias (AGI), Audiencia de México,
        legajo 616, expediente 65, folios 4r–16r.

1689 Expedition

89-A   Archivo General de la Nación (AGN), Ramo de Provincias
        Internas, volumen 182, folios 428r–440v.

89-B   Archivo General de Indias (AGI), Audiencia de México,
        legajo 616, expediente 65, folios 37v–50r.

89-C   Biblioteca Nacional de México (BNMx), Archivo Franciscano,
        caja 1, expedientes 13 y 14, folios 133v–141v.

89-D   Archivo General de la Nación (AGN), Ramo de Historia,
        volumen 27, folios 51r–66r.

89-E   University of California–Berkeley, Bancroft Library,
        M-M 278–281, document 24, folios 305r–318r.

1690 Expedition

90-A   Archivo General de la Nación (AGN), Ramo de Provincias Internas, volumen 182, expediente 6, folios 418r–426v.

90-B   Archivo General de Indias (AGI), Audiencia de México, legajo 617, folios 4v–18r.

90-C   Biblioteca Nacional de México (BNMx), Archivo Franciscano, caja 1, expedientes 12 y 13, folios 126v–133v.

90-D   Yale Collection of Western Americana, Beinecke Rare Book and Manuscript Library, MSS S-327, folios 1r–13r.

90-E   Gilcrease Museum, Tulsa, Oklahoma, Hispanic Documents Section, item 67.1, folios 1r–9r.

90-F   Gilcrease Museum, Tulsa, Oklahoma, Hispanic Documents Section, item 67.2, folios 1v–11r.

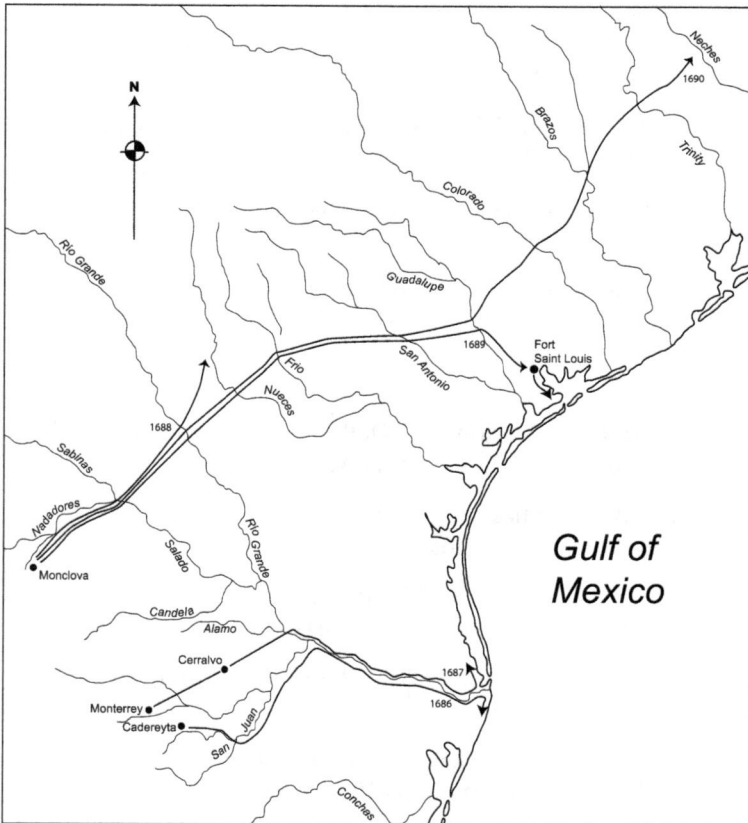

Likely routes of Alonso de León's five expeditions (map by Ana Clamont)

Introduction

In Herbert E. Bolton's seminal work *Spanish Exploration in the Southwest, 1542–1706*, readers learn that during the 1689 expedition into Texas in search of La Salle's colony, General Alonso de León distributed "cotton garments, blankets, beads, rosaries, knives, and arms" to five Indian nations gathered near the Río Grande ([1908] 1916, 389). While giving gifts to members of indigenous groups was common practice on exploratory journeys, readers may be surprised to discover that "arms" were included as gifts. Supplying arms to Indians was outlawed by royal decree. Moreover, at the end of the seventeenth century, New Spain was in a constant state of war with the natives of her northern frontier. Indian raids on colonial settlements were frequent and Spanish punitive attacks numerous. Thus, it would appear to have been ill-advised to place weapons in the hands of potential enemies. The assertion seems even more startling in that, just a year prior to this 1689 expedition, de León himself had led a protracted campaign against various belligerent groups of natives and crushed yet another bloody uprising in the region. When preparing to undertake said 1689 *entrada* to locate the French fort on the Texas coast, the general expressed concern that warring Indian bands might attack the new settlements in Coahuila during his absence. This begs the question: why would he supply them with weapons?

A careful reading of the oldest extant manuscripts of de León's 1689 expedition diary, which the explorer kept in his native Spanish, makes it perfectly clear that he provided the five Indian nations with *harina*, which means "flour," not "arms" (89-A 429r17; 89-B 39r20; 89-C 134v21).[1] How could these two

---

1. Five manuscripts have been identified for the 1689 expedition: (1) Archivo General de la Nación, México, Provincias Internas, vol. 192, folios 428r-440v (cited hereafter as 89-A); (2) Archivo General de Indias, Spain, Audiencia de México, leg. 616, folios 37v-50r (cited hereafter as 89-B); (3) Biblioteca Nacional de México, Archivo Franciscano, caja 1, expedientes 13 y 14, folios 133v26–141v (cited hereafter as 89-C); (4) Archivo General de la Nación, México, Ramo de Historia, vol. 27, folios 51r-66r (cited hereafter as 89-D); and (5) University of California–Berkeley, Bancroft Library, M-M 278–281, doc. 24, folios 305r-318r (cited hereafter as 89-E). The first three, 89-A, 89-B, and 89-C, are the oldest copies. No original diary is extant.

terms be confused? How is it possible that such an obvious mistake appeared in the English translation?

Bolton, an eminent scholar in the history of Spanish North America, had knowledge of at least two copies of de León's original 1689 diary (89-A and 89-D). The two manuscripts and their respective locations were listed in his extensive *Guide to Materials for the History of the United States in the Principal Archives of Mexico* (Bolton [1913] 1977, 28, 123). However, in *Spanish Exploration in the Southwest, 1542–1706* ([1908] 1916), Bolton did not include his own English translation of either 1689 manuscript. Instead, he reprinted a translation by Elizabeth Howard West[2] that had been previously published in the *Quarterly of the Texas State Historical Association* (1905, 199–224). Unfortunately, West's translation was based on manuscript 89-D, the least reliable copy of de León's diary. This manuscript, contained in volume 27 of the collection *Memorias de Nueva España*, which is often referred to as *Archivo General de la Nación (AGN) Historia 27*, had been copied in 1792—over a hundred years after the actual expedition—from one of the earlier copies of the diary by Fray Francisco García de la Rosa Figueroa,[3] and it was fraught with transcription errors. In this particular case, the scribe had misread *[h]arina* "flour" as *armas* "arms," providing the foundation for West's erroneous rendition (89-D 52v3).

It cannot be discerned whether West was cognizant of the problems that manuscript 89-D posed. She was aware that other documentary sources existed but stated that she had no access to them at the time (West 1905, 200–201). The only additional contemporary documents she consulted were Fray Damián Massanet's[4] letter to Carlos de Sigüenza y Góngora[5] and Sigüenza y

2. Elizabeth Howard West (1893–1948) was an archivist and librarian from Pontotoc, Mississippi, who held various positions at important libraries. She worked at the Library of Congress, the Texas State Library, the Carnegie Library in San Antonio, and the Texas Tech Library. In 1918, she became Texas state librarian and the first woman in Texas to head a state department. West published frequently in the journal of the Texas State Historical Association, known until 1912 as the *Quarterly of the Texas State Historical Association* and afterward as the *Southwestern Historical Quarterly* (Winfrey 2010).

3. Francisco García de la Rosa Figueroa, a Franciscan friar from the Archdiocese of Mexico, had been entrusted with selecting and copying all manuscripts pertaining to the history of New Spain by royal order in 1790. Father Figueroa produced thirty-two volumes of copies from collected originals. One set of the entire collection was sent to Spain, and the other remained in Mexico. Volume 27, entitled *Documentos para la historia civil y eclesiástica de la Provincia de Texas*, contains the friar's copy of General Alonso de León's 1689 expedition diary (89-D). This volume is also frequently referred to as *AGN Historia 27* (Crivelli 1909).

4. Fray Damián Massanet (alternative spellings: Masanet, Mazanet, or Manzanet) was a Franciscan friar from Mallorca, Spain, who arrived in Mexico in 1683. He was one of the founders of a missionary college, Colegio de Santa Cruz de Querétaro. Later, he moved to the northern

Góngora's map of de León's 1689 *entrada*. While these documents provided West with important additional information about the journey, which she included in her footnotes, they did not help her detect the Franciscan scribe's transcription errors or avoid her own misinterpretations and mistranslations. Consequently, West's rendition was seriously flawed and presented major mistakes, textual inaccuracies, and distortions of meaning.

Bolton's inclusion of West's translation in his vastly influential book had a burgeoning effect. In spite of its many flaws and serious factual errors, the translation was legitimized. In fact, since Bolton's publication in 1908, West's translation has stood as the main source for historical English-language accounts of de León's 1689 expedition (e.g., Dunn [1917] 1971; Castañeda 1936). Even more-recent works have relied, at least in part, on Bolton's edition (e.g., Bannon 1970; Ashford 1971; Hickerson 1994; Foster 1995; Chipman and Joseph 1999, 2001). No other comprehensive English rendition of the 1689 diary has been published. To this day, this faulty translation has informed historians' interpretations of de León's most successful expedition.

This example highlights a frequent problem faced by North American historians and other scholars working with historical sources of early colonial Texas and the US Southwest. Primary archival documents are among the most important resources for humanities research. For scholars interested in the early exploration and settlement of the region, original Spanish-language manuscripts constitute the cornerstone of scholarship. Surprisingly, as Jerry R. Craddock observed, few critical editions of these documents exist in their original Spanish language (1996, 352). Held at different archives, libraries, and museums in Spain, Mexico, and the United States, the manuscripts are not always readily accessible. Although many of the larger repositories nowadays employ modern technology to preserve their manuscripts and make them electronically available, this is not the case for smaller archives. Even at the well-funded prominent archives, complete digitization is still very much a work in progress because of the sheer volume of existing documents. An additional hurdle to accessibility is the archaic Spanish language and difficult script, which further complicate their readability. Hence, many North American

---

frontier and established the mission of Caldera near Nuevo León. He accompanied General Alonso de León on the 1689 and 1690 expeditions and founded the first mission on Texas soil, San Francisco de los Tejas, in 1690 (Gómez Canedo 1988, 46).

5. Carlos de Sigüenza y Góngora (1645–1700) was one of most outstanding scholars and scientists born in the viceroyalty of New Spain. A professor of mathematics at the University of Mexico, he was also a cosmographer and drew some of the earliest maps of Mexico and Texas (Dunn [1917] 1971, 158).

researchers have preferred to base their studies on existing English translations or narrative summaries rather than the Spanish source documents. In many instances, as in the case in point, this has led to historical inconsistencies, misinterpretations, and substantive errors (cf. Craddock 1996; Imhoff 2002, 2006; Cunningham 2004).

Translations are invaluable tools for scholars who are not fluent in Spanish or are less experienced in Spanish paleography, but compared to the primary documents, they are always imperfect means of transmission (Imhoff 2002, 1). A translation can never fully capture all the nuances of the original, and the dangers of misreading and misinterpreting the text are very real. Hand-written documents are even more likely to be misread, misinterpreted, and mistranslated.

Spanish colonial texts present an additional level of complexity. The problem of reliability is frequently exacerbated by the existence of several contemporary and subsequent copies of the same document. Because of the ponderous nature of Spanish colonial bureaucracy, manuscripts were customarily copied several times, for provincial and vice-regal authorities in the Americas as well as for the Consejo de Indias in Spain (Polzer 1999, 155). Over time, additional copies might have been fashioned for numerous other reasons. Manuscript 89-D, for instance, was a copy produced a hundred years later to be included in a multi-volume compilation of the history of New Spain. Copies, and copies of copies, augment the likelihood of scribal errors, making them almost unavoidable. With so many contemporary and later copies of the same manuscript, which one is the most reliable? When the original document bearing the autograph signature of the author is unavailable to scholars or no longer exists, it is often very difficult to ascertain which one of the copies is the archetype closest to the original. Scribal errors and misinterpretations in early copies tend to be perpetuated in later ones, further complicating the situation. Philologists are best suited to disentangle linguistic conundrums and determine the original manuscript or the copy closest to the original document. Thus, the philological approach becomes indispensable in rendering Spanish-language texts more accessible to other scholars.

But colonial manuscripts are also of utmost importance to language historians themselves. Scribes hailed from different regions and diverse social and linguistic backgrounds, so manuscript copies often present different spellings and significant language variation. While these differences may cause frustration for historians and other scholars, they are of vital importance for philologists. Language variants are important elements in the analysis of linguistic features and are essential when documenting language change. In addition, these differences, minor as they may appear, often contain substantive information that can prove important for other researchers too. Narrative summaries or English translations simply cannot include this information or re-create these nuances. Thus, it is essential that the text be available in authoritative editions in Spanish.

However, traditional Spanish-language publications of early Texas documents have also proven to be problematic. Typically, these texts have been edited with historians in mind. The Spanish has been modified and adapted to conform to modern language standards (cf. de León, Chapa, and Sánchez de Zamora [1961] 2005; Gómez Canedo 1988). These publications are of limited use to philologists. The adaptation to modern Spanish makes it impossible to discover paleographic and linguistic information from orthography (Craddock 1996, 351; Kania 2000, 7; Imhoff 2002, 1).

For linguists, the original manuscripts are vital primary sources, essential for the study of linguistic features and the documentation of language change. Hence, it is crucial that colonial documents be approached in a philological manner. Only competent paleographic transcriptions can safeguard the reliability and authenticity of the texts. In addition, a rigorous philological treatment takes all known versions of the manuscripts into consideration and establishes a genetic relationship between them. This is critical when it comes to identifying the original or the archetype closest to the original. It constitutes an important step that should precede any translation, summary, or analysis. Moreover, when treated philologically, Spanish-language documents become accessible to a wider audience of scholars, providing reliable textual platforms for multiple disciplines.

In the case of General Alonso de León's five expeditions in search of La Salle's colony, archival research in Spain, Mexico, and the United States led to the identification of sixteen manuscripts: fifteen diaries and one narrative summary. The sigla (e.g., 86-A, 88-B, 89-C), which are used henceforth to identify the manuscripts, reflect the year of the expedition as well as the chronological relationship of the manuscripts. For instance, manuscript 89-A is older than manuscript 89-D. These sixteen documents hold major importance for early Texas scholarship. Thus, it is imperative that they be studied together because they form a distinct corpus, and information from earlier expeditions is required to fully comprehend subsequent ones.

For purposes of cohesion and corpus manageability, this book analyzes only expedition diaries and *autos*[6] attributed to General Alonso de León, with the notable exception of Chapa's short summary of the 1687 expedition

6. *Autos* are official declarations or signed statements.

(87-A), for which no other documentary evidence exists. Father Massanet's narrative summary of the 1689 and 1690 expeditions, which is the crux of his letter to Sigüenza y Góngora, is not included in this study for two reasons. The report was not written during the respective journeys but over a year after the conclusion of the first expedition and months after the second one. In addition, it does not present an unbiased account. During the 1690 expedition, Massanet, a zealous missionary and recent arrival from Spain, had a serious falling out with the more experienced de León, a native of Mexico and lifelong resident of the northern frontier. Espousing a rather vindictive tone, the friar seized every opportunity to contradict and criticize the general in his letter. On several occasions, he assigned himself more importance and agency while diminishing de León's leadership. Massanet's letter does incorporate some supplementary information that will be referenced in this book.

Historical accounts of General Alonso de León's exploratory journeys have been published in separate English-language translations and narrative summaries (Chipman 1992; Foster 1995; Chapa 1997; Weddle 1999; Chipman and Joseph 1999, 2001) or in modernized Spanish transcriptions (de León, Chapa, and Sánchez de Zamora [1961] 2005; Gómez Canedo 1988).[7] Several of the 1690 expedition diaries have been transcribed and analyzed in two unpublished master's theses (Branum 1974; McLain 2005). However, no study has ever included all extant manuscripts, and no paleographic transcription of this corpus has ever been published. The manuscripts have never been presented or studied together as an interconnected body of work. In addition, none of the known publications offer both Spanish transcriptions and English translations.

The purpose of this book is twofold: to establish authoritative paleographic transcriptions of the Spanish manuscripts in order to make the texts accessible to a wider audience and promote further studies; and to produce faithful, annotated English translations of each diary's archetype. This may help clarify existing misconceptions about the journeys and correct certain aspects of the historical canon that were based on faulty translations.

The book is divided into three sections. The first section sets the stage. It comprises several subsections starting with a literature review of prior publications about de León's expeditions and a look at large-scale projects dedicated to the philological treatment of colonial manuscripts. Subsequent subsections

---

7. Robert S. Weddle's *Wilderness Manhunt* (1999) provides the most complete account of La Salle's journey and the vicissitudes of his colony as well as the ensuing Spanish exploratory missions, including de León's.

offer a brief narrative summary of the earliest exploration efforts in Texas, a biographical sketch of Alonso de León, and the trajectory of his five expeditions. Bibliographic data along with detailed descriptions of the sixteen manuscripts and their archival locations conclude the section with key background information. Section 2 contains a paleographic transcription of the six Spanish colonial manuscripts that have been identified as archetypes: 86-A, 87-A, 88-A, 89-B, 90-B, and 90-D. For the sake of corpus manageability, only one transcription per expedition is included in this section, with the exception of the 1690 journey, for which two distinct versions of the diary exist. Annotated English translations of the six archetypes are included in section 3. The translations are kept very close to the source texts. Their literality, although strange at times to modern readers, is a purposeful attempt to better render the tone and formulaic style of official Spanish colonial correspondence. In addition, the translated texts are compared to existing scholarship, and discrepancies, linguistic errors, misinterpretations, inaccuracies, and mistranslations are noted and explained.

It is hoped that these paleographic transcriptions and authoritative translations will serve to correct factual errors based on earlier faulty transcriptions and translations. The interdisciplinary character of this book will serve English- and Spanish-speaking scholars alike. Linguists, historians, ethnographers, anthropologists, and others might benefit from this information, thus fostering further multidisciplinary scholarship.

General Alonso de León's
Expeditions into Texas,
1686–1690

1.

Archival Records and the
Exploration of Texas

1.1 The Study of Archival Records of the Colonial Southwest

In recent years, great strides have been made toward publishing full-length editions of Spanish colonial records. Several large-scale projects have contributed to the recovery and publication of the vast corpus of colonial documents of the Spanish Southwest. Through the guidance and perseverance of these programs, important manuscripts from the sixteenth, seventeenth, and eighteenth centuries documenting the Spanish presence in the Southwest have been identified, recovered, and published in authoritative editions.

The Documentary Relations of the Southwest (DRSW hereafter), housed at the Arizona State Museum in Tucson, Arizona, is possibly the oldest of these key research projects. It was founded by Charles W. Polzer, SJ, who directed it until his death in 2003. According to its website, the DRSW owns fifteen hundred reels of microfilm pertaining to the Spanish colonial history of the Southwest culled from the extensive holdings of numerous libraries and archives. The DRSW's most important achievement is without a doubt the creation of indexes to facilitate research within this immense sea of Spanish documents. The electronic master indexes provide categorical archival information and allow searches for persons and places; however, "full text" documents are not available (Polzer 1999, 155). The project has published a research guide and several volumes on the establishment of military presidios, as well as one book on the Seri Indians and another on the Rarámuri or Tarahumara (Sheridan and Naylor 1971; Barnes, Naylor, and Polzer 1981; Naylor and Polzer 1981, 1986; Hadley, Naylor, and Schuetz-Miller 1997; Polzer and Sheridan 1997; Sheridan 1999). While all publications, except the very first volume, offer both Spanish transcriptions and annotated English translations, Craddock criticizes the editors' decision to modernize the spelling, punctuation, and language of the original in the Spanish transcriptions (1998, 483).

The Vargas Project, as the name indicates, deals exclusively with the journals of Diego de Vargas (1644–1704) and his private correspondence. Vargas was appointed governor of New Mexico in 1690 and was in charge of its reconquest in 1692, twelve years after the Pueblo Revolt of 1680 ousted the Spaniards. Led by John L. Kessell of the University of New Mexico, the Vargas Project has published an impressive six-volume collection documenting Vargas's endeavors (Kessell 1989; Kessell and Hendricks 1992; Kessell, Hendricks, and Dodge 1995; Kessel et al. 1998, 2000, 2002). While the first printed volume included Spanish transcriptions of the documents as well as English translations, the subsequent volumes were published only in English (Craddock 1998, 2). Microfiche editions of the Spanish transcriptions are available for the first three volumes (Hendricks 1988, 1992; Hendricks, Avellaneda, and Dodge 1993). As with the publications of the DRSW, the Vargas Project's preference for English translations versus complete paleographic transcriptions and facsimile copies of the original documents could be considered a weakness. However, both projects have contributed significantly to the recovery of the colonial history of New Spain.

The Cíbola Project, directed by Jerry R. Craddock and now under the auspices of the Research Center for Romance Studies, International and Area Studies, at the University of California–Berkeley, has taken the most inclusive approach to Spanish-language colonial manuscripts. In its beginnings, the project, which describes itself as "an association of scholars devoted to the publication primarily of documents concerning the exploration and settlement of the Hispanic Southwest during the colonial period," worked chiefly with documents pertaining to New Mexico, its foundation in 1598, and the Pueblo Revolt of 1680. However, it has expanded in recent years to include primary sources from other parts of the colonial Southwest. Initiated in 1996, the project fostered numerous publications, culminating in the two-part special issue of *Romance Philology* (vol. 53, 1999–2000): "Documenting the Colonial Experience with Special Regards to Spanish in the American Southwest," edited by Barbara De Marco and Jerry R. Craddock. Since then, the Cíbola Project has continued to publish a number of important monographs, critical editions, and scholarly articles expounding on the importance of the philological approach to colonial manuscripts (e.g., Craddock 2008; Craddock and Polt 2008, 2010, 2014; Carlin, De Marco, and Craddock 2009; Coll et al. 2009; Nostas, Coll, and Imhoff 2013; Baranowski 2011; Yengle 2013; Hough-Snee 2013). The ever-growing collection encompasses seventy-seven articles published between 2008 and 2015. This project stresses the publication of documents in their original Spanish language. The editions may include facsimile copies of the manuscripts, paleographic transcriptions, lists of variants, annotated commentary, and so forth. Through eScholarship, its accessible online electronic repository, the Cíbola Project makes its studies available to interested scholars and the public alike.

The Vargas and Cíbola Projects have centered their efforts on the vast corpus of documents from colonial New Mexico. There are no parallel projects with exactly the same focus on paleographic transcriptions of manuscripts from early Spanish Texas. The Hispanic History of Texas Project (HHTP) encompasses a much wider range of recovery that includes literary as well as historical texts from colonial times to 1960. An offshoot of Recovering the US Hispanic Literary Heritage Project conceived and directed by Nicolás Kanellos of the University of Houston, the HHTP has the overarching objective of recovering, preserving, disseminating, and studying any kind of Hispanic text produced in or about Texas. The project also provides resources and research opportunities for the study of colonial documents via HHTP grants. In addition, it organizes biannual international conferences to share new scholarship. One of those conferences was held in 2008 in collaboration with the Texas State Historical Association (TSHA).[1] The Recovering the US Hispanic Literary Heritage Project has compiled an impressive bibliography of books and other artifacts. Its holdings include original books and manuscripts as well as microfilmed and digitized historical newspapers and photographs. However, the project's scope is very broad, and there is no focus on paleographic transcription or philological treatment of the oldest Spanish-language manuscripts of colonial Texas.

Philologically oriented publications dealing with archival documents of early Spanish Texas, however, are rather sparse. *The Diary of Juan Domínguez de Mendoza's Expedition into Texas (1683–1684)* (Imhoff 2002) is, to the author's knowledge, the only comprehensive, book-length critical edition of a Spanish-language manuscript that includes paleographic transcriptions, variant lists, and facsimile reproductions of the originals. It was published by the Clements Center for Southwest Studies at Southern Methodist University. The center had previously issued an excellent critical edition of a New Mexican manuscript (Craddock and Folt 1999). Several journal articles have also contributed to the field, addressing diverse aspects of the Mendoza expedition of 1683–1684 (Imhoff 2006), Mendoza's inquisitorial process (Nostas, Coll, and Imhoff 2013), and the Ramón-Espinoza expedition of 1716 (Cunningham

---

1. The 2008 TSHA annual meeting, cosponsored by the Recovery Project, took place in Corpus Christi and offered more than sixty scholarly panels and other events. A collection of essays culled from the conference papers and edited by Monica Perales and Raúl A. Ramos was published in 2010 by Arte Público Press under the title *Recovering the Hispanic History of Texas Project* (Perales and Ramos 2010).

2004, 2006). In addition, two unpublished master's theses analyze various aspects of Alonso de León's 1690 expedition (Branum 1974; McLain 2005). In general, Spanish-language manuscripts pertaining to the colonial history of Texas have not been the subject of many paleographic or philological studies.

Conversely, de León's five *entradas* into Texas have received ample treatment throughout the years from Southwest historians (e.g., Bolton [1908] 1916; Dunn [1917] 1971; Castañeda 1936; Ximenes 1963; Bannon 1970; Ashford 1971; Weddle 1991, 1999; Chipman 1992; Foster 1995, 1997). Mexican scholars have also studied the expeditions (e.g., Portillo 1886; García 1909; Alessio Robles [1938] 1978; Cavazos Garza [1961] 2005; Del Hoyo 1979; Gómez Canedo 1988). The majority of these historical accounts—whether in English or Spanish—consist of narrative summaries based on primary and secondary sources, interwoven with occasional citations from the manuscripts, published Spanish transcriptions, or the corresponding English translations. De León's journeys are recognized as vastly important to the settlement of Texas and to the larger picture of the French-Spanish conflict in the Gulf of Mexico region. As primary sources, the expedition diaries hold foremost importance. However, only seven publications have been identified that contain unabridged versions of some, but not all, of de León's diaries. Four of them were published in Spanish and three in English. They are reviewed in more detail below.

The first Spanish-language publication appeared as early as 1886. Mexican local historian Esteban L. Portillo edited a transcription of Alonso de León's *autos* and diary of the 1688 expedition (corresponding to 88-A) in the fourth chapter of *Apuntes para la historia antigua de Coahuila y Texas* (1886, 182–238). He also included some bibliographical information about General Alonso de León. Since, as Guadalupe Curiel indicates, Mexican historiography in the nineteenth century generally lacked interest in the exploration, conquest, and settlement of northern New Spain, and of Texas in particular, Portillo's publication was especially relevant (1994, 14). In spite of its methodological deficiencies, Curiel considers this work to be one of the pillars of the colonial historiography of Texas because it presents the historical processes that led to the settlement of Coahuila and Texas. Portillo's publication served as a vital source for Alessio Robles's seminal *Coahuila y Texas en la época colonial* ([1938] 1978). In *Apuntes*, Portillo includes the transcription of de León's 1688 *autos* and expedition diary embedded in a lengthy narrative summary and discussion of related events. While he maintains some of the orthographic cues of the original manuscript, it is not a paleographic transcription.

In 1909, Mexican bibliographer Genaro García included the transcription of a formerly unknown seventeenth-century manuscript on the history of Nuevo León in volume 25 of his *Colección de documentos inéditos o muy raros para la historia de México* (cited in Cavazos Garza [1961] 2005, xvii). The compilation consists of three separate chronicles: (1) three discourses on the history of Nuevo León before 1650, written in chapter form by Captain Alonso de León, the general's father; (2) forty-two chapters on the history of Nuevo León from 1650 to 1690 by an anonymous author; and (3) seven chapters on the discovery of the Río Blanco region by General Fernando Sánchez de Zamora (Cavazos Garza [1961] 2005, xviii). The second chronicle contains a transcription of the only known copy of the 1686 diary (corresponding to 86-A) and the only known record of the 1687 expedition (corresponding to 87-A), a short summary. The *entradas* of 1688, 1689, and 1690 are included in the form of narrative summaries. Very few copies of this book are extant in rare book collections, and they were unavailable for consultation for this volume. The above information was culled from Cavazos Garza's account and description of the source ([1961] 2005).

Under the auspices of the university and government of Nuevo León, Israel Cavazos Garza reedited García's publication in 1961 to commemorate the three hundredth anniversary of the death of Captain Alonso de León— the general's father and namesake. *Historia de Nuevo León con noticias sobre Coahuila, Tamaulipas, Texas y Nuevo México* ([1961] 2005) includes an extensive preliminary study in which Cavazos Garza identifies the anonymous author of the second chronicle as Juan Bautista Chapa.[2] Chapa, originally from Italy, had served both the elder and the younger de León as secretary. Like García's 1909 publication, *Historia* ([1961] 2005) also contained the 1686 diary (corresponding to 86-A) in unabridged form and narrative summaries of the 1687 (corresponding to 87-A), 1688, 1689, and 1690 expeditions. The 1689 expedition summary includes a list of the participants' names and additional information Chapa possessed because he had accompanied de León on his journey as his secretary. The summary for the 1690 expedition is less detailed, which reflects the likelihood that Chapa did not accompany de León on this journey. As in the earlier edition, the Spanish

---

2. Juan Bautista Chapa (1627–1695) was born in Albisola, Italy, and left his country for New Spain in 1647. His Italian name was Giovanni Battista Schiappapietra. "Schiappapietra" is an occupational name that means 'stone mason' in Italian. In northern New Spain, he served as secretary for several governors and important leaders, among them the de Leóns, both father and son. For more information on Chapa's connection to Italy, see *Da Albisola al nuovo regno di Leon*, the first Italian translation of Chapa's *Historia del Nuevo Reino de León*. The book was published in 2013 in Neive, Italy, by Fondazione Schiappapietra and contains a foreword by Israel Cavazos Garza (Schiappapietra 2013).

transcriptions are not paleographic, but modernized and adapted to modern language usage.

The first publication to contain full-length Spanish-language transcriptions of de León's expedition diaries of 1688, 1689, and 1690 based on archival sources was Fray Lino Gómez Canedo's *Primeras exploraciones y poblamiento de Texas, 1686–1694*, which was published in 1968 and reedited in 1988. In this significant comprehensive contribution, the author includes transcriptions of ancillary documents, such as letters, plans, and reports by de León and other contemporaries. The book also comprises diaries and letters pertaining to the two subsequent expeditions into Texas in 1691–1692 and 1693, which were undertaken after de León's death. Most importantly, Gómez Canedo documents the existence and location of other manuscript copies besides the ones he transcribes. However, he is selective in his choice of documents. For example, he does not transcribe all of the *autos* or the complete diary from 88-B, but rather selected passages. Also, in his transcription of the 1690 journey, he coalesces information from both the 90-A and 90-B manuscripts and notes divergent information from 90-D. Unfortunately, Gómez Canedo's book does not include the 1686 diary or the 1687 summary. As with the other earlier publications, the Spanish transcriptions have been modernized and adapted to modern Spanish orthography, punctuation, and capitalization.

No Spanish-language publications containing full-length paleographic transcriptions of all of de León's extant expedition diaries exist.

English-language publications of the complete diaries are even scarcer. As discussed in the introduction, at the turn of the last century, the *Quarterly of the Texas State Historical Association* published Elizabeth H. West's English translation of de León's 1689 expedition diary based on manuscript 89-D (1905, 199–224). Although the *Quarterly* invariably offered important contributions on the early history of Spanish Texas, La Salle's journey and settlement on Matagorda Bay, and de León's expeditions, none of them included full-length transcriptions or translations of the general's diaries. Besides West's translation, there was only one other document pertaining to these expeditions, which appeared in facsimile accompanied by an unabridged translation. It was Friar Damián Massanet's letter to Carlos Sigüenza y Góngora, translated into English by Lilia M. Casis (1899, 253–312).[3]

3. Lilia M. Casis (1869–1947) was born in Jamaica and was of Spanish, French, and German descent. She was a Spanish professor, scholar, and later dean at the University of Texas–Austin (Bolton [1908] 1916, 353; Cottrell 2010). For a long time, her translation of Massanet's letter to Sigüenza y Góngora was regarded as the most complete account of de León's 1689 and 1690 expeditions. Later comparisons to de León's journals have shown several disparities.

The only two book-length English-language publications that incorporate unabridged translations of some of de León's diaries are *Spanish Exploration in the Southwest 1542–1706* ([1908] 1916) by Bolton and *Texas and Northeastern Mexico, 1630–1690* (1997), William C. Foster's English edition of some of the documents previously transcribed by Genaro García in 1909 and reedited by Israel Cavazos Garza in 1961 (Chapa 1997). Bolton's historical oeuvre, organized by region, presents English translations of vital colonial documents from California, New Mexico, Texas, and Arizona. Chapter 3 is dedicated to the exploration and settlement of Texas but includes only full-length annotated English translations of de León's 1689 and 1690 diaries. Bolton mentions that he fashioned the translation of the 1690 expedition himself, with some assistance ([1908] 1916, v). The text of the diary corresponds mainly to 90-A, but at times Bolton resorts to 90-B and 90-D to fill in the blanks.[4] In addition, he confirms the inclusion of West's previously published translation of the 1689 diary.

Foster's edition offers an introductory study by the author and a comprehensive English translation by Ned F. Brierley (Foster 1997, xii) of the entire second chronicle, which appeared in García's volume (1909) and was attributed to Juan Bautista Chapa in *Historia* (Cavazos Garza [1961] 2005). Thus, it contains an English rendition of the unabridged 1686 diary (corresponding to 86-A), the narrative summary of the 1687 expedition (corresponding to 87-A), and summaries of the journeys of 1688, 1689, and 1690. Most importantly, appendix A presents the English translation of a previously unpublished version of the 1690 diary (corresponding to 90-D), whose existence had been alluded to in prior publications (Bolton [1908] 1916, 352; Gómez Canedo 1988, 152). Foster was the first to identify this document as a revised manuscript, highlighting significant instances of divergence from the other known copies of the 1690 diary. He asserts that "no other seventeenth-century diary of a Spanish expedition into Texas was subsequently revised and extended by the author in the manner and to the extent that de León altered his 1690 diary" (Foster 1997, 23).

Neither Bolton's volume nor Foster's edition of Chapa (1997) contains a translation of the 1688 diary. In fact, the *autos* and diary pertaining to the

---

4. Bolton mentions the existence of three documentary sources: "(A) one from the Archivo General y Público of México, lacking the first few entries; (B) one from the Archivo General de Indias at Seville; and (C) one from a manuscript in the collection of Genaro García, the noted Mexican editor" (corresponding to 90-A, 90-B, and 90-D, respectively). He notes the differences between the prior two and 90-D, indicating that "there are many minor differences, and some essential ones" and referring the reader to the footnotes for further comments ([1908] 1916, 352).

1688 expedition have never been published in a full-length English translation. Furthermore, no publication, in English or Spanish, contains the diaries of all five expeditions in their unabridged form.

Although no paleographic transcriptions or critical editions have been published about any of de León's five expeditions, two unpublished master's theses analyze various aspects of de León's 1690 *entrada* (Branum 1974; McLain 2005). Lawanda Carter Branum studied a previously unknown manuscript of the 1690 expedition (90-E) that she located at the Gilcrease Museum in Tulsa, Oklahoma. She attempts to generate a paleographic transcription but is inconsistent and does not follow specific norms. For instance, she does not indicate foliation or manuscript line division. Scribal abbreviations are not expanded and omissions or emendations are not indicated as such. Branum's linguistic study consists of a general description of the orthography, and two alphabetical lists: the first records all the words that appear in the manuscript and the other contains all the names and locations mentioned. Conversely, Jana McLain, following guidelines adapted from the *Manual of Manuscript Transcriptions* (Mackenzie 1997), produces rigorous paleographic transcriptions of three of the 1690 manuscripts (90-B, 90-D, and 90-E) and compares all six extant copies to establish significant differences between them. After a careful analysis, following Foster's example, she classifies them into revised and unrevised manuscripts. McLain's thesis does not include a linguistic analysis of the corpus. However, her paleographic transcription and comparative analysis provide valuable information.

To sum up, scholarship on de León's five expeditions is fragmented and consists chiefly of narrative summaries, modernized Spanish transcriptions, and English translations of several individual manuscripts and other documentary sources. Except for McLain's study, Spanish transcriptions do not follow paleographic criteria, and several of the English translations are fraught with errors. The historical and linguistic importance of these documents is undisputed and dictates the most scholarly rigor. It is crucial that manuscripts be transcribed in unabridged form and studied as an interconnected corpus. These accounts of the systematic exploration of South and East Texas provide firsthand descriptions of the flora and fauna and document early contact with the Native Americans of the region. Besides discovering the ruins of Fort Saint Louis on the Texas coast and repatriating some of the French survivors, the expeditions established routes for subsequent journeys, which resulted in the founding of missions and the settlement of Texas.

1.2. The Earliest Exploration of Texas

At the end of the seventeenth century, the region that would later become Texas, although claimed by the Spanish Crown, remained without permanent settlements. Not that it had been overlooked. Because of its dimensions and strategic location between Florida and Mexico, Spanish conquistadores had encountered Texas country early on during their exploration. Alonso Álvarez de Pineda was most likely the first Spaniard to lay eyes on Texas during his 1519 voyage along the northern Gulf Coast. Sailing from the Florida Keys to Veracruz, he explored the Texas coast and claimed the land for the Crown. He sketched the first map of the region, which he called Amichel, outlining rivers and bays and naming the Mississippi River, Río del Espíritu Santo (Chipman 1992, 24; Weddle 1999, 25). Historians today doubt that Pineda disembarked on the Texas coast. Consequently, it was Álvar Núñez Cabeza de Vaca and the other survivors of the ill-fated Narváez expedition who first set foot on Texas soil. Shipwrecked on Galveston Island in 1528 and enslaved by coastal Indians, the last four surviving castaways later traversed vast stretches of the Texas plains before reaching Culiacán, Mexico, almost eight years later (Chipman 1992, 29–33; Calvert, de León, and Cantrell 2002, 14–15). Upon returning to Spain, Cabeza de Vaca published his *Relación*, later known as *Naufragios*, the earliest book to offer descriptions of Texas landforms, fauna and flora, and indigenous populations. In the 1540s members of the Coronado expedition explored the West and North Texas region, while survivors of the Moscoso/de Soto expedition penetrated East Texas from Florida. It is believed that around 1542, Luis de Moscoso Alvarado reached the Trinity River and established the first documented contact with members of the Hasinai Confederacy (Chipman 1992, 40). Thus, Moscoso encountered the Tejas Indians,[5] a people of major significance for Alonso de León's later journeys and for the early history of Spanish Texas.

However, the reports these explorers brought back were not encouraging. No precious metals or magnificent cities had been found. Certainly, the region to the north of New Spain was "of continental proportions . . . but its size was formidable, its people often inhospitable, and its soil unpromising to

---

5. "Tejas" and "Hasinai' were names used interchangeably to refer to Caddo Indians. The term "Techas," often spelled "Teshas," "Thechas," "Tejas," or "Texas," was derived from a Caddo expression meaning 'friend,' according to Massanet in his letter to Sigüenza y Góngora (Bolton [1908] 1916, 359).

treasure-seeking adventurers" (Chipman 1992, 42). Exploration of the area, now called Tierra Nueva, was no longer desirable or encouraged. The Florida peninsula had become the primary focus of Spain's military and missionary efforts. Texas had to wait.

The extension of New Spain's northern boundary toward Texas would develop gradually from the Mexican interior northward. The discovery of rich silver deposits in Zacatecas and subsequent expansion of the mining frontier into the land of the Chichimeca[6] led to protracted warfare. It also led to the establishment of fortified towns, presidios, and missions. Bolton (1917), Bannon (1970), Weddle (1992), and other historians have highlighted the importance of the mission as a frontier institution in the colonization of Spanish America. The coupling of military garrisons and missionary endeavors had proven very effective during Spain's own Reconquista; now, in New Spain, the same agencies developed into a successful system of colonization (Calvert, de León, and Cantrell 2002, 17). As the frontier advanced northward to Santa Bárbara, located in modern-day Chihuahua, and the headwaters of the Conchos River, so did the missionaries.

In fact, many of the journeys into New Mexico and Texas at the end of the sixteenth century were initiated by missionaries and aimed at Christianizing Indians. Spain had overextended its military resources during the conquest and early exploration and now lacked the necessary manpower to subdue the fierce nomadic tribes of the north (Smith 1995, 17). It was content to let the missionaries push the frontier northward and eastward. Several missionary efforts by Franciscan friars eager to proselytize advanced north along the Río Grande, while others reached West Texas and the Trans-Pecos region and possibly even as far as the Texas Panhandle. The Chamuscado-Rodríguez-López expedition of 1581–1582, for instance, brought three Franciscan friars,[7] accompanied by Francisco Sánchez Chamuscado and a small military escort, down the Conchos and north along the Río Grande to modern-day El Paso and upriver to the Indian Pueblos of New Mexico. A year later, another friar, Fray Bernardino Beltrán, was the driving force of the Espejo-Luxán expedition into New Mexico and Arizona. This expedition returned to Santa Bárbara via the Pecos River and established contact with the Jumano Indians (Bannon

6. "Chichimeca" was a generic term applied to the diverse groups of fierce seminomadic Indians in the northern part of Mexico. The literal meaning of the word was 'People of Dog Lineage' (Meyer, Sherman, and Deeds 2010, 31).

7. The missionaries were Fray Agustín Rodríguez, Fray Francisco López, and Fray Juan de Santa María (Bannon 1970, 31–32).

1970, 30–33; Chipman 1992, 55–58).[8] Although these expeditions were not officially sanctioned and did not result in permanent settlements, they did produce an effect: they piqued the colonial government's interest in the upper Río Grande region. Finally, under the leadership of Juan de Oñate, the official colonization of New Mexico occurred in 1598 (Chipman 1992, 59). Again, Texas was left alone. Spain, it seemed, did not have an urgent interest in Texas, or in settling the vast land east of the Río Grande that was inhabited by numerous and diverse Indian nations.

As the frontier moved slowly northward throughout the seventeenth century, settlements and missions were established closer to the Río Grande. Minor incursions into the western fringes of Texas, either to indoctrinate Indians or to avenge attacks on Spanish settlements, continued sporadically. However, they remained close to the Río Grande and did not result in permanence. The Indian peoples were strong and numerous and remained "the rulers of these lands" (Barr 2007, 5). The first authenticated exploratory journey into south-central Texas did not occur until 1675. Again, the Bosque-Larios *entrada* was chiefly a missionary endeavor. Heeding an apparent request for missionaries from representatives of Indian tribes along the Río Grande—the Indians were probably interested in trading, not conversion—the expedition traveled forty leagues beyond the river into modern-day Edwards County. Bosque took copious notes on the land and the Indians they encountered. Upon their return, they recommended establishing three missions and presidios among the Indians in Coahuila and Texas (Hoyt 1992, 22). Conditions, however, were not favorable at the time (Chipman 1992, 68). Once more, Texas remained unexplored and uncolonized.

Two events in the 1680s, almost a century after the colonization of New Mexico, changed the pattern of Texas exploration drastically: the Great Pueblo Revolt of 1680 and La Salle's landing at Matagorda Bay in 1685. When the Pueblo Indians ousted the Spaniards from New Mexico, incursions into Texas from the west increased. The Spanish survivors established themselves in El Paso del Norte, modern-day Ciudad Juárez, and planned the reconquest of New Mexico. Soon they realized that it would be a lengthy process and looked toward the lands to the east of the Río Grande. In 1682, Antonio de Otermín and Fray Francisco de Ayeta established a separate settlement and mission for

8. The name "Jumano" (also Jumenes, Humana, and other variants) was used to identify several Indian groups that lived in the southern plains, including Texas. The Jumano were buffalo hunters and skilled traders who became middlemen between the Spaniards and many Indian nations (Hickerson 1994, vi).

Tigua Indians who had fled with the Spaniards after the Pueblo Revolt. The mission, named Corpus Christi de la Ysleta,[9] was located east of modern-day El Paso. Thus, it could be considered "the first permanent European settlement" within the boundaries of what would later become Texas (Chipman 1992, 68–69).

A year later, following a request by Jumano Indians for missionary presence and protection against the Apache, the Mendoza-López expedition traveled south along the Río Grande to the junction with the Conchos and established a mission at La Junta de los Ríos. The Jumano were more interested in military protection than in Christian teachings, but they recognized the important role missionaries played on expeditions. The invitation extended to the padres meant something different to them than to the Indians. The missionaries understood it as a plea for Christianization, the Indians as a way to forge alliances and obtain trade goods (Smith 1995, 15). Mendoza explored a large area beyond the Pecos and Concho Rivers, reaching the Colorado in 1684 and establishing a bastion and chapel in San Clemente, near present-day Ballinger (Imhoff 2002, 3). But it was the arrival of the French on the Gulf Coast in 1685 that radically changed the dynamics of exploration and settlement in Texas.

In 1682, French explorer René-Robert Cavelier, Sieur de La Salle (1643–1687), traveling from Canada, descended the Mississippi River and reached the Gulf of Mexico. He claimed the entire river valley for France, naming it La Lousianne in honor of King Louis XIV. After returning to Québec, he sailed to France to garner support for his plan to establish a French fort on the mouth of the Mississippi River. This was in full disregard of Spain's claim to the entire Gulf of Mexico. With France and Spain at war at the time, his bold endeavor was approved, and in 1684 La Salle returned to the Americas with four ships and around three hundred settlers (Weddle 1991, 9–19). Because of failed calculations or insidious intentions—historians disagree on this—he overshot the Mississippi delta and ended up on the coast of Texas in January 1685. Landing at Matagorda Bay, La Salle constructed Fort Saint Louis and a small settlement on Garcitas Creek off Lavaca Bay, in fact making the French, not the Spanish, the first European settlers of the Texas coast (Weddle 1991).

9. Ysleta, possibly the oldest continuously inhabited town within the modern boundaries of Texas, was initially located south of the Río Grande until flooding between 1829 and 1831 created a new, deeper river channel farther south. Initially Ysleta was under the jurisdiction of Nuevo México and later Chihuahua. It became part of the United States and Texas after 1848, upon the signing of the Treaty of Guadalupe Hidalgo (Hamilton 2010).

The vicissitudes of La Salle's journey and settlement in Texas were meticulously recorded by Henri Joutel, a member of the expedition who later returned to France. Joutel's journal is considered the most comprehensive and accurate account of La Salle's expedition (Foster 1998, 4).[10]

Rumors of the French presence caused much concern in New Spain. When they were confirmed by captured deserters, pirates, and friendly Indians, the viceroy immediately ordered several land and sea missions in search of La Salle's colony (Weddle 1991, Chipman 1992). The charge was explicit: find the colony and eradicate it. All attempts, however, proved unsuccessful until Alonso de León's expedition of 1689.

1.3 General Alonso de León's Five Expeditions to Texas

General Alonso de León (1639 or 1640–1691) was the offspring of a prominent *criollo*[11] family. He was born in Cadereyta, a town founded in 1637 by his father and namesake near Monterrey, Nuevo León, in northern New Spain. The general's name was often appended with "El Mozo," the younger, to distinguish him from his famous father. The elder Alonso de León had been born in Mexico City in 1608 of Spanish parents and was schooled at the prestigious Jesuit Colegio de San Ildefonso before moving to the frontier as a *ganadero*, or stockman (Cavazos Garza 1994, 7; Chipman and Joseph 1999, 24). A distinguished man, the senior Alonso de León was soon named *alcalde mayor*[12] of Cadereyta and captain of its presidio by Governor Martín de Zavala (Cavazos Garza 1994, 8). He participated in numerous campaigns against hostile Indians and in several important exploratory journeys. He is best known for writing the very first chronicle of the discovery and settlement of Nuevo León (Chipman and Joseph 1999, 24).[13] Following in his father's footsteps, Alonso de León, the younger, would also rise to prominence as a soldier, entrepreneur, and explorer before being named governor of Coahuila in 1687.

10. For the only English translation of the journal of Henri Joutel, 1684–1687, see Foster's edition *The La Salle Expedition to Texas* (Joutel 1998). The book also includes a translation of the interrogation of Pierre Meunier, another member of the La Salle expedition, who was apprehended by Alonso de León on his 1689 expedition.

11. A *criollo* is a person born in the Americas, whose parents, grandparents, or ancestors are from Spain.

12. There is no true English equivalent for the term *alcalde mayor*. It cannot be translated as 'mayor,' since the *alcalde mayor* was a form of magistrate who exercised jurisdiction over a municipality and was also commander of the local presidio (Gerhard 1993, 350).

13. This is the first of the three chronicles published by Genaro García.

Not much is known about El Mozo's birth or youth. Israel Cavazos Garza, a well-known de León scholar, asserts that no birth record exists of the general (1994, 9). The only documentary evidence of his youth appears in Chapa's *Historia*, which states that as a sixteen-year-old, young de León accompanied his father on official business to Spain on behalf of Governor Zavala in 1655 ([1961] 2005, 142). Chipman (1992, 78) and Chipman and Joseph (2001, 47) convey that young Alonso had been sent to Spain as a teenager to study at the Naval Academy. Cavazos Garza disputes this notion (which was also proposed by Regino F. Ramón) as implausible and lacking documentary evidence (1993, 10–11). He refers to Chapa's account, which records that father and son de León, having completed the negotiations at the Spanish court, traveled south to the port city of Cádiz. However, as they were getting ready to return to Mexico, English ships attacked Cádiz and the sea voyage was postponed. El Mozo asked permission from his father to join the Spanish fleet impromptu as a volunteer without pay (Chapa [1961] 2005, 142).[14] It is not known whether young Alonso remained in the service of the fleet in Spain and for how long, or whether he returned with his father to Mexico upon averting the English threat.

However, when the elder de León died in 1661, only six years after his journey to Spain, El Mozo was already married and living in Cadereyta with his family (Cavazos Garza 1993, 14). His wife bore him seven children, and for the next twenty years, Don Alonso dedicated himself to ranching, farming, and exploration of the region (Cavazos Garza 1993). He held a number of important governmental and military positions, ascending to the rank of general. In 1667 he was named *alcalde mayor* of Cadereyta and captain of its presidio, a position

14. "Todas estas negociaciones hizo, en el Real Consejo, el capitán Alonso de León; quien, habiendo llegado de Cádiz, de Madrid, para embarcarse en la flota, se aparecieron a la vista de la ciudad ochenta naos de Inglaterra; con que fue forzoso suspenderse al salir la flota de la bahía. Antes sí, se descargó y se formó armada para seguir a la de Inglaterra. Y el general Alonso de León (que hoy es gobernador de la provincia de Coahuila); que había ido con su padre a España; habida su licencia; se embarcó en las naos para servir a S.M. por aventurero y sin sueldo, comenzando a hacerle este servicio de edad de diez y seis años; como consta de las certificaciones que tiene en su poder" (Cavazos Garza [1961] 2005, 142). My translation: "All these negotiations were conducted by Captain Alonso de León in the Royal Council. He had arrived from Cádiz, from Madrid to embark with the fleet, when eighty English ships arrived within sight of the city, which made it necessary to cancel because the fleet left the bay. Before that, it was unloaded and an armada was formed to pursue that of England. And General Alonso de León (who today is governor of the Province of Coahuila); who had gone with his father to Spain; having received his [father's] permission, embarked on the ships to serve His Majesty as an unpaid adventurer, starting this service at the age of sixteen; as is stated in the certifications that he has in his possession."

Alonso de León (drawing by Scott Harshbarger)

he held for eight years (Cavazos Garza 1993, 14; 1994, 14). Seventeen years later, he was named interim governor of Nuevo León (Weddle 1999, 55) and in 1687, governor of the new Provincia de Coahuila (Weddle 1999, 133). A seasoned frontiersman, entrepreneur, and *encomendero*,[15] he explored northern New Spain and participated in many military campaigns against hostile Indian nations as well as other exploratory journeys. When the initial maritime and land explorations failed to discover the French fort and settlement, Spanish officials

15. An *encomendero* was granted an *encomienda* by the Spanish Crown. The *encomienda* was a labor system established during the conquest and colonization of America. Initially conquistadores and later some other colonists were given trusteeship over the indigenous people they colonized. *Encomenderos* did not own the Indian land, but they had the right to receive tribute and free labor from the natives. In return, Indians were entrusted into their care, and the *encomenderos* were required to protect them, maintain order, and provide Christian teachings. In practice, the *encomienda* system was severely abused and caused much hardship among the Indians. New laws were enacted in the early and mid-sixteenth century to reform the system and redress the abuse. The *encomienda* system was officially abolished in the eighteenth century, but it was already inefficient, having been in decline for a long time (Simpson 1982; Meyer, Sherman, and Deeds 2010).

turned to the experienced de León, who knew the frontier region so well, to lead an overland search. But the French settlement on the Gulf Coast was elusive and not easily found. Over the next five years, Spain expended considerable time and resources to locate La Salle's ill-fated colony and eliminate any vestiges of French presence in Texas.

All five of de León's expeditions commenced in northern New Spain, and all but one reached the lands of what is now Texas. The general's often terse but carefully kept diaries have allowed historians to follow the trajectory of the journeys. He noted the leagues and directions in which they traveled daily and provided other important information, such as descriptions of the terrain and the plant and animal life, notes on the availability of water for the expedition party and their horses, and observations about the Indian nations they encountered.

On his initial reconnaissance, Alonso de León left Cadereyta on June 27, 1686 (86-A 48v25). Two companies—one from Monterrey and another from Cadereyta—with a total of fifty soldiers, had passed muster and received an official send-off from the governor of Nuevo León, the Marqués de San Miguel de Aguayo. It was a rather large-scale endeavor, complete with eighteen mule drivers, servants and pages, three Indian scouts, a chaplain, forty loads of supplies, and 468 horses (86-A 47r20–48v22). The governor also assigned three special members to the expedition: his brother, Pedro Fermín de Echeverz, Francisco de Benavides, and Juan Bautista Chapa (86-A 48v22–24). The large party traveled along the San Juan River to its confluence with the Río Grande. Forty-four Caurame Indians on the warpath joined them on July 1, just before they reached the junction. They were friendly and tried to help the Spaniards obtain Indian guides from other tribes, but most of the other natives fled as soon as they saw the company approach (86-A 49r21–26). The terrain proved difficult for the large expedition party. Dense woods slowed them down and called for repeated detours. De León made frequent sorties with smaller detachments of men to reconnoiter the land before continuing with the entire *real*.[16]

---

16. *Real* is the Spanish term used to signify a military expedition party that traveled under the official flag, on a mission from the king. However, it can also refer to the location where the company camped overnight or to a named stopping place where the company remained for a longer time. In this book, "company" is generally used to refer to the full expedition party, and "camp" for the overnight location. When a detachment separates from the expedition party for reconnoitering purposes, "main company," "main body," or "main force" is used to refer to the larger group, and "detachment" is used for the smaller party.

They reached the Río Grande and tried to cross it on July 3, but it proved to be too wide and deep. De León noted that the river was navigable with a small vessel (86-A 49v2). As they pressed forward along the river, they encountered a large group of Indians, who, having fled their *ranchería*,[17] jumped in the stream and swam across to the other side of the river, the north/east bank, escaping from the Spaniards. One Indian approached the riverbank and shot arrows at the soldiers (86-A 49v10–19). The expedition party continued along the often impenetrable banks of the river with much difficulty. De León's attempts to obtain Indian guides were unsuccessful, as they fled and hid as soon as they spied the soldiers on horseback. On July 10, the expedition party was threatened by a large group of Indians from the other side of the river. The natives followed the Spaniards along the opposite bank but never attacked (86-A 50v26–51r2). Not knowing the land, de León was forced to make frequent forays with smaller detachments before moving the entire company. On one of these sorties, after having come upon an abandoned encampment, the general captured three Indian women. He questioned them but was unable to glean any information about the French; language barriers made communication impossible (86-A 51r30–51v9). On July 14, a small detachment finally reached the mouth of the Río Grande and explored its delta and eight leagues of coastline to the south. The height of the sun was measured with an astrolabe[18] and the latitude computed as 25°45'(86-A 52r10). De León found remains of some ships and three dilapidated canoes, but no sign of the French fort (86-A 52r15–29).

On July 17, the detachment joined the main force, which was camped at an estuary some eight leagues from the ocean; together they began the trek home the next day (86-A 52v7–12). When they reached the *ranchería* where the Indians had shot arrows at them two weeks earlier, the Spaniards encountered a group of fifty natives and attacked. One soldier was injured, two natives killed, and two Indian youths captured (86-A 52v21–27). Without further incident, the company reached Cadereyta on July 26. De León himself appeared before the governor to report that no evidence of the French fort had been found.

Disappointed but convinced that the French had settled on the Gulf Coast, the Marqués de San Miguel de Aguayo ordered de León to undertake a second *entrada* in 1687 (Weddle 1999, 64–65). This time, de León was to cross

---

17. *Ranchería* is the Spanish term for a native seasonal or temporary encampment (Barr 2007, 5).

18. De León noted that the astrolabe may have been flawed. This was the same astrolabe employed during subsequent expeditions, and several references were made to its defectiveness.

the Río Grande and reconnoiter the land on the other side of the river. No detailed diary exists of this expedition. The only documentary record consists of a scant narrative summary in Chapa's *Historia* (87-A), which provides the following information. Three companies set out from Monterrey at the end of February 1687. They were led by General Martín de Mendiondo, Don Pedro Fermín de Echeverz, and Captain Nicolás de Medina, respectively. All three were under de León's overall command (87-A 53r25–29). They proceeded to Cerralvo and crossed the river at a known ford, twenty leagues from town (87-A 53r22–24).[19] It is not stated what route the soldiers took across the southern tip of Texas. They encountered many warlike Indian nations who gave them ample signs of their animosity. They reached the coast on March 20 (87-A 53r29) and wandered in different directions but could not find the French fort. A large salty river prevented their passage farther north.[20] Again, they were forced to return home without having found a trace of the French. The governor of Nuevo León was particularly frustrated with another unsuccessful expedition because his term had ended and he was to return to Spain.

Three more maritime reconnaissance missions were sent along the Gulf Coast in 1687 and 1688. The new viceroy, the Conde de la Monclova, was adamant about finding the French invaders. But New Spain's fears were allayed when careful sea exploration discovered only a sunken ship[21] at Matagorda Bay, and reports seemed to indicate that the French endeavor had failed (Weddle 1999, 132).

Shortly after returning from his second expedition in 1687, de León had been named governor of Coahuila and was occupied with the settlement of the new province and its defense from hostile Indians. His third expedition was brought about by a report that a white chief was living among Coahuiltecan Indians on the other side of the Río Grande (88-A 17v12–17). Agustín de la Cruz, a Tlaxcalan[22] Indian sent by de León to gather friendly

19. According to Weddle, the fording took place near either modern-day Zapata-Guerrero or Rio Grande City–Camargo (1999, 67). Chipman favors present-day Roma–Los Saenz (1992, 78).

20. Chipman (1992, 78) and Weddle (1999, 65) posit that de León was referring to Baffin Bay near Kingsville.

21. The wreckage sighted by the various expeditions and first recorded in Juan Enrique Barroto's diary was that of *La Belle*, La Salle's last ship, which had run aground in 1687. The ship was discovered in 1995 and excavated in 1997 by archaeologists from the Texas Historical Commission. See *From a Watery Grave* (Bruseth and Turner 2005). The ship and artifacts recovered are exhibited at the Bullock Texas State History Museum in Austin.

22. The indigenous Tlaxcalan, Tlaxcaltecan, or Tlascaltecan people were of Nahuatl ethnicity. They became allies of the Spaniards and assisted Cortés in the conquest of the Aztec empire.

natives who were willing to fight with the Spaniards against other Indians, had encountered the white man himself and learned that he was French (88-A 17v22–23). Perceiving an imminent threat, the governor quickly assembled a small party of eighteen men, three mule drivers, and eighty horses and set out to investigate (88-A 20r10–33). The expedition started on May 18, 1688, taking de León from Monclova to the Río Grande. Leaving five soldiers at the river, he pressed on with thirteen men (88-A 22v25–26). But his Indian guides could not find the *ranchería*, and the governor was told to return to the Río Grande. On its way there, the small party encountered a group of over five hundred Indians[23] on a buffalo hunt. When asked about a white man among them, the natives took the Spaniards to the Frenchman, explaining that he was their chief (88-A 22r10–25). At a large Indian settlement on top of a hill,[24] they found Jean Henri[25]—de León spells his name "Yan Jarri," in an attempt to imitate French phonetics—likely a French deserter from La Salle's colony. The Spaniards noticed that the Frenchman was treated with much reverence and protected by a guard of forty-two warriors. Completely adapted to the Indian way of life, Jean Henri was wearing buckskin clothing and sporting Indian tattoos on his face and body (88-A 17v15–16).

In spite of the Frenchman's initial resistance and the opposition of the Indians, de León was able to convince Jean Henri to return with him to Coahuila. They arrived in Monclova on June 6 (88-A 21r32). De León questioned the Frenchman and took his sworn statement before sending him

---

Because of their support, they were granted privileges such as the right to ride on horseback, bear firearms, keep their last names and noble titles, and govern themselves. Several Tlaxcalan communities were resettled in northern Mexico to help with the pacification of the hostile northern tribes. They were to serve as examples of sedentary model subjects of the Spanish Crown.

23. Ben Cuellar Ximenes erroneously states that de León "came upon more than 1,500 Indians hunting buffalo" (1963, 84).

24. Weddle states that the region was called Sierra Sactasol or Yacasol and identifies it at Anacacho Mountain near Brackettville, in Kinney County (1999, 134).

25. The name "Yan Jarri" has often been rendered as "Jean Géry" in English translations. A linguistic analysis strongly suggests that the Frenchman's name was Jean Henri, as some historians have noted (e.g., Ximenes 1963). De León, who did not speak French, recorded the name in a Spanish phonetic approximation of the French pronunciation he heard when the prisoner stated his name. Had the name been "Jean Géry," de León would have spelled it "Yan Yeri," since in French the sound of *j* and that of *g* before the vowels *e* and *i* are identical. The Spanish *j*, on the other hand, sounds like a harsh English *h*, very different from the Spanish *y*. Additional support for this argument can be found in other primary sources. When the French prisoner was sent to Mexico City to be questioned by French-speaking Spaniards, his name was invariably given as "Juan Enrique" in the manuscripts, the fully Hispanicized form of "Jean Henri."

to Mexico City for further interrogation. However, the more the prisoner was questioned, the more he contradicted himself and the more confused he became. The Spaniards grew convinced that he was demented (Weddle 1999, 150). Although unreliable and fraught with contradictions, Jean Henri's statements seemed to confirm the French presence and threat on the Texas coast. The viceroy called for a new exploratory journey under Alonso de León's command. In the meantime, while preparations were underway for the large-scale land expedition, another maritime search was ordered. Two ships reconnoitered the mouth of the Río Bravo[26] and the entrance to Matagorda Bay, but again they returned to Veracruz without having located the French colony (Weddle 1999).

De León's fourth and successful expedition set out on March 23, 1689, from Monclova down the Coahuila River to its junction with the Nadadores (89-B 38r9). The company was joined by the Nuevo León troops four days later, near the junction of the Nadadores and Sabinas Rivers (89-A 38r21). A general muster was held and the names of all the participants listed.[27] There were a total of 113 men: eighty-five soldiers (including de León and Juan Bautista Chapa, the historian); the French prisoner, Jean Henri; two priests, Toribio García de la Sierra and Damián Massanet; twelve mule drivers; and thirteen servants (Weddle 1999, 176; Chapa [1961] 2005, 213). Eighty-two mule loads of supplies, three loads of gifts for the Indians, and 721 horses and mules rounded out the expedition (Chapa [1961] 2005, 213).[28] An unidentified number of Indian scouts also traveled with them (Weddle 1999, 176).

On March 28, the company set out toward the Río Grande, advancing in a northeasterly direction. Before reaching the river, the expedition was guided to a nearby *ranchería* by one of the Indians accompanying Jean Henri. Again, the Frenchman was heartily welcomed by the natives and invited to a special dwelling covered with buffalo hides (89-B 39r10–11). Five nations were camped at this location, and the Spaniards counted 490 people and eighty-five huts. De León distributed gifts of clothing, blankets, beads, knives, and

26. Río Bravo and Río Grande are used interchangeably throughout the Spanish manuscripts. The same river was also known as Río Turbio at its delta and Río del Norte in New Mexico. Massanet mentions these names in his letter to Sigüenza y Góngora (Bolton [1908] 1916, 353–54).

27. The names of the participants are not included in the expedition diary. However, they are all listed individually in Juan Bautista Chapa's *Historia* ([1961]2005, 212–14). Chapa indicates that he copied them verbatim from de León's list (212).

28. Weddle states that "there were 720 horses and mules and eighty-five mule loads of provisions" (1999, 176).

flour[29] among the natives and had five cows slaughtered to feed the people (89-B 39r21–22). The Río Grande was forded on April 2 at what would be known as Paso de Francia from that day on (Weddle 1999, 178). The expedition was led by a faithful Indian guide who had visited the French settlement before and knew its location (89-B 39v13–19). Finding himself in uncharted territory, de León named every stopping place and every stream he encountered from then on, mostly after salient features or events that transpired.[30] A sun shot was taken on April 3 with the same defective astrolabe, and the latitude was calculated as 26°31' (89-B 40r15). The governor mentions problems with the instrument and the antiquated tables he applied in an effort to explain possible inaccuracies of the reading.

De León's descriptions of the land they traversed provide a picture of areas dense with prickly pear cactuses, mesquite trees, scrub live oak, and other vegetation that required frequent clearing to allow the large expedition force to pass. He also mentions petroglyphs on large rocks on the banks of the Río Sarco (89-B 41r4).[31] Although the company followed what seemed to be established Indian routes (Foster 1995, 11), no natives were sighted for several days. A stampede on April 9, the day before Easter, forced them to stop for a day to recover the horses. Another observation of the sun's elevation rendered a latitude of 25°55' (89-B 42r22–23).[32] They reached the Guadalupe River on April 14. Six buffalo had been killed on the way, the first ones encountered in over one hundred leagues (89-B 43r12–13). Upon learning that the French fort was nearby, de León advanced with a detachment of sixty soldiers to reconnoiter the area (89-B 43v4–5). He encountered several Indian *rancherías* where he was able to gather information about the French settlement and its inhabitants. He was also repeatedly told that four Frenchmen were living among the Tejas Indians (89-B 43v22–24). After determining that it was too

29. As stated elsewhere, Bolton ([1908] 1916) and West (1905) included "arms" instead of "flour" in the list of gifts as a consequence of scribal error in 89-D.

30. In fact, most of the names de León gave were descriptive and referred to characteristics of the rivers or events that occurred, for example, Paraje de los Cuervos, Arroyo de Ramos, Río de las Nueces, Río Zarco, Río Hondo, Arroyo del Vino, and so on. Later expeditions, namely the 1690, 1691, and 1693 expeditions, named locations and rivers almost exclusively after saints or other Catholic entities. In fact, on the 1689 expedition, only three rivers had names associated with religion: Arroyo de Ramos, Río de Guadalupe, and Río de San Marcos.

31. The adjective *zarco* means 'blue.' The word is misspelled here as "Sarco."

32. Manuscript 89-A records a pole elevation of 27°55' (89-A 431v22–24). Manuscripts 89-C, 89-D, and 89-E, being copies of 89-A, show the same elevation. The expedition party was traveling mostly in a northeasterly direction after having taken the latitude as 26°31' on April 3; thus, 27°55' makes more sense. This appears to be a scribal misreading while copying.

far to pursue them, he wrote a missive to them and sent it to the land of the Tejas with an Indian messenger (89-B 44v8–10). De León returned to the main camp, and together the entire company set out to search for the French fort and settlement.

On April 22, the expeditionary force finally discovered the ruins of La Salle's ill-fated colony (89-B 46r2). Abandoned, Fort Saint Louis still stood, surrounded by the deserted dwellings of the colonists, with broken belongings strewn everywhere (89-B 46r4–8). De León noted that it was a depressing sight. The settlement had been sacked and everything was in a deplorable state. The governor took careful note of the destroyed buildings and of the items found scattered about. Eight iron artillery pieces, too heavy to be carried away, were buried on location (Ximenes 1963, 100).[33] The Spanish friars gave Christian burial to three skeletons,[34] including one of a woman, the only human remains they found (89-B 46r24–46v1). With Jean Henri's guidance, the general and a detachment of thirty men reconnoitered the Bay of Espíritu Santo (89-B 47r6–7). Upon returning to the main camp on April 25, he received a reply from two of the French survivors, informing the Spaniards that they would join them within two days (89-B 48r12–18). De León moved the camp to a better location and, while waiting for the Frenchmen, set out to discover the Río de San Marcos (89-B 48r25–48v26). Another sun shot with the defective astrolabe provided a reading of 29°3' by the bay.[35] When the two Frenchmen did not appear after two days, the general set out with a detachment of thirty men to look for them. On May 1, the soldiers returned to camp with the two foreigners and a group of Tejas Indians. De León then learned the details of the French colony's demise at the hands of the coastal Indians from Jean L'Archevêque[36] and Jacques Grôlet,[37] two members of La

33. These iron cannons were unearthed in 1999 by archaeologists with the Texas Historical Commission.

34. These skeletal remains of two men and one woman were uncovered in 2000 by archaeologists with the Texas Historical Commission.

35. Manuscript 89-A again shows a divergent latitude of 26°3', as do 89-C, 89-D, and 89-F for obvious reasons; they are copies of each other. Bolton notes the discrepancy and states that that the "figures of the diary are evidently a misprint" ([1908] 1916, 402).

36. Jean L'Archevêque (1672–1720) was a servant of Sieur Duhaut, La Salle's murderer. L'Archevêque had been an accomplice in the explorer's murder in 1687 and had remained among the Hasinai without returning to the French settlement. It is not clear how he knew what had occurred there in the last few years or during the massacre. His answers to de León's questions were guarded (Weddle 1999, 196). Although he was imprisoned in Mexico City and Spain, he was later allowed to return to the Americas after swearing to serve the Spanish Crown. He

Salle's settlement who had been living among the Hasinai at the time of the attack (89-B 49r20–49v21).

It was ironic that such a large-scale military expedition had been mounted to discover a thrashed, abandoned fort. But the journey had not been in vain. De León captured two more French intruders and met the delegation of Tejas Indians that accompanied them. Visibly impressed with the friendly and civilized Hasinai, the governor invited them to come to Coahuila (89-B 50r7–8). He also promised to return and bring priests to instruct them in the Christian faith. With the destruction of the French settlement at the hands of the coastal Indians, the French threat seemed to be averted. However, after a four-year search for the elusive colony, the Spanish appeared to have learned their lesson. To avoid any other intrusion into their lands, they had to occupy and settle the region (Weddle 1999, 203).

De León's report to the viceroy presented suggestions for securing the area with military presidios at strategic locations: on the Río Grande, on the Río Zarco, on the Guadalupe River, at the Bay of Espíritu Santo, and within the province of the Tejas Indians (Weddle 1999, 207; Chapa [1961] 2005, 252). Conversely, Father Massanet advocated for an exclusively missionary presence and disparaged the governor's recommendations at every occasion (Weddle 1999, 209). The Franciscan's religious zeal had been stoked by the apparent interest of the Tejas in Christian teachings and the claims that the Indians' ancestors had been visited by a "Lady in Blue" and had received religious instruction (Weddle 1999, 205; Chapa [1961] 2005, 226; Barr 2007, 37).[38] The padre's insistence bore fruit. The viceroy and his council viewed the dismal failure of the French colony as proof of divine intervention (Weddle 1999,

---

settled in Santa Fe, New Mexico, and had several children. He became a successful trader after retiring from the military (Blake 2010).

37. Jacques Grôlet (ca 1660–?) had deserted from La Salle's colony in 1686 during one of the marches. He had been living alone among the Tejas and had taken several Indian wives (Weddle 1999, 197). In 1687 he joined a group of Frenchmen who had remained among the Hasinai after being involved in La Salle's murder. Together with Jean L'Archevêque he was located by Alonso de León and imprisoned in Mexico City and Spain. He petitioned to return to America to serve the king of Spain. Like L'Archevêque, he was permitted to settle and marry in New Mexico. His name was Hispanicized to Gurulé. Some of his descendants still live near Albuquerque today (Weddle 2010b).

38. The "Lady in Blue" refers to María de Jesús de Ágreda, a Spanish nun born in 1602. Through bilocation, she is said to have engaged in spiritual travels among the Indians of the American Southwest, although physically she never left Spain. Jumano Indians reported having seen a woman dressed in blue who taught them the Catholic faith in the 1620s (Weddle 1999, 205; Barr 2007, 37).

206). Thus, Massanet's religious mission was favored over the governor's proposal to maintain a strong military presence in the region that would prevent any further foreign incursions into Texas.

Alonso de León's fifth and last journey was to commence in February 1690. However, problems gathering the necessary horses and the required number of soldiers from the surrounding presidios delayed the expedition for another month. By mid-March, only forty men had been enlisted from Zacatecas and Sombrerete, twenty from Nuevo Reino de León—including four from Cerralvo—and twenty from El Parral, Nueva Vizcaya (Chapa [1961] 2005, 253).[39] Without waiting for all the soldiers to congregate in Monclova, the governor moved out the pack animals on March 26 and the entire *real* a day later. On March 30, they were joined at the junction of the Coahuila and Sabinas Rivers by the men from Nuevo Reino de León and the four missionaries: Fathers Damián Massanet, Miguel de Fontecuberta, Antonio Bordoy,[40] and Francisco de Jesús María (Ximenes 1963, 110; Weddle 1999, 211; Chapa [1961] 2005, 258). The latter three had been selected to become the first missionaries among the Tejas Indians. The company from Nueva Vizcaya would not join the expedition until a month later, near the Guadalupe River. Upon orders by the viceroy, the exploratory force had been supplied with "150 loads of flour, 200 cows, 400 horses, fifty long firelocks, twelve hundredweight of powder, and three hundredweight of shot" (Ximenes 1963, 110). According to Father Massanet, an additional twenty mule loads had been sent along with supplies for the missionaries, containing necessary items such as wine, candles, clothing to distribute among the Indians, and six loads of tobacco (Gómez Canedo 1988, 59).

The expedition party followed the same northern route as the year before, crossing the Río Grande at Paso de Francia on April 6[41] and continuing northeast and east until they reached the old French fort on April 26 (90-B 8r13–15). Along the way, they had forded the same rivers and camped mostly at the known stopping places from 1689, adding only a few more names to the ones given on the earlier expedition. Once more, de León explored La Salle's ill-fated settlement and found it in the same condition as the year before (90-B 8r16–17). The entire compound was set afire as required by his superiors.

39. Weddle states that the expedition force consisted of 110 soldiers (1999, 209). However, Juan Bautista Chapa reports only 80, that is, 10 fewer than the 90 that were requested ([1961] 2005, 253).

40. Chapa renders this name as "Bordey" ([1961] 2005, 258).

41. Weddle writes that the river was crossed on April 2 (1999, 209), but the diary states that it was on April 6 (90-C 6r5).

The governor reconnoitered the mouth of the Río de San Marcos and saw two logs, which he mistook for buoys that marked the entry channel. This observation and his failure to remove the putative markers would bring much criticism upon him on his return (Weddle 1999, 209).

Along the way, they had received reports that two other Frenchmen were living in nearby *rancherías*. With a detachment of sixteen men, the governor set out to search for the French survivors. Pierre Talon (Pedro Talón)[42] was located on May 10 and Pierre Meunier (Pedro Muñi)[43] two days later. Now the full expedition force headed northeast into uncharted territory to the province of the Tejas. De León discovered the Trinity River and named all the new valleys and rivers he encountered. When the expedition reached the land of the Tejas ten days later, the Indians welcomed him with their legendary hospitality. De León was impressed with their agricultural skills, commenting on their well-tended fields of corn, beans, squash, and watermelons (90-B 12r4–6, 12r23–24).[44] He noted their many villages with permanent dwellings, their cleanliness, and their organization.

On May 24, the feast of Corpus Christi was celebrated for the first time in East Texas (90-B 13r3–8). A procession and an official ceremony followed during which de León awarded the Tejas chief a governor's staff on behalf of the viceroy. Father Massanet was recognized as the friar in charge of the religious conversions. While searching for a suitable location for a mission, the natives showed the Spaniards the graves of two Frenchmen who had died while staying among them. Weddle surmises that they were the graves of two

42. Pierre Talon (1675–?) was born in Canada as the oldest son of Jean and Isabelle Talon, who joined the La Salle expedition with their six small children (the youngest child was born on the ship en route). Pierre had been sent to live among the Hasinai to learn their language and customs. He was absent when the coastal Indians attacked the French settlement, killed his mother, and took four of his siblings. His father and one of his older sisters had perished earlier while living in the settlement. Rescued by de León, Pierre and his siblings became servants of the viceroy. Pierre and two of his brothers were later enrolled as soldiers in the Spanish navy but were captured by the French, who showed great interest in them and their experiences in the Spanish frontier. Pierre reappeared in Texas with Louis Juchereau de St. Denis around 1714 and assisted the explorer as translator. It is believed that Pierre died in France (Weddle 2010e)

43. Pierre Meunier (1670–?) was a member of the La Salle expedition. He was born in Paris and was only fourteen when he arrived at Matagorda Bay. He accompanied La Salle on his last journey in search of the Mississippi and witnessed the events surrounding the leader's assassination. He remained among the Hasinai but was captured by de León on the 1690 expedition. He later served as interpreter for the Terán expedition of 1691 and went to New Mexico with the second Diego de Vargas expedition (Weddle 2010c).

44. Watermelons were not native to the Americas. The Caddo must have acquired the seeds through trade.

of La Salle's men who had turned on each other after slaying La Salle's murderers (1999, 210). De León was also told of other Frenchmen, who had come to the Tejas from a settlement in the east.[45] Meanwhile, a small church and a dwelling for the friars were built within the main Indian *ranchería*. On June 1, 1690, de León officially gave possession of the San Francisco de los Tejas mission to Fray Massanet (90-B 14r717–20). The governor had planned to leave fifty men behind to guard and protect the mission. Owing to Father Massanet's vehement opposition, only three soldiers were allowed to be stationed with the three missionaries who remained among the Tejas (Weddle 1999, 211).

The company retraced the same route to return to Coahuila. On the way, the governor ransomed three of Pierre Talon's siblings who were being held by the coastal Indians not far from the old French settlement. Marie-Madeleine,[46] Lucien,[47] and Robert Talon[48] had been abducted by the Karankawa during the Fort Saint Louis massacre (Weddle 1999, 212). These children were among a handful of surviving eyewitnesses of the attack. The last two survivors, Jean-Baptiste Talon and Eustache Bréman, would not be rescued until a year

45. This was the Henri de Tonti expedition. Tonti, an old associate of the French explorer, had searched unsuccessfully for La Salle's colony at the mouth of the Mississippi. In 1690 he arrived in the land of the Caddo, coming from the Illinois River in the east. The Indians did not aid him in locating the lost French settlement, and Tonti returned to the Mississippi. De León did not pursue Tonti's retreating expedition and was criticized for it upon his return to New Spain (Chipman 1992, 89; Smith 1995, 25–26; Weddle 1999, 208; Barr 2007, 22).

46. Marie-Madeleine Talon was the second-oldest child and second daughter of Jean and Isabelle Talon. She was born in Canada in 1673 and made the trip to La Salle's colony on the Texas coast with her parents and family. During the massacre, she was abducted by the Karankawa together with brothers Jean-Baptiste, Lucien, and Robert. After being ransomed by de León, she became a servant to the viceroy and his wife and traveled to Spain with them when they retired. She returned to France and married in 1699. She is said to have returned to her native Canada (Weddle 2010e).

47. Lucien Talon was the fifth child of Jean and Isabelle Talon. He is believed to have been born in Canada just before the family left for France and joined the La Salle expedition of 1684. Lucien was abducted during the massacre at Fort Saint Louis and lived with the Karankawa until he was rescued by de León in 1690. Like his siblings, he bore Indian tattoos and had forgotten his native French language. With his three brothers, he was enrolled as a Spanish soldier in the Armada de Barlovento. Captured by the French, he was sent to the island of Oléron in 1698. Nothing is known of him after that date (Weddle 2010e).

48. Robert Talon (1684–?) was the youngest son of Jean and Isabelle Talon. Born on one of the four ships during the voyage to Matagorda Bay, he was named after La Salle. Robert was taken by the Karankawa Indians during the massacre at Fort Saint Louis. He bore Indian tattoos on his face and arms and had forgotten how to speak French by the time he was rescued by de León in 1690. Like his sibling, he became a servant in the viceroy's household and went to Spain with them upon their retirement. He reappeared in Texas with his brother Pierre and Louis Juchereau de St. Denis around 1714. Robert settled in Mobile, where he married and had children (Weddle 2010e).

later by the Domingo Terán de los Ríos expedition of 1691 (Weddle 1999, 228). Traveling back to Coahuila, de León and his men encountered flooding rivers that slowed them down for days. At the Río Grande they were detained for over a week. The governor finished his report to the viceroy and swam across the river with a handful of soldiers, Father Massanet, and Pierre Meunier. They reached Monclova on July 15. De León dispatched Captain Gregorio de Salinas Varona to Mexico City to hand-deliver the report of the journey. Pierre Meunier, one of the French prisoners, accompanied the officer to provide further information to the viceroy and his council.

In spite of his achievements, de León fell out of grace with the authorities because of two minor issues that appeared in his diary. The viceroy's advisers criticized the governor's failure to remove the "buoys" at the mouth of the Río de San Marcos and his inaction in ascertaining the location of the alleged French settlement to the east. A scathing letter from Father Massanet only added fuel to the fire (Weddle 1999, 216). The padre criticized several of de León's decisions during the two expeditions. Questioning the general's leadership, Massanet also accused him of leniency toward his men and inappropriate behavior toward the Indians. A new exploratory journey was planned to pursue the two unresolved issues, but de León was not entrusted with it. Instead, Domingo Terán de los Ríos, a newcomer to the region who had never crossed the Río Grande, was chosen to head the 1691 overland expedition (Weddle 1999, 225). De León died in March of that year, before the new trek was even underway.

Alonso de León's five expeditions obeyed the Spanish Crown's mandate to find La Salle's colony, destroy it, and put an end to French encroachment in New Spain. Because each journey was a military mission, de León was ordered to keep official expedition diaries, in which he meticulously recorded the miles and direction traveled each day. He was required to list fauna and flora; name rivers, streams, and campsites; describe geographical features; and document encounters with Indian tribes. In spite of the formalistic style and official quality of the reports, his accounts also reveal an important human dimension of the first encounters between the Spaniards, Indians, and French on the Texas plains.

The Spanish had solidified their presence in New Spain and held a superior position as a colonizing power, and de León's expeditions clearly reflected that. These were large-scale, well-planned military endeavors, complete with armed soldiers of all ranks, padres, horses, cattle, pack animals, muleteers, servants, pages, and Indian scouts. While they were well equipped, outfitted with compasses and astrolabes, and technically advanced, the explorers had not been successful in reaching their goal. Not knowing the lay of the land, the Spaniards were often lost and sought out local Indians as guides. However, because they did not speak the native languages, communication was difficult if not impossible, and misunderstandings sometimes led to violent altercations.

The situation seemed to improve when de León made contact with the Tejas Indians in 1689. The Hasinai had seen periodic visits from La Salle's men and had welcomed the French into their villages. Some Frenchmen, displeased with La Salle, even deserted the colony to live among the friendly Tejas. Members of the Caddo confederacies, the Hasinai had a thriving agriculture and a well-developed political system (Newcomb 1961, 284; Barr 2007). They were successful traders who had established extensive networks with other Indian groups across Texas, most notably the Jumano. Interested in fostering a relationship with the Spaniards, the Tejas invited them to return to their lands. However, what Father Massanet understood as an invitation to Christianize was actually an offer to develop alliances and establish trading ties (Smith 1995, 15). Nevertheless, this led to the founding of San Francisco de los Tejas, the first Spanish mission in East Texas, in 1690. Father Massanet's vehement opposition to de León's proposed establishment of a presidio to protect and support the missionary endeavors left the fledgling mission alone and disconnected from the rest of New Spain.

Although another mission was founded within the same year, initial Indian goodwill soon turned to disappointment and later to open enmity. The Hasinai had no interest in Christian teachings and proved to be more difficult to convert than had been expected. When Terán de los Ríos returned to New Spain from his 1691–1692 expedition to the missions, he reported on the dismal conditions in East Texas (Chipman 1992, 98). Even a resupply expedition by Gregorio de Salinas Varona in 1693 could not avoid the obvious. Failed crops, diminished food supplies, and spreading diseases rendered the Indians less than indifferent to the domineering ways and religious doctrine of the Spaniards (Chipman 1992, 99). The Tejas became openly hostile. Three years after the founding of the first mission, the Indians forced the missionaries out of their land. One of the last to leave, Father Massanet reached Monclova in February 1694 after a torturous journey (Foster 1995, 19). Spain made the retreat official: "In March of 1694 the viceroy of Mexico formally recognized the state of affairs by ordering the abandonment of the province of Tejas" (Newcomb 1961, 287). De León had been right. Without the supporting structures of presidio and settlement, the missions could not stand on their

Statue of René-Robert Cavelier, Sieur de La Salle, at Indianola, Texas

own. East Texas would not see any Spanish attempts at colonization for another two decades.

1.4. The Expedition Diaries

The corpus consists of sixteen manuscripts located at various archives. Each of these documents is presented in detail, with information on their known history, important characteristics, present location, and other elements of interest.

The 1686 Expedition

Manuscript 86-A   archetype

The 1687 Expedition

Manuscript 87-A   archetype

Manuscripts 86-A and 87-A are the only documents pertaining to the 1686 and 1687 expeditions known to exist. They consist of a contemporaneous copy of the 1686 diary and a narrative summary of the 1687 expedition and are included in chapters 31 and 32 of Chapa's chronicle. Chapa had access to de León's original 1686 diary and copied it verbatim. No reference has been found in the literature to a diary from the 1687 expedition. Either de León did not keep a record during his second exploratory journey in search of La Salle, or it was lost before it could be copied and sent to the proper authorities. It is also possible that records of this expedition were among the documents that were destroyed during the 1692 Corn Riot, when the archives at the Secretaría del Virreinato in Mexico City were set afire. Chapa's chronicle, together with the elder Alonso de León's history of Nuevo León, was published for the first time in 1909 by Genaro García.[49] According to Cavazos Garza, García obtained the manuscript from Vicente de Andrade ([1961] 2005, xviii). Cavazos Garza surmises the existence of four other manuscripts of the chronicles;[50] he was, however, unable to locate or consult any of them. For this book, an extensive search for these documents in Mexico, following Cavazos Garza's leads, was equally fruitless. Thus, the only extant manuscript is the one García used. According to Bolton, Yale University purchased García's collection at the beginning of the twentieth century ([1908] 1916, 352). Hence, manuscripts 86-A and 87-A, which are in fact different chapters of the same document—Chapa's chronicle—are located in the Yale Collection of Western Americana, Beinecke Rare Book and Manuscript Library, MSS S-327, folios 46r–53r and 53r–53v, respectively.

49. This is the same manuscript by Juan Bautista Chapa that was transcribed into modernized Spanish by Israel Cavazos Garza and translated into English by Ned F. Brierley for William C. Foster's edition of *Texas and Northeastern México, 1630–1690* (Chapa 1997).

50. Besides Genaro García's manuscript, Israel Cavazos Garza mentions the following: (1) Chapa's original chronicle, which would either be in the hands of his descendants or was (2) the manuscript alluded to by governor Arriaga y Brambila, located in the Archivo Municipal de Monterrey in 1725; (3) the manuscript sent to Mexico for publication by the elder de León himself; and (4) the manuscript cited by Beristáin, who claims to have located it at the library of the Universidad de México ([1961] 2005: xviii). Efforts to locate these manuscripts at these locations for this volume were unsuccessful.

The two manuscripts are easy to read and virtually error-free. They do not appear to be damaged. Of the three small ink splatters on folios 50v, 52r, and 52v, only one hampers legibility of the affected word. Since 86-A and 87-A are part of the same document, they are written in the same hand and show the same characteristics. A chapter heading and a short introduction precede the actual expedition diary in 86-A. The author of the manuscript states that he copies the original diary "a la letra," verbatim. The document contains very few marginal notes on the left and none on the right. "Diario" is the only word that appears in the margin to indicate the beginning of the expedition diary. The remaining marginalia are numbers that correspond to the leagues traveled each day and appear at the beginning of each entry. Manuscript 87-A has no marginal notes.

The 1688 Expedition

Manuscript 88-A	archetype
Manuscript 88-B	
Manuscript 88-C	

Three copies of the 1688 expedition documentation have been located: 88-A, 88-B, and 88-C. In all three documents, the diary proper is very short but is accompanied by several *autos* providing important ancillary information about the journey. Although not strictly part of the expedition diary, these *autos* are included in this book because most of them have never been published, although they contribute important details that expand our understanding of the expedition.

A detailed linguistic analysis of the three manuscripts renders the following textual transmission stemma:

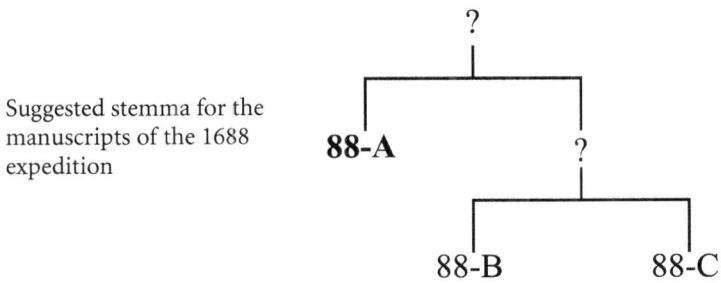

Suggested stemma for the manuscripts of the 1688 expedition

Manuscript 88-A was likely a direct contemporaneous copy of the original expedition diary, but it includes original *autos* signed by de León. Manuscripts 88-B and 88-C both appear to be concurrent copies of another lost copy of the original, most likely fashioned within a short period of each other. Manuscript

88-A is held in Austin, Texas, at the University of Texas, Nettie Lee Benson Latin American Collection, William B. Stephens Collection 2053, folios 17r–22r. It is part of a larger bundle or *legajo* with a cover folio that shows the year 1687 and the following heading: "Auttos de Guerra fechos por el jeneral Alonso de Leon gobernador y capitan del presidio de esta probincia de Coauguila desde catorze de octubre deste año de 1687 años con motivo de los daños causados por los indios barbaros."[51] The last two lines of this heading appear to have been written by a different hand. The first folio of the bundle bears an official seal accompanied by a typeset text, "Un quartillo, sello qvarto, vn qvartillo, años de mil y seiscientos y ochenta y seis, y seiscientos y ochenta y siete," which is characteristic of official correspondence. The bundle contains a chronological collection of official records that document important events that occurred in the Province of Coahuila from October 17, 1687, to July 17, 1688. It includes a large number of *autos*, each immediately followed by original signatures of Alonso de León and two witnesses. The names of the witnesses vary throughout the *autos*. This appears to be the same *legajo* that was first transcribed by Portillo (1886, 182–238). According to Alessio Robles, the manuscript was held at the Archivo de la Secretaría de Gobierno del Estado, in Saltillo, Coahuila ([1938] 1978, 340). A visit to this archive in Coahuila in 2008 did not succeed in locating the *legajo*. It must be assumed that this is the same manuscript 88-A, now located in the Benson Collection. However, it has not been ascertained when it was purchased by the University of Texas. A meticulous comparison of Portillo's transcription and the original held in the Benson Collection seems to confirm that this is the same document.

Manuscript 88-A is in good condition and is easy to read. Folios 21r–22v are torn on the top right or left corner, respectively; however, the tear does not affect the actual text. Marginal notes on the left indicate the beginning of each separate *auto*. They include "Auto p*ara* la salida a buscar al francés" (17r1)[52] and "Declara*cion* del prisionero frances" (19r31).[53] Right-hand marginalia in the diary proper appear at the end of each entry, showing the number of leagues traveled each day. Ornamentation is included at the top of each folio. Next to de León's autograph signature at the end of each *auto* are the signatures of José Gutiérrez and José Antonio de Ecay y Múzquiz. The latter

51. "War documents by General Alonso de León, governor and commander of the presidio of this Province of Coahuila, from October 14 of this year 1687 owing to the damage caused by barbaric Indians." (This and all other translations are the author's unless stated otherwise.)
52. "Official document of the journey to search for the Frenchman." As noted in section 2.1, "Transcription Methodology," italics indicate expansions of scribal abbreviations in the original.
53. "The French prisoner's statement."

also seems to be the scribe, judging from the similarity between his signature and the text. The names of these witnesses are important to note because they are not identical to those that appear in the other two manuscripts (88-B and 88-C).

Manuscripts 88-B and 88-C were found in the Archivo General de Indias (AGI) in Seville, Spain. Evidently, two official copies of the report were sent to Spain. The two documents form part of the same *legajo* or bundle but not of the same *expediente* or folder. Manuscript 88-B's exact location is AGI, Audiencia de México, legajo 616, expediente 62, folios 3v–12r. Manuscript 88-C is located at AGI, Audiencia de México, legajo 616, expediente 65, folios 4r–16r. Although written by the same hand, the manuscripts are not identical. They show several discrepancies, all the result of scribal error. They also do not appear to be copies of 88-A since the name of one of the witnesses does not coincide. Instead of José Gutiérrez, who signs as witness in each of the *autos* and the diary of 88-A, manuscripts 88-B and 88-C show Carlos Cantú[54] as a recurring witness for all entries. Besides the divergent signatures, there are several other discrepancies between 88-A, 88-B, and 88-C. Most of them are not very significant and can be attributed to scribal error. These discrepancies are pointed out in the English translations. Manuscript 88-A appears to be an original written by José Antonio de Ecay y Múzquiz and bears autograph signatures by Alonso de León and his two witnesses. The portion that corresponds to the actual expedition diary was most likely copied from de León's original journal and attached to the *autos*. The existence of another lost source text can also be assumed. Culled from entries of "Autos de Guerra" (which includes 88-A) and signed by de León and two witnesses (Ecay y Múzquiz and Cantú) before it was sent on to the viceroy in Mexico, this lost manuscript is the archetype for documents 88-B and 88-C that were sent to Spain.

Individually, 88-B and 88-C show the following characteristics. Manuscript 88-B is part of a long *expediente* on official paper with a characteristic official seal and typeset heading, which includes the year of issue and tax: "Un quartillo, sello qvarto, vn qvartillo, años de mil y seiscientos y ochenta y ocho, y seiscientos y ochenta y nveve." It is preceded by a letter directed to "Excelentisimo señor," which does not precede 88-A, and it is followed by additional documents associated with the expedition, which are also lacking in 88-A. The manuscript is in good condition and is not difficult to read. It seems to have been written by the same hand that wrote 88-C. Right and left

54. Captain Carlos Cantú appears as one of the members of the expedition party. It is very likely that he was one of de León's in-laws, since his wife's name was Agustina Cantú.

marginalia are generally the same as in 88-A, though some illegible symbols appear on the margins of several pages. Small ornamentation decorates the top and bottom of each folio. Other than the discrepancy in the names of the witnesses and a few scribal errors, 88-B is very close to 88-A.

Manuscript 88-C is also part of a longer document, *expediente* 65, which contains a title folio with the following text: "Jesus – Maria – Joseph. Auttos y diligencias que se an executtado por el capitan Alonsso de Leon governador de la provincia de Coaguila en la Nueva [E]spaña sobre el descubrimiento de la vna poblazon de franzeses que se dijo havia en el Seno Mexicano y la aprehenzion de tres dellos y lo obrado sobre todo."[55] The seal and typeset heading that appear on the first folio of the full *expediente* are identical to the ones in 88-B. The preceding letter and some subsequent documents are also the same as in 88-B. The entire *expediente* 65, however, is much more extensive than *expediente* 62, and it also includes a copy of the 1689 expedition (89-B). Besides the two diaries, it contains records of the interrogations of Jean Henri and Jean L'Archevêque, lists of supplies for the 1689 expedition, and other pieces of communication pertaining to the search for the French colony. This confirms that 88-C was copied after the conclusion of the 1689 expedition. The 1688 diary and ancillary *autos* that form 88-C show fewer marginal notes than 88-B. Ornamentation at the top and bottom of the pages is also present.

The 1689 Expedition

Manuscript 89-A
Manuscript 89-B   archetype
Manuscript 89-C
Manuscript 89-D
Manuscript 89-E

Five manuscripts have been located for the 1689 expedition, but none of them bear de León's original signature. Manuscripts 89-A, 89-B, and 89-C appear to be contemporaneous copies of the original diary. As mentioned elsewhere, manuscript 89-D was fashioned in 1792, over one hundred years after the expedition took place. Manuscript 89-E is an even later copy, from the 1850s. Owing to their late dates of replication, manuscripts 89-D and 89-E were not included in the philological analysis to establish archetypes.

55. "Jesus – Mary – Joseph. Official documents and proceedings that have been executed by Captain Alonso de León, governor of the Province of Coahuila in New Spain, concerning the discovery of a settlement of Frenchmen that was said to exist on the Seno Mexicano and the apprehension of three of them and all that was done."

Based on a linguistic analysis and comparison of the manuscripts, the following stemma has been created to explain the textual transmission from a lost original to the extant manuscripts:

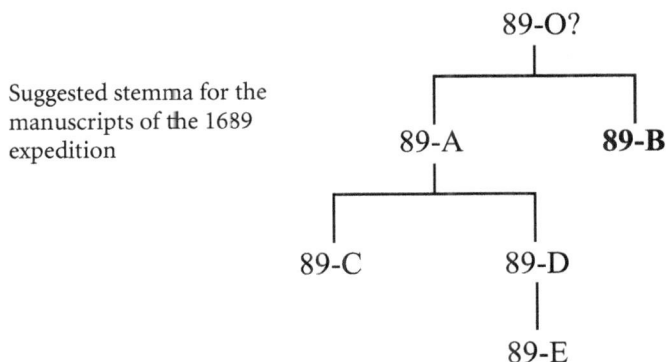

Suggested stemma for the manuscripts of the 1689 expedition

```
                    89-O?
              ┌───────┴───────┐
            89-A             89-B
       ┌──────┴──────┐
     89-C          89-D
                     │
                   89-E
```

Manuscript 89-A is located in the Archivo General de la Nación (AGN), Ramo de Provincias Internas, volumen 182, folios 428–440v, in Mexico City. It appears to be a contemporaneous copy of the 1689 original diary and it is one of the two oldest manuscripts of the 1689 expedition. Although it does not bear de León's original signature, it was likely reproduced directly and immediately from the original journal, 89-O, upon his return. Volume 182 contains a somewhat jumbled collection of seventeenth- and eighteenth-century documents connected to Spanish Texas, including several of Massanet's papers. The location of 89-A has been known to researchers since at least the beginning of the twentieth century. It was listed in Bolton's guide to the archives in Mexico ([1913] 1977, 123). However, it has been neglected as a source in favor of manuscript 89-D, a very legible copy that was not contemporaneous and is exceedingly problematic, as discussed elsewhere. An explanation for this preference might be that the documents within volume 182 are badly organized and the order is quite confusing. Manuscript 89-A, for instance, is misplaced behind 90-A, which in turn is misdated as a 1689 document. Another, more obvious reason for the preference of 89-D over 89-A is the clean, crisp script and excellent readability of the former. Manuscript 89-A itself is in good condition. The copy is neat and carefully written. It is easy to read and virtually free of scribal errors. The manuscript contains ornamentation on the top of each folio and a long line at the end of several folios. The headings on the first page are darker and somewhat more ornate than the rest of the text. On the left margin, a dash marks the beginning of each daily entry. Marginalia on the left are numbers that correspond to the daily distance traveled.

Manuscript 89-B is held at the Archivo de Indias in Seville, Spain. Its exact location is AGI, Audiencia de México, legajo 616, expediente 65, folios 37v–50r. This is the same comprehensive document described above that also includes 88-C, which precedes 89-B within the folder. It is part of a wide-ranging report sent to Spain after the discovery of La Salle's colony in 1689. The extensive *expediente* 65 was ostensibly the work of several scribes. Indeed, 89-B appears to have been written by a hand other than the one that produced 88-C. Two affidavits on the last page of the *expediente*, certifying the faithfulness of the copy, attest that they were "fecho en Mexico" on the twenty-eight and twenty-ninth of June 1689, respectively. This confirms that this contemporaneous copy was produced approximately one month after de León's return from his expedition. It is highly probable that it was reproduced directly from the original diary. Thus, this manuscript has been selected as the archetype for the 1689 expedition. The document remains in good condition and is highly legible. Left marginalia include "Diario de Leon" (37v13) at the beginning of the diary and several unidentified symbols throughout. The right margin contains numbers that correspond to the distance traveled each day. At the bottom, the sum of the leagues traveled up to that date is stated. This number is carried over to the top of the right margin in the next folio. Small ornamentation adorns the top and a long line appears at the bottom of each folio.

Manuscript 89-C is located in the Biblioteca Nacional de México (BNMex), Archivo Franciscano, caja 1, expedientes 13 y 14, folios 133v–141v, in Mexico City. It is evidently a copy of 89-A. The diary is immediately preceded by 90-C, to which it is joined, replicating the inverse chronology evident in volume 182 of AGN's Provincias Internas, where 90-A appears before 89-A. This further confirms that 89-C was written subsequent to the conclusion of the 1690 expedition, after manuscripts 90-A and 89-A were coalesced into one document and misdated. Both 89-C and 90-C are written by the same hand and display the same characteristics. The manuscript is in good condition and easy to read. The scribe who copied the document used the margins to restate dates and distances covered: the dates of the daily entries appear in the left margin, while the leagues marched each day are noted in the right margin.

Manuscript 89-D can be found in the AGN, Ramo de Historia, volumen 27, folios 51r–66r, in Mexico City. A certification at the beginning of the volume states that it was copied in 1792 by Fray Francisco García Figueroa. The scribe was a Franciscan friar from the Archdiocese of Mexico, who in 1790 had been charged by royal order with the selection and reproduction of all manuscripts pertaining to the history of New Spain. These dates coincide with the viceroy's project to reorganize the Secretaría del Virreinato as an archive to hold New Spain's important documents, no doubt inspired by the establishment of the AGI in Seville just five years earlier. Two sets of thirty-two volumes were produced; one was sent to Spain and the other was kept in Mexico. Volume 27 is entitled *Documentos para la historia civil y eclesiástica de la Provincia de Texas*. Besides 89-D, the volume also contains copies of numerous other documents about Texas from 1689 to 1767. Manuscript 89-D is in excellent condition and is very easy to read. The scribe's goal was clearly to produce a highly legible copy. Thus, the writing is very neat and the excessive use of abbreviations and marginalia has been avoided. In fact, only the dates of the daily entries appear in the left margin, and the number of leagues traveled daily is noted in the right margin. Unfortunately, the copy contains several significant scribal errors and omissions that render it unreliable as a historical source. Regrettably, manuscript 89-D has served as the basis for most English-language accounts since 1905. This has resulted in misinterpretation and distortion of historical facts.

Manuscript 89-E is held at the University of California–Berkeley, Bancroft Library, M-M 278–281, document 24, folios 418r–426v. It is undoubtedly a copy of 89-D, as the same substantive errors and omissions are present. However, 89-E is written in a much more contemporary hand and shows modernized spelling, capitalization, and punctuation. Several nonnative-speaker errors are also evident, such as "jeuves" (305r5), "trienta" (312r9), "asimisimo" (312r10), "teirra" (315r9), "Gaudalupe" (315r15), and so on. Marginalia are scant; only the daily traveling distance is noted in the right margin. According to the Bancroft Library catalog, 89-E is part of Manuscritos Mexicanos, 1715–1842, a collection of transcripts "made chiefly in 1850 from archives in Mexico, of various documents relating to California, Texas, Louisiana, Canada, and Mexico, largely in the handwriting of Robert Greenhow,[56] although a portion is in that of his wife, Rose."[57]

56. Robert Greenhow (1800–1854) was a sophisticated gentleman, physician, and scholar from a wealthy Virginian family. Although he was a medical doctor, his passion was history, and he devoted much of his time to studying maps, deciphering old handwritten accounts, and engaging in other scholarly endeavors. In 1835, he married Rose O'Neale. Widely traveled and fluent in several languages, he worked as a translator and librarian at the State Department. In 1850, when California became a state, the Greenhows moved to San Francisco, where Robert worked as an associate law clerk for the US Land Commission. On their way west, they spent six months in Mexico City researching documentation to settle land claims of American citizens after the Treaty of Guadalupe Hidalgo. He died in California from an accident (Blackman 2005).

57. Rose O'Neale Greenhow (1817–1864) was born in Maryland, the daughter of a planter and slave owner. As a teenager, she went to live with her aunt in Washington, DC, where she

Through comparison of various handwritten documents, it was ascertained that 89-E was indeed written by Rose O'Neale Greenhow, the famous Confederate spy (see Blackman 2005). In 1850, Robert and Rose Greenhow spent almost six months in Mexico City before moving to California, which had just become the thirty-first state and was experiencing gold rush fever. Robert Greenhow had worked as a translator and librarian in the State Department for a number of years. He had been sent to Mexico on a diplomatic mission "with instructions to settle claims of American citizens that had been assumed by the United States on the signing of the Treaty of Guadalupe Hidalgo" (Blackman 2005, 152). Robert's duty was to find proof for the legitimate land claims and identify the fraudulent ones. Although toward the end of their stay in the Mexican capital, he sent a dispatch to Washington stating that "the Mexican government had failed to provide the documents necessary to settle U.S. claims" (Blackman 2005, 154), the Greenhows must have had access to the archives and were in a position to copy the documents held at the Bancroft Library today. Blackman does not make mention of this in her book. Nevertheless, given Robert's keen interest in historical manuscripts and Rose's support of her husband's endeavors, it would not come as a surprise that she lent her hand in the transcription task. It appears that she was not as fluent in Spanish as her husband, which would explain some of the transcription errors.

The manuscript's relatively recent provenance renders 89-E inconsequential for the linguistic analysis and comparison. Nonetheless, it is fascinating to know that it was transcribed by such a prominent, if later notorious, American woman, who went on to become a spy for the Confederate cause after her husband's death.

---

met the most important figures of the Washington elite. She moved among the highest circles of society and became friend and confidante to presidents, congressmen, and high-ranking officers. In 1835, she married Robert Greenhow. When her husband died in California in 1854, Rose settled in Washington and became enmeshed in politics. A fervent southerner, she used her influence to help the Confederate cause. As a spy, she provided General Beauregard with information that resulted in the victory at First Bull Run. She was tried for espionage, imprisoned, and later deported to Virginia. Jefferson Davis sent her to Europe as an envoy of the Confederacy to gather intelligence. On her return to America, her ship ran aground when chased by a Union ship. She tried to escape in a rowboat but drowned when it capsized, as she was weighed down by the $2,000 in gold she was carrying for the Confederate treasury (Blackman 2005).

The 1690 Expedition

    Manuscript 90-A
    Manuscript 90-B   archetype
    Manuscript 90-C
    Manuscript 90-D   archetype
    Manuscript 90-E
    Manuscript 90-F

Six manuscripts have been identified for the 1690 expedition: 90-A, 90-B, 90-C, 90-D, 90-E, and 90-F. Foster (1997) first identified 90-D as a revised manuscript. McLain (2005) discovered 90-E and 90-F and divided the diaries into two categories: revised and unrevised. She identified 90-A, 90-B, and 90-C as unrevised manuscripts and 90-D, 90-E, and 90-F as revised copies. The first three appear to be copies of a lost original, 90-O, that was either kept by de León or forwarded to the viceroy at the end of the expedition in July 1690. The latter three are believed to be revised copies, written after the return of the exploratory force to Monclova, Coahuila. Owing to the existing controversy between Massanet and de León, a number of revisions were made. However, it is not clear what primary source was used. In addition, 90-E and 90-F are not complete copies of 90-D. There are several substantive differences between them. Many questions on the genesis and motive for 90-D, 90-E, and 90-F remain unanswered. None of the manuscripts bears de León's original signature.

The genetic relation between the manuscripts can best be visualized through the following stemma:

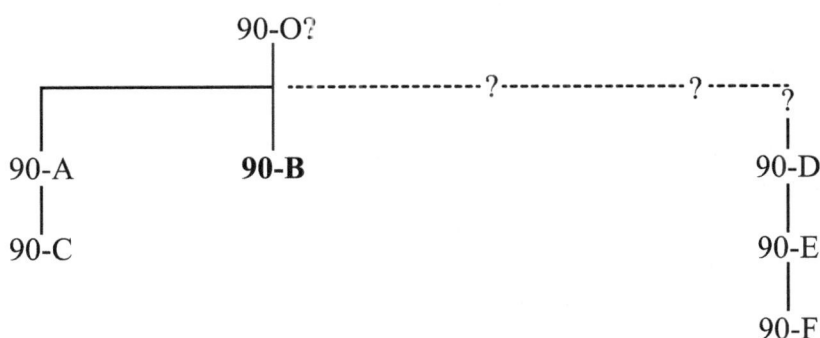

Suggested stemma for the manuscripts of the 1690 expedition

Manuscript 90-A is located in the AGN, Provincias Internas, volumen 182, expediente 6, folios 418–426v. It appears to be the oldest of the manuscript copies, but it is an incomplete document because it is missing an unknown number of folios and lacks the first fourteen entries, from March 26 through April 8, 1690. The diary begins with the last sentence of the entry of April 8[58] and ends with the entry of July 5–11, 1690, when the expedition was unable to cross the swollen Río Grande. Within volume 182, manuscript 90-A immediately precedes manuscript 89-A, even though this is chronologically incorrect. Because 90-A lacks the first folios and was placed ahead of the diary of the earlier expedition, it has been misdated as a document from 1689. The word "Texas" and the year "1689 [sic]" appear on the top and right margin of the first page. Also written in the right margin is "No 1," and just below, a small paper strip has been pasted vertically with the following text, written in a different hand: "Numero 1 de los papeles | del Superior Govierno." Another small paper with the number 1277 is pasted in the left margin and the same number is written twice on the top of the folio. These all seem to be subsequent archival annotations.

The ink on the first two folios is faded and the paper shows some damage, but subsequent folios are intact and easy to read. The manuscript contains marginalia throughout: an unidentified symbol in the left margin marks the beginning of each daily entry, while the right margin contains numbers at the end of each entry that correspond to the leagues traveled each day. Additional marginal notes on the left and right are written in a different hand and were most likely added at a later date. These notes point out important events of the expedition: "Francesitos" (420v21), "Pedro Talon Francesito" (420v33), "Pedro Muni Francesito" (421r18), "Governador de Tejas" (421v19), "se celebro la fiesta del corpus en Tejas año de 1689 [sic]" (423v5), and "Posesion al Padre Damian Masanet" (423v25). The document appears to have been written by at least two different hands.

Manuscript 90-B is held at the AGI, Audiencia de México, legajo 617, folios 4v–18r. Although not the original diary, it is part of a more comprehensive official report that was sent to authorities in Spain soon after the conclusion of the 1690 expedition. The accompanying documents as well as the official seal and stamp on the first folio confirm that the document was written in either 1690 or 1691. Besides the diary, the complete *expediente* includes ancillary documents such as letters, testimonies, and detailed lists

58. McLain erroneously states that the first entry is May 8, 1690 (2005, 16), instead of April 8, 1690.

of expedition members and supplies. Unlike 90-A and 90-C, 90-B is a complete copy of the diary, beginning on March 26, 1690, the very first day of the journey, and ending with the entry of July 5–11, when the company was stalled at the Río Grande. The manuscript is in good condition and is very easy to read. It is neatly written and appears to be almost error-free. Some marginalia are noted throughout: dashes in the left margin point to the beginning of each daily entry; and numbers in the right margin, at the end of each entry, indicate the leagues traveled. Typical ornamentation adorns the top and bottom of each folio.

Bolton examined copies of both 90-A and 90-B while working on his translation for *Spanish Exploration in the Southwest, 1542–1706* ([1908] 1916, 352). He was also familiar with 90-D and noted discrepancies with the other two diaries in his footnotes. He based his English translation on 90-A, but because the manuscript was incomplete, he utilized 90-B to reconstruct the missing entries from March 26 through April 8. Indeed, 90-A is arguably the oldest of the extant manuscripts and is likely the closest to the original. However, because it presents a truncated text, manuscript 90-B has been chosen as the archetype for this analysis. Thus, this manuscript is the one that has been paleographically transcribed and translated into English.

Manuscript 90-C is located at the BNMex, Archivo Franciscano, caja 1, expedientes 12 y 13, folios 126v–133v, in Mexico City. It is a copy of 90-A and therefore represents an incomplete record of the 1690 exploratory journey. Manuscript 90-C begins with the April 9[59] entry and ends with the one for July 5–11, 1690. In the archival folder, this diary immediately precedes 89-C, replicating the previously mentioned jumbled chronology evident in volume 182 of AGN Provincias Internas. This further confirms that 90-C is indeed a copy of 90-A. The manuscript is in good condition and is not difficult to read. It shows abundant marginalia in both margins. Marginal notes on the left include an introduction to the document on the first folio: "Derrotero del viage que se principio [en] 9 de abril y finalizo en 11 de junio [sic] por Alonso de Leon como general y cabo principal" (126v1);[60] and later, "Pedro Talon Frances" (128v29). All other left-hand marginalia correspond to the chronological dates of each entry. The scribe noted the leagues traveled each day at the end of every day in the right margin. Other marginalia on the right include "Pedro Muni Frances" (129r15) and "Año de [1]689 [sic]

---

59. McLain misstates the first entry as having been on May 9 (2005, 17), instead of April 9, 1690.

60. "Route of the journey which started on April 9 and ended on June 11 by Alonso de León, general and main leader."

se celebro la fiestta de Corpus en Texas" (130v6).[61] This last note contains an obvious error and is further proof that 90-C is a copy of 90-A, as the same mistake appears in the latter manuscript.

Although manuscripts 90-A, 90-B, and 90-C show numerous scribal variants, there are no significant factual discrepancies. This is not the case with the remaining three documents. Manuscripts 90-D, 90-E, and 90-F differ considerably from the prior three. McLain's thesis (2005) is a comprehensive study of the differences between what she identifies as revised and unrevised manuscripts.

Manuscript 90-D is located in the Yale Collection of Western Americana, Beinecke Rare Book and Manuscript Library, MSS S-327, folios 1r–13r. This is the same collection that contains manuscripts 86-A and 87-A, although 90-D is not part of Chapa's chronicle; rather it is an adjunct document. Like the other manuscripts in the collection, 90-D was purchased from Genaro García at the beginning of the twentieth century (Bolton [1908] 1916, 352). Foster first noted the discrepancy between 90-D and both 90-A and 90-B, the manuscripts used for Bolton's translation, and identified the document as a revised expedition diary (1997, 23). McLain (2005) further analyzed these diaries and discovered numerous substantive differences. Foster (1997, 23) and McLain (2005, 15) surmised that de León himself and others rewrote whole segments of the diary, fine-tuning distances, adding clarifications, and including names of Indian tribes encountered in order to counteract the controversy that surrounded the 1690 expedition after their return, triggered by the declarations of Friar Massanet. However, the revisions, changes, additions, and omissions are so numerous that additional sources might have been used.

Like 90-B, manuscript 90-D begins with the first day of the expedition, March 26, 1690, but, unlike any of the other manuscripts, it ends with the entry for July 15. In fact, 90-D is the only manuscript that includes entries for the days from July 12 to 15, the days after the company managed to cross the swollen Río Grande and return to Monclova. This seems to indicate that de León dispatched the original expedition diary with his assistant Gregorio de Salinas Varona[62] and the Frenchman Pierre Meunier directly from the Río Grande before the general even reached Monclova. The last few days of the

61. "Year of 1689 [*sic*] the feast of Corpus was celebrated in Texas."
62. Gregorio de Salinas Varona (ca. 1650–?) was a Spanish soldier who came to New Spain in 1687 after having served in Flanders for nineteen years. He participated in three expeditions into the land of the Tejas: in 1690 with Alonso de León, in 1691 with Domingo Terán de los Ríos, and in 1693 as commander of his own relief expedition to the East Texas missions. He also served as governor of Coahuila (Weddle 2010d).

journey are recorded only in manuscript 90-D, as they are also missing in 90-E and 90-F. Nonetheless, 90-D is incomplete because it lacks entries in the middle, for May 23, 24, and 26.[63] During these days, the Spaniards held processions and celebrated the feast of Corpus Christi before ceremonially raising the standard in the name of the Spanish king, investing the Indian leader as "governador" of his people, and selecting a location to build the mission. It appears that this information was to be added later, as the diary includes an entire blank folio 8v,[64] as well as blank spaces at the bottom of folio 8r and at the top of folio 9r. The diary is not signed. Additional folios contain incomplete lists of Indian nations and leagues traveled from river crossing to river crossing. These lists are not addressed in the transcription.

The manuscript is written by two distinct hands and is often very difficult to read. Hand A, the more challenging of the two to decipher, writes from folio 1r1 until folio 5v15 and from folio 9r to the end of the diary. Hand B records the entries from folio 5v16 to folio 8v25 and stops right before the blank folio that truncates the report. Curiously, hand B appears to be identical to the one that wrote manuscript 88-C, which has been identified as belonging to José Antonio de Ecay y Múzquiz, the scribe who composed de León's "Autos de Guerra" from October 1687 to July 1688. It is possible that Ecay y Múzquiz, who appears as a witness on many of de León's *autos*, was in fact one of the two scribes engaged in the revision of the 1690 diary.

Calligraphically, hand A presents an interesting case. Throughout, scribe A utilizes what appears to be a unique hybrid letter, a *z* with a cedilla tail, which resembles a blend between graphs *z* and *ç*. This *z* with a tail appears in addition to the *ç*—not in lieu of it—in words such as "nuezes" (2v1), "franzes" (2v21), "pedazos" (4v14), "nazion" (11r2), "desberguenzas" (11r6), "zerca" (11r27), and so forth. It is clearly differently shaped than the cedilla, which is also present in the text in words such as "çarco" (2v10) and "neçessario" (3r24). The cedilla is used less frequently. Although interesting, this graph does not appear to be phonologically significant. Rather, it seems to represent a caprice of scribe A. Thus, it was decided to transcribe this graph as a simple *z* throughout since it is definitely a *z* and not a *ç*.

Marginalia in 90-D are scant and limited to the leagues traveled each day, which appear in the right margin at the end of each entry. These marginal

63. McLain states that it "lacks entries from May 23 until May 26" (2005, 19). However, there is a short entry for May 25 (90-D 9r4–5).

64. McLain (2005) fails to identify the blank folio 8v and consequently numbers the remaining folios incorrectly.

notes are often essential for gleaning complete information for each day's march. Unlike other manuscripts, where marginalia stating the daily distance traveled are but a repetition of information already contained in the daily entry, in 90-D the leagues are frequently recorded only in the margin. Several erasures and emendations are noted throughout the manuscript.

Manuscripts 90-E and 90-F are both located in the Gilcrease Museum in Tulsa, Oklahoma. Published literature about the 1690 expedition makes no reference to these two documents. Branum's (1974) and McLain's (2005) unpublished master's theses are the only studies that address these manuscripts. McLain categorizes both as revised manuscripts (2005, 14). They appear to be copies of 90-D, with 90-F being a copy of 90-E. However, they present extensive substantive differences. For example, in 90-E and 90-F the name of one of the captured Frenchmen appears as Pedro Molinero (90-E 6v18, 90-F 8v9), whereas in 90-D it is Pedro Mone (12v19). The French name was actually Pierre Meunier. Indeed, Pedro Molinero is the literal Spanish translation of the French, namely the equivalent of Peter Miller in English. It appears that the scribe who wrote 90-E either understood French and translated the name into Spanish or consulted additional sources that might have presented a Hispanicized version of the name. Another significant discrepancy is that in 90-E and 90-F the main valley of the Tejas is named San Francisco de los Tejas (90-E 8r40, 90-F 10v24–25) as in 90-A, 90-B, and 90-C, whereas in 90-D it receives the name Madre Jessús María de Ágreda (8r24). More importantly, 90-E and 90-F include entries for May 23, 24, and 26, which are lacking in 90-D, as well as a completely different entry for May 25. Interestingly, these entries are not identical to the ones in 90-A, 90-B, or 90-C, either. It is not known from which manuscript these last three entries were copied. Clearly, 90-E and 90-F are incomplete records of the 1690 journey, as they end with the entry for May 26 and do not include the remainder of the expedition from May 27 through July 15, 1690.

The exact location for manuscript 90-E is the Gilcrease Museum, Tulsa, Oklahoma, Hispanic Documents Section, item 67.1, folios 1r–9r. The first folio consists solely of the heading "K (^D) H. 1, Leg*ajo* 1 / 1a entrada a Texas, año de 1690 / Diario." As stated above, the diary records only part of the expedition, from March 6 to May 26, 1690. It ends just as the Spaniards and Indians were identifying the best location for the mission. The manuscript does not include the search for the Talon siblings or the violent altercation with the Indians who held them. The document is not signed, and several blank pages follow the last entry. It is quite possible that the scribe was unable to complete the full transcription. Marginalia are scant. The only notes that appear in the right margin are numbers corresponding to the leagues traveled for each entry.

The document is at times very difficult to read and contains many scribal deletions and emendations. The handwriting is often quite challenging to decipher. In addition, several of the folios are damaged. The manuscript shows signs of having been folded horizontally and vertically for a long period. This has created deep creases in the center of the folios. In particular, the last few pages show a great deal of damage. In fact, the paper is so worn at the center, where the creases meet, that small holes have appeared. These tears make it impossible to read several of the words that have been completely worn away.

Manuscript 90-F is held at the Gilcrease Museum, Tulsa, Oklahoma, Hispanic Documents Section, item 67.2, folios 1v–11r. It is a copy of 90-E and includes the same type of marginalia, with the leagues traveled at the end of each daily entry. The diary documents only part of the exploratory journey, from March 26 to May 26, 1690. It ends at the same spot as 90-E, just as the Spaniards were preparing to build the first mission. Diverging from 90-E, the word "fin" is written at the end of manuscript 90-F, although it is evidently not the end of the expedition. This confirms that the scribe who copied 90-F from 90-E was not aware of any other versions of the expedition diary. Manuscript 90-F has been categorized as an incomplete revised manuscript. The manuscript is in good condition and is highly legible. The scribe wrote very neatly and exerted great care in the process of reproduction. The document is virtually error-free. It varies very little from 90-E; the few cases can easily be attributed to scribal errors.

Manuscript 90-D and its partial copies 90-E and 90-F still leave many questions unanswered. Why was such an extensive revision needed after the fact? After all, the original diary had already been read by the viceroy and the council, and copies of it (90-B, 90-C) had been sent on to Spain. What sources were used for the revision, since some entries contain vastly different information? Who were the people involved in the revision process and when was it completed? What purpose did the incomplete copies 90-E and 90-F serve?

In conclusion, the sixteen manuscripts of this corpus provide significant insights into Alonso de León's five expeditions into Texas in search of La Salle's colony. The archival documents are essential for our complete understanding of the historical processes. However, they also offer a textual platform essential for the analysis of linguistic features and documentation of the development of the Spanish language.

2.

Transcription of
the Spanish Manuscripts

2.1 Transcription Methodology

This chapter contains paleographic transcriptions of the six documents that
have been identified as archetypes: 86-A, 87-A, 88-A, 89-B, 90-B, and 90-D.
The transcriptions of 86-A, 87-A, and 90-D were fashioned from a microfilm
of the original manuscripts furnished by the Beinecke Library at Yale, holder of
the originals. The microfilm is of excellent quality and the documents remark-
ably legible. For manuscripts 88-A, 89-B, and 90-B, photocopies of the texts
were used for initial transcription. Subsequently, the author traveled to the
archives in Austin, Mexico City, and Seville to consult the originals and personally compare the transcriptions to the seventeenth-century manuscripts
held at the Benson, the AGN, and the AGI, respectively.

The transcription is paleographic, which means that the orthography
and appearance of the original text are maintained. As such, it adheres to
an adapted version of the norms formulated by the Hispanic Seminary of
Medieval Studies in Madison, Wisconsin (Mackenzie 1997), which have become the normative guide for paleographic study. Modified guidelines and
best-practice norms have been established by scholars in the field (Craddock
1996, 1997; Frago Gracia 1999; Imhoff 2002) to guarantee high standards of
textual integrity while facilitating readability.

In the following explanation, specific clarifications are provided as well as
the exceptions to the norms adopted herein (see Imhoff 2002 and McLain
2005): Capitalization, punctuation, and word division have been modernized. Words are divided as necessary, except in contractions such as *del* 'de
él,' *della* 'de ella,' *dellos* 'de ellos,' *desta* 'de esta,' and *asial* 'hacia el,' which have
been kept intact.

The original spelling has been meticulously maintained, but accent marks
have not been included. Variation between the graphs *b/u/v* is retained: *embie*

(90-B 10v21); *cauallo* (88-A 18v28); *vaia* (89-B 37v22). The distinction between the graphs *i/j/y* is recognized: *indios* (90-D 1r9); *jndio* (90-D 10v11); *yndio* (86-A 48v17). Graphs *x/j/g* are maintained: *abaxo* (89-B 38r6); *jentte* (89-B 38r4); *trugeron* (89-A 433r15). Variation between the graphs *s/ss/z/c/ç* is also respected: *antesedentte* (89-B 43v4); *passo* (89-B 43r13); *zerca* (86-A 49r14); *pricionero* (89-A 437r20); *deligençias* (89-B 45r22). Manuscript 90-D presents an interesting case. As stated in subsection 1.4, in some sections, an unusual hybrid letter appears. It consists of a graph between a *z* and *ç*, resembling a *z* with a cedilla tail. The author has determined this to be a capricious tendency of this particular scribe and has decided to transcribe it as a *z* since the *ç* is shaped differently.

A pilcrow sign "¶" designates paragraphs and marks the beginning of each entry. Line numbers in increments of five have been placed in the left margins to enhance readability and facilitate references to the study. Braces "{}" record marginalia and mnemonics: "{LM}" is used to indicate marginalia found in the left margin, and "{RM}" for marginalia in the right margin; "{HD}" precedes headings and "{SIG}" signatures. Brackets "[]" are employed to indicate foliation and editorial insertions, while parentheses "()" are used for editorial deletions. Virgules "/" designate line breaks. Carets "^" in combination with parentheses "(^)" indicate scribal deletions; carets surrounded by brackets "[^]" indicate scribal insertions. A caret followed by a single parenthesis "^(" or "^)" signifies parenthesis by scribe. Italics are used to expand scribal abbreviations. Question marks denote illegibility. Single question marks "?" indicate a word-internal missing letter, double question marks "??" a missing word, and triple question marks "???" multiple missing words.

To avoid redundancy, marginalia that repeat the number of leagues traveled have been eliminated when this information is provided in the diary entry. In 90-D, the distance is occasionally missing in the entry and is entered only in the margin. This has been resolved with a bracket, as in "6 [leguas]."

toda esta orilla es piedra. la costa corre de norte a sur
algo mas al norueste, la mar es muy brava aunque no hace
viento al en su orilla muchos sauinos Piños palmas y totoral
gruesos como la pierna y otros mas que sacados de la mar
la costa es muy sombra sin Peñasco alguno y muy amoda-
ble la orilla acalado que no se atascan. Tres leguas que
nauego al norueste

Lunes 15 de Julio estando en la mesma loca del Rio en el pun-
to del medio dia se tomo la altura de sol con astrolauio y
se hallo en veinte y tres grados y quarenta y cinco minutos
de altura de norte (salvo yerro por estar clara esta lauio o lo que
parece mala sumtada y algo descompuesto) por el poco jas de-
dribase saber si el Real de que de medio dia esta donde
alcanza aquel dia que el siguiente parece en cierto
to donde estubo el dia sabado y lo con veinte y un
soldados para a querer ver de nuebo la costa arial Rio
de Palmas en distancia de mas de ocho leguas en la qual
hallamos alguna tablazon de costados de naueo vergas maste-
leros y pedazos de quilla y el timon todos de pino y dos
las becas y quatro cauduillas de piesa de artilleria una
pieza con los aros de uimbres, tres caras quebradas una
de cemento de Pedro Redonda muy gruesa, tapada con un
conclo que destapada allie en ella un poco de Pino ya co-
rrupto el Pino es mas blando y parece no fue labrada
en los Reynos de Castilla segun su forma y finalmente hallo
en esta orilla a todo genero de madera y ruinas de naueo
con que sin duda se robaron algunos en ella por la diuersi-
dad de ellas ruinas y la madera ser una mas antigua que la
otra, lo que mas me admiro fue ver alguna cañas de maso
que traia la Resaca dela mar al parecer dela sum brardue
año que amonzaba a Pilotear con sus Paises, la cañas
sobre que discurri que ay alguna poblacion cercana y que el

Folio 52r of manuscript 85-A (Yale Collection of American Literature, Beinecke Rare Book and Manuscript Library)

[folio 46r]

{LM} Diario

Derrotero, diario y demarcacion del viaje que yo el
general Alonso de Leon, theniente de gouernador y de capitan general
de este Nuebo Reyno de Leon hise al descubrimiento de la
30   costa del Mar del Norte y boca del Rio Brauo

[folio 46v]

los fundamentos y motibos que para ello hubo con
todo lo suzedido en el, cantidad de jente, caballos y va-
gaxe [etcetera].

¶ Hauiendo el señor marques de San Miguel de Aguayo,
5   gouernador y capitan general de este Nuebo Reyno de Leon reze-
uido en 8 del mes de junio despacho del excelentisimo señor virrey
de la Nueba España este año de 1686, en que le encar-
ga que, por la noticia que le han dado los oficiales reales
de la ciudad de la Vera Cruz que los franzeses estaban
10   poblados en la Baia del Espiritu Santo y que estaba
sei(^?)s o siete jornadas de este reyno, que se hiziese
descubrimiento por esta parte y se ynquiriese la verdad
con toda yndiuidualidad para poner el remedio que com-
biniese, mandando hazer junta el dia onze de dicho mes
15   en la ciudad de Monterrey, cabezera de dicho reyno, anti-
cipando el auiso a todas las juri(^?)sdicciones, y siruiendose de
llamarme para dicha junta, que fecha, se resoluio
hazer la dicha jornada para el dia veinte y cinco del
dicho mes de julio [sic],[1] saliendo este dia de la dicha ciudad
20   de Monterrey vna compañia de treinta soldados, que
hauia de conduzir el capitan Nicolas Ochoa asta la
villa de Cadereyta; y que se alistase otra en la jurisdiccion
de dicha villa que conduxese el capitan Antonio Leal; y que
su señoria vaxaria de la ciudad dicho dia a ella para que
25   pasasen muestra y se entregasen a los capitanes que nom-
braria; y que dichas dos compañias fuesen a mi cargo,

1. This is obviously a scribal error. The copyist wrote "julio" 'July' instead of "junio" 'June.' The
expedition started on June 26, as is attested on the same folio.

aziendome en esto merzed mas por su grandeza que

no por mis meritos; y dispuesto todo en la forma refe-

rida fue su señoria seruido baxar de la ciudad

30   de Monterrey con la dicha compania el dia 26

[folio 47r]

de junio, delatandose este dia mas de lo propuesto

por los accidentes de las aguas que vbo. Y este mismo

dia llegue a dicha villa con la compa[ñ]ia de los veinte

soldados de la dicha jurisdiccion, la qual y la de Monterrey

5   se juntaron zerca de dicha villa para que el dia siguiente,

27, pasasen muestra; que hauiendose juntado dicho

dia en la dicha villa con toda orden militar en forma

de marcha, y teniendo dicho señor marques los titulos

echos de los capitanes, aferez y sarxentos para

10   entregarlos por su mano a los electos, mando pasar

la dicha muestra en su presencia, que se hizo en la

manera siguiente:

¶ Passo la compañia que conduxo de la dicha ciudad

de Monterrey el capitan Nicolas Ochoa con los

15   soldados de ella y su jurisdiccion, en la forma siguiente:

Primeramente al pasar el susodicho, saco su señoria

el titulo de capitan, fecho en Carlos Cantu, el qual

mando leer en alta boz y se lo entrego y fueron pasan-

do por sus yleras a caballo los soldados en esta forma:

20   el dicho capitan Carlos Cantu

el alferez Diego Rodriguez

el sarxento Nicolas Ochoa

el sarxento mayor Lucas Caballero

el capitan Nicolas Garzia

25   el sarxento Lorenzo de Ayala

el sarxento Gaspar de Lerma

Gonzalo de Treuiño

el sarxento Juan de la Garza

Jacinto de la Garza

[folio 47v]

Joseph de Treuiño

Francisco de la Garza

Joseph de la Garza

Alonso Garzia de Quintanilla

5   Marcos Flores
     Alonsso de Olibares
     Andres Fern*andez* Tijerina
     Nicolas de Montaluo
     Juan Perez de la Garza
10   Fran*cisc*o de la Garza
     Juan de la Garza
     Diego Martin
     Joseph Perez
     Antonio Perez
15   Joseph Gonzalez
     Fran*cisc*o Gonzalez
     Matheo de Peña
     Santiago de Leon
     Nicolas Cantu
20   Y suzesibamente passo muestra la compañía de
     di*c*ha villa de Cadereyta conduzida por el capitan
     Antonio Leal, la qual entrego al capitan Nicolas
     de Medina, capitan electo de ella, cuio titulo se
     leyo y entrego, y fueron pasando en esta forma:
25   el di*c*ho capitan Nicolas de Medina
     el alferez Thomas de la Garza
     el sarx*en*to Miguel de Leon
     Alonso de Leon, el mozo
     el sarx*en*to Lorenzo de la Garza
[folio 48r]
     el sarxento Juan Cantu
     el sarxento Agustin Garzia
     el sarxento Thomas Cantu
     Joseph Gutierrez
5   Sebastian de Villegas
     Fran*cisc*o Falcon
     Lucas de Betancur
     Fran*cisc*o de Escamilla
     Luis Perez
10   Nicolas de Lira
     Miguel Gonzalez
     Mathias de Herrera
     Santiago de la Garza.

Pasada la muestra en esta forma, su señoria entrego
15   los titulos de alferez y sarxentos a las personas elec-
tas de la compañía de Monterrey: alferez Diego
Rodriguez y sarxento Nicolas Ochoa, el mozo (^??).
De la compa[ñ]ia de la villa de Cadereyta: alferez Thomas de la Garza y sarxento Miguel de Leon.
20   Assimismo fue pasando el bagaxe de las dos compañias en esta forma:
quarenta cargas de bastimento: entre arina, vizcocho, carne y chocolate; quatrocientos y sesenta y ocho caballos; arrieros, mozos de seruicio
25   y paxes de estas compañias:
Diego Monita
Pasqual de Gumendio
Matheo Esteban

[folio 48v]

Juan Rodriguez
Juan de Olibarez
Juan de Villagran
Juan Rendon
5   Thomas de Torres
Nicolas de Losa
Mathias de Munguia
Juan Cabazos
Christobal de Auila
10   Juan de Ochoa
Bernabe de la Garza
Miguel
Juan
Joseph
15   Juan
Alonso, yndio capitan de la rancheria zacatil, nues-
tro guia; Bernabe, yndio; Matheo, yndio.
  ¶ Despues de lo qual su señoria mando leer mi titu-
lo en que fue seruido nombrarme por cauo de estas com-
20   pañias con plena comision y ynstrucion y nombro por
capellan al padre presidente de esta villa, fray Diego
de Orosco y me agrego su senoria a don Pedro Fer-
min de Echeberz, su hermano; al alferez Francisco

de Benauides; y Juan Baptista Chapa. Este mismo dia
25   veinte y siete de junio, juebes, pasada la muestra, sali
con el real a dormir al puesto que llaman de San Diego,
que esta quatro leguas en distansia de dicha villa arrimado al rio, tierra llana, al rumbo del leste.

    ¶ Viernes 28 de junio sali con el real a dormir
30   mas aca del Rio de San Juan en vnos charcos, camino
[folio 49r]

    llano aunque hubo como vna legua de montecillos. Ca-
mino el real este dia ocho leguas al rumbo del leste.

    ¶ Sabado 29 de junio sali con el real al rumbo del nordes-
te llebando la mira a vn zerrito punteagudo que esta co-
5   mo media legua mas aca del Rio de San Juan, el camino algo montuoso aunque penetrable. Llegamos
al passo del rio que fue mui bueno, anduuimos dos leguas
mas despues de hauerlo pasado; anduuimos este dia 4 leguas al
nordeste.

10   ¶ Domingo 30 de junio sali con el real, siendo nezesario andar al rumbo de sueste como legua y media, por no poder
atrabesar vn monte grande; anduuimos cinco leguas lo
mas al leste quarta al nordeste. Paramos este dia en vnos
charcos de agua zerca de la rancheria de mis yndios. El
15   rio enderezo azia el norte por esta parte.

    ¶ Lunes 1º de julio salimos del dicho puesto y fuimos la
derrota de leste y quarta al nordeste, tierra llana; anduuimos distancia de seis leguas; paramos en vnos charcos en
tierra llana; el agua de ellos es llobediza como la de los de-
20   mas que ban mencionados.

    ¶ Martes 2 de julio, dia de la Visitacion de Nuestra Señora, sa-
limos con quarenta y quatro yndios, Caurames de nacion, que
se nos juntaron el dia antes, y la noche dicha hauian
espiado vna rancheria de enemigos suios; y por ver si podia
25   coxer dos yndios para guia, me adelante con veinte hombres; deuieron de tener auiso y la hauian desamparado.
Este dia caminamos lo mas la derrota del norte y nordeste ocho leguas; nos dio razon el yndio Alonso que
el Rio Grande estaba zerca. No pudo el real con las cargas
30   y caballada penetrar vn monte grande por lo qual paramos en vna cieneguilla. Penetre por vn ailadero el dicho

monte, que fue vien penoso, a no mas de dos leguas

[folio 49v]

al rio, que ba en esta parte vien ancho y mui turbia el agua.
A lo que pareze es nabegable con em[b]arcacion pequeña;
no hubo forma de sondearlo; tiene de ancho vn tiro de arcabuz y corre en esta parte azia el norte.

5   ¶ Miercoles tres de julio. no hallando passo fue forzoso ∧(aunque con mucho trabaxo∧) pasar con el real el monte espesso;
no anduuimos mas que dos leguas este dia porque dispusse
salir a la lixera, a reconozer el rumbo por donde hauiamos
de yr el siguiente dia. Sali con efecto con doze compañeros

10   y yendo el rio abaxo topamos ynpensadamente con vna
rancheria bazia de jente que hauiendonos sentido, la hauian desamparado y dexado todas sus alaxas, que mande
no se les llegase a cossa. Voluimos a seguir el rio abaxo y vimos como algunos yndios y yndias lo yban pasand[o] a nado,

15   como con efecto lo pasaron; y aunque los llame de paz, no
pude conseguir viniese ninguno, antes si vno se benia a lo
mas angosto a flecharnos, a menos de tiro de arcabuz, con que
discurrimos que no hauian visto españoles, pues no temia el
tiro de arcabuz. El rumbo fue al leste.

20   ¶ Juebes 4 de julio sali con el real al rumbo del nordeste distancia de quatro leguas: paramos en vna laguna y cañada
apartados del rio como vna legua, porque el rio en lo mas
tiene montes mui espesos en su orilla. Passe con doze compañeros a la lixera a reconozer el dicho rio, que por su mu-

25   cho monte fue nezesario andar tres leguas para reconozer-
lo. En esta parte ba mui ancho y a lo que pareze [es] nabegable;
lleba mucha corriente, no vbo forma de ber puesto a proposito para que pudiese la caballada baxar a beber.
¶ Viernes 5 de julio caminamos quatro leguas azia el leste,

30   pasando vn ailadero de media legua, auierto a mano de
los yndios; paramos junto al rio y vnas lomas largas;
la caballada beuio con dificultad; es nabegable de embar-
cacion pequeña. Sali con diez compañeros a la lijera

[folio 50r]

a descubrir la tierra; segui vna bereda que se encamino
en vn monte tan espeso que no pudimos penetrar.
¶ Sauado 6 de julio sali con el real por el rumbo descuuier-

to el dia antes, pasando vn ailadero de vna lomita mui corto

5 y espesso; anduuimos quatro leguas por vn llano asta que topamos vna cienega seca que a tener agua fuera imposible,
llena de hoios y descomodidades. No hallamos salida a vn monte que se nos ofrecio; seguimos vna cañada asta que se
diuidio en dos y seguimos la del rumbo del norte asta que

10 llegamos al rio con dificultad por los muchos jarales
espinosos que tiene. Hubo estremado abrebadero; pareze menos nabegable y con menos agua que en lo antes visto. Sali
con vnos compañeros a buscar salida para el siguiente dia
y ver si allaba algun yndio para guia; ai muchas beredas

15 aunque no trilladas. Anduuimos este dia al rumbo del
nordeste.

¶ Domingo 7 salimos al rumbo del nordeste a vista del
rio; hubo algunos montes que desechar; fuimos a topar el
rio que pareze nabegable; proseguimos a su orilla como vna

20 legua asta vnos arboles grandes que estan en vn llano, donde
hallamos vn aguaxe pequeño que parecio manantial. De aquí
sali con doze compañeros a buscar passo para el siguiente
dia. Diuisamos vnas lomas largas, suuimos a la mas alta;
diuisamos grandes llanos y el rio como en distancia de dos

25 leguas. Me quede en esta loma con siete compañeros con
yntencion de dormir en ella aquella noche; y antes que se pu-
siera el sol se fueron apareciendo como quarenta yndios que, assi que los diuisamos, suuimos a caballo y ellos
echaron a juir. Les dexe vn paño blanco, vizcocho, tabaco

30 y otras cossas y me vine al real. Anduuimos seis leguas
este dia a lesnordeste.

¶ Lunes 8 salimos por el rumbo de lesnordeste por el rastro
[folio 50v]
del dia antes. Me adelante con veinte compañeros por si
podiamos coxer algun yndio de los del dia antes, y a
distancia de tres leguas ∧(pasando por la loma del dia antes,
donde hauia dexado el paño y demas cossas, las quales ha-

5 llamos en el mismo lugar∧) salieron zerca de vn monte como
cinquenta de ellos. Les hize muchas carizias y no quiso venir
ninguno. Les puse en vn arbolito vn paño y vn cuchillo de mi
estuche y me retire, y con efecto lo vinieron a coxer, y en
recompensa de ello me rebolearon vna bandera de plumas

10   y pusieron vn plumero para que lo coxiese, aziendo señas
      lo fuese a coxer como lo hize. Fui siguiendo el rumbo, y
      siempre nos fueron siguiendo, amparados del monte. Anduui-
      mos este dia ocho leguas por diferentes rumbos, lo mas al
      leste, y topando vn monte espesso y no hallando agua, nos fue
15   forzoso voluer atras tres leguas a buscar el rio, que lo
      hallamos con buen abrebadero aunque menos nabegable.
      ¶ Martes 9 de julio fue nezesario parar con el real en estte
      paraxe del rio. Sali con veinte y cinco compañeros a descu-
      brir la tierra para el dia siguiente. Me fue nezesario andar
20   ocho leguas para dar con el, en cuia orilla ay muchos montes
      espesos que salen a llano tres y quatro leguas, y sin hallar-
      se otro aguaxe, despache seis compañeros el dia mier-
      coles siguiente para que saliese el real y siguiese nuestro
      rastro.
25   ¶ Miercoles 10 salio el real por el rastro, guiando los sol-
      dados que despache, y poco antes de empezar a aparexar la
      requa, dieron alarido de la otra vanda del rio como treinta
      yndios, aziendo señas que se viniesen o que se hauian de
      juntar y matarnos a todos. Tocaban dos flautas, y
30   hauiendo salido poco trecho, salio otra esquadra como
      de sesenta; aunque nunca acometieron, siguieron el real
      asta vn llano, en donde hauia vn gran rastro, donde
[folio 51r]
      al parezer se juntaron a algun baile mas de trecientos
      yndios. Paro el real en vn llano sin agua, como cinco leguas
      anduuimos al rumbo de lessueste este dia.
      ¶ Juebes 11 salio el real por mi rastro y llego a distancia de tres
5   legua[s] rumbo del lesncrdeste al rio, donde los estaba espe-
      rando; ba en esta parte mui ancho y nabegable de pequeña
      embarcacion, aunque con demasiada corriente; la tierra fue
      llana y a lo que se pudo duisar nos pronosticamos buen cami-
      no para el siguiente dia.
10   ¶ Viernes 12 de julio salio el real del rio; me adelante con
      quinze compañeros a buscar derrota; allamos vn estero que
      haze el rio en distancia de seis leguas al rumbo del les-
      sueste; parado el real, volvi a salir con doze compañeros a bus-
      car passo para el dia siguiente y a distancia de quatro
15   leguas hallamos dos lagunas de sal, aunque no la hauia

por hauer poco que hauia llouido. Tiene la vna legua y
media de largo y media de ancho; el agua es mui salada
que no se pudo beber.

¶ Sauado 13 de julio salio el real del estero donde durmio
20 y lo encamine al principio por el rumbo del dia antes, y anduuimos este dia diferentes rumbos distancia de quatro leguas
aunque lo mas al lessueste. Pare con el real junto al
rio zerca de vn gran rastro que dexo vna rancheria de
yndios que hauia quinze dias que la hauian despoblado. Aquí
25| hallamos vna duela de barril. Sobre tarde me adelante con
veinte y ocho compañeros por juzgarme ya mui zerca de la
mar. Anduuimos seis leguas con mucho recato, buscando
siempre el rio, y a las seis de la tarde ynpensadamente dimos
en vna rancheria de yndios, que por hauernos diuisado, tuuie-
30 ron lugar de desampararla. Con que no se coxieron mas que
tres yndias, que acariciadas y preguntadas por zeñas don-
[folio 51v]
donde hauia españoles y jente bestida, señalaron la parte
del norte y que hauia en dos partes, con que discurri no
los habria en la boca del rio que seguiamos por caer a leban-
te. Nombraron muchas vezes los dos puestos donde estaban
5 diziendo se llamaban Taguili el mas zercano al norueste y el otro al norte Zaguili ∧(decian en su ydioma,
sin duda∧). No supieron dar razon de las distancias, aunque hizimos dilijencias, porque ni aun por conxeturas nos enten-
dian ni las entendiamos. Hallamos en esta rancheria vn
10 pedazo de fondo de pipa, vn perno de nauio quebrado, vn
eslabon de cadena y vn pedazillo de vidrio y no otra ala-
xa alguna. Quedeme esta noche con los compañeros a dormir
orillas del rio, y con el sosiego de ella se hoio el bramido de la
mar.
15 ¶ Domingo 14, dia de San Buenabentura, despache quatro {LM} 4
soldados a que saliese el real y viniese caminando a parte señalada. Passe con los demas compañeros a descubrir
la mar, venciendo cienegas, carrizales, espesuras de mimbres
y montes espessos de la orilla del rio; y a distancia de dos leguas
20 lo hallamos azia al nordeste; y andubo este dia quatro
leguas el real. No hubo bestijio de hauer jamas llegado a esta
boca del rio españoles ni estranxeros. Costee vna legua para

llegar a dicha boca. Entra mui turuio en la mar, como vna legua
de distancia la mar adentro el agua es de color bermexo; tiene
25   la boca de ancho vn tiro de mosquete poco mas. Mande hazer
vna balssa y sondear en cinco o seis partes, y la mas honda
fue de siete brazas y media y ocho; con que puede entrar
nao de alto bordo, a lo que pareze, como dos leguas a dentro.
Este dia costee la orilla de la mar quatro leguas azia el
30   Rio de Palmas; vbo algunos rastros de yndios fresco[s] y algunos
palos parados en distintas partes donde hauian estado
rancheados, aunque de mucho tiempo, no se hallara en

[folio 52r]

toda esta orilla vna piedra. La costa corre norte a sur,
algo mas al nordeste; la mar es mui braba, aunque no hace
viento. Ai en su orilla muchos sauinos, pinos, palmas y otates
gruesos como vna pierna y otros mas que ha echado la mar.
5   La costa es mui limpia, sin peñasco alguno, y mui anda-
ble la orilla a caballo, que no se atascan; creze y mengua
mas de vn estado.
      ¶ Lunes 15 de julio estando en la misma boca del rio en el pun-
to del mediodia, se tomo la altura de sol con astrolauio y
10   se hallo en veinte y cinco grados y quarenta y cinco minutos
de altura de norte ^(saluo yerro por estar el astrolauio, a lo que
pareze mal apuntado y algo descompuesto^). Por el poco pasto
dispuse saliese el real despues de mediodia asta donde
alcanzase aquel dia, y que el siguiente parase en el este-
15   ro donde estubo el dia sauado. Y yo con veinte y cinco
soldados passe a reconozer de nuebo la costa azia el Rio
de Palmas en distancia de mas de ocho leguas, en la qual
hallamos alguna tablazon de costado de nauio, bergas, maste-
leros y pedazos de quilla de timon, fondos de pipas, due-
20   las, boias y quatro ruedecillas de pieza de artilleria, vna
pipa con los aros de mimbre, tres canoas quebradas, vna
redomita de vidr[i]o redonda, mui gruesa, tapada con vn
corcho que, destapada, alle en ella vn poco de vino ya co-
rrupto. El vidr[i]o es mui bis[to]so y pareze no fue labrada
25   en los reynos de Castilla segun su forma. Y finalmente hubo
en esta orilla de todo jenero de madera y ruinas de nauios,
con que sin duda zozobraron algunos en ella por la diuirsi-
dad de dichas ruinas y la madera ser vna mas antigua que la

otra. Lo que mas me admiro fue ber algunas cañas de maiz

30   que traia la resaca de la mar, al parezer de la siembra de este
año que comenzaba a jilotear, con sus raizes las cañas,
sobre que discurri que ay alguna poblazon zercana y que

[folio 52v]

alguna abenida les llebo alguna milpa.

    ¶ Martes 16 sali de zerca de la orilla de la mar en busca del
real y no pude atrabesar vnas lagunas ni pasar vnos atolladeros, con que fue forzoso boluer al camino de la orilla de la

5   mar y salir por el rastro en su busca. No le alcanze aquel
dia.

    ¶ Miercoles 17 de julio llegue al real temprano y por lo maltratado de la caballada, no pasamos aquel dia. Lo halle en el estero
donde paro el viernes 12 de este presente mes. Esta distante el estero

10   de la mar ocho leguas.

    ¶ Juebes 18 sali con el real asta el rio distancia de seis leguas
largas.

    ¶ Viernes 19 fui con el real a parar al manantial del llano, donde
paramos a la yda el domingo 7 del corriente. Anduuimos este

15   dia onze leguas, hauiendolas andado en tres a la yda. Hubo muchos rastros de yndios que se encaminaban al passo del rio en donde nos amenazaron.

    ¶ Sauado 20 salimos del puesto de arriba y venimos a dormir
con el real adelante del mal abrebadero del rio en vna lomita

20   sin agua. Anduuimos ocho leguas.

    ¶ Domingo 21 salimos de la lomita, venimos a dormir zerca de
la rancheria donde nos flecharon los yndios, y diuisando algunos, acometimos a ellos, hauia mas de cinquenta. Queriendo coger
vno el sarxento mayor Lucas Caballero se metio en vn chaparro y le

25   tiro vn flechazo que se metio la flecha debaxo de la tetilla
por no tener cota. Mataronse dos, se coxieron dos muchachos. Anduuimos ocho leguas.

    ¶ Lunes 22 de julio salimos de este puesto; anduuimos cinco leguas;
salimos por el hailadero espesso por donde descubrimos el rio.

30   Por escusar mucho camino, quisimos benir por otro rumbo y nos
lo ympidio otra laguna. Dormimos en vn llano y charcos de
agua.

    ¶ Martes 23 de julio sali con el real por diferentes rumbos
del que vine, por hauer entonzes baxado mucho a dar

[folio 53r]

en la rancheria de los Paxaritos. Anduuimos siete leg*uas*
largas; paramos en el charco de las Calaberas.

¶ Miercoles 24 sali con el real del d*i*cho puesto pasando por su
rancheria de los Caurames, quienes nos estaban esperando en el
5   camino; benimos a pasar en el passo del Rio de San Juan. Anduuimos doze leguas.

¶ Juebes 25 de julio salimos del d*i*cho puesto, venimos al real de San
Simon, de alli pasamos al real de San Diego. Vbo de distancia
cartorze leguas.

10   ¶ Viernes 26 estando en d*i*cho real, llego la orden de su señoria
para que las compañias fuesen a descansar y estuuiesen
aperciuidos, para assi que fuese nezesario voluer a salir. En
descansando la caballada, por hauer benido maltratada, pasamos a la villa este dia, y yo luego a dar quenta al *señor* marques

15   de la jornada. Fecha en Cadereyta en 27 de julio de 1686 años,
Alonso de Leon.

53

en la Rancheria delos Pajaritos anduimos siete leg.s
largas paramos en el Charco delas Calabazas =
Miercoles 24 sali con el Real del dho puesto pasando por el
Rancheria delos Cauzanes quienes nos estauan esperando en el
camino benimos a gazar en el paso del Rio de San Juan anduui
mos doze Leguas =
Jueves 25 de Julio salimos del dho puesto benimos al Real auan
Simon de alli pasamos al Real de San Diego Ra de distancia
Catorze Leguas =
Viernes 26 estando en dho Real llego la orden de su Señoria
para quelas Compañias fuesen a descansar y estubiesen
apercibidos para asi que fuese necesario boluer a salir en
descansando la Cauallada por hauerse venido maltratada para
mos ala Villa ese dia y lo luego a dar quenta al S.r Marques
de la Jornada fha en Cadereyta en 27 de Julio de 1686 a.s
Alonso de Leon =

                Cap.o 32 en que se ban prosiguiendo
                Los Sucesos en adelante =

El Marques de San Miguel de Aguayo siempre estubo
firme en la opinion de que los franceses estauan poblados
en el mar del norte y asi dispuso que se repitiese jornada
por la otra Vanda del Rio hauiendo pasando por la Villa de
Tizalotes por estar ya Ausencia de esto este Reyno tener
buen lado a distancia de Veinte leguas de ella formo a
principio del año de 87 tres Compañias las ha hecho cargo
del S.r Martin de Mendiondo. La otra de Don Pedro
fermin de echeleza y la terzera del Capitan Nicolas de
Medina y por Cauo Principal el General Alonso de Leon
que salieron desta Ciud.d a fin de febrero y a los Veinte de Marzo
llegaron ala Costa del mar atravesando por muchas naciones
de Indios belicosos que le dieron aviso en que entender
aun anduuieron bajando por diferentes Costas hasta hallar
ron poblazon de franceses ni quien les pudiese dar noticia

2.3 Manuscript 87-A

[folio 53r continued]

{HD} Capitulo 32 en que se ban prosiguiendo / los suzesos en adelante

    El marques de San Miguel de Aguaio siempre estubo

    firme en la opinion de que los franzeses estaban poblados

    en el Mar del Norte; y assi dispuso que se repitiese jornada

20   por la otra vanda del Rio Brauo, pasando por la villa de

    Zerraluo, por estar ya reconocido por este reyno tener

    buen bado a di[s]tancia de veinte leguas de ella. Formo a

    principios del año de 87 tres compañias; la una fue a cargo

    del jeneral Martin de Mendiondo; la otra de don Pedro

25   Fermin de Echeberz; y la terzera del capitan Nicolas de

    Medina; y por cauo principal el jeneral Alonso de Leon,

    que salieron de esta ciudad a fin de febrero, y a los veinte de marzo

    llegaron a la costa del mar atrabesando por muchas nasiones

    de yndios belicosos que le dieron arto en que entender, y

30   aun anduuieron bagando por diferentes rumbos. No halla-

    ron poblazon de franzeses ni quien le pudiese dar noticias

[folio 53v]

    antes si les ympidio un rio grande salado el que pudiese pa-

    sar azia el norte; con que quedaron frust[r]adas las esperanzas

    del descubrimiento con arto sentimiento de todos y maiormente

    del dicho marques, quien deseaba que en su tiempo se descu-

5   briese vna cossa que tanto ciudado hauia costado, y que

    ya se le yba acabando el gouierno, respecto a que hauia em-

    uiado a hazer dexacion d'el a su majestad para pasarse a España,

    como con efecto, hauiendolo conseguido el dicho año de ochenta

    y siete, probeio el señor conde de la Moncloua por governador ynte-

10   rino al general don Francisco Cuerbo de Baldes, cauallero mon-

    tañez de mui buenas prendas, que entro a su gouierno por

    el mes de septiembre; en cuio gouierno, que fue poco mas de

    nuebe meses, tuuieron mucha suxecion los indios, mediante

    a que fue anticipada prebencion de que para conserbarse

15   las haciendas, assi de minas como de labores, era medio muy

    nezesario el temor y castigo con esta jente natural.

con los Indios donde le allamos ó si el ay²d a la d̄ha poblaçion aber los y en
las ocasiones que le tinieron a ber diga y declare lo que le comunicaban ?
consultaban y a que Intento Venian aque² Vbo de que desde que bino Ir
a aque² con los Indios donde le ballamos no a id̄o a la d̄ha poblaçion pero
que los de ella si le an benido a ber como lo hizieron a tiempo de Vn año que
tinieron diez y seis franzes con el Capitan Monsiur Vaxe a bisitarle ? que
aora dos mes² pos mas tinieron otros al mismo efecto con solo ocasion de
comunicar con el con tenido el estado que tenia en la agreaçion de los Indios
y que no comunicaban otra cosa nin guna y esto Respon de =
Pregunta do si el puesto y sitio de la d̄ha poblaçion y su ar cadio es tierra llana ó ai
tierras ó algunas Lomas Çienegas o laguñas que Impidan Llegar a ella Dixo que
todo es tierra llana y sin ningun Impedim̄ para poder Llegar a ella y que es mui
a proposito para su semen tera y aun que se le pregunto si Sauia ojos de agua
ó arroios con que Regaban las sementeras no supo dar razon de ello y esto Respon
de = fuerõ le f̄ā otras pregunta y Representas al caso tocante y pertenecien
te por medio del d̄ho yntessete y dixo que no saue otra cosa y que es la ber̄, se
cargo del husam̄ que se tiene en que leiendole su conferion se afirmo y Ratifico ?
Leiendole que firmase y sauiendo ynstançia para ello se escuso con decir que no
sauia ni lo firmo el ynterprete por que dixo no sauia ni lo firmo el ynterprete
por que dixo no sauia firmelo yo d̄ho gobern̄ con dos t̄ē, de mi asistençia =

                                        tt̄, Joseph Anto de Leai Z Murguin
   A d̄o Alonso de leon
                                              tt̄, Joseph gutieres

ausso =   En el pueblo de n̄ s̄ra Sr̄ā de coauquela en nueve dias del mes de Junio de mil s̄cos ochenta
          y ocho años El General Alonso de Leon gobern̄, y cap̄n, del sur² d̄o de esta probinçia ā
          uiendo hecho la declar, y conferion fa por fran̄, de naçion franzes y por otro nombre
          monsiur San Jase su socorio y los demas autor de esta Causa y que de ellos Reruba
          la certidumbre de la poblaçion de los franzes en el n̄o ar de abaxo del espiritu santo
          mando que estos autos y el d̄ho pleso se remitan al ex̄mo, S̄r, conde de la Monclova
          Virei y Capitan Seneral de la nueba españa y presidente de la Real aud̄ienḡa de
          ella para que su ex̄a, con bista de ellos disponga lo que fuere seru²d̄o y en estas
          fronteras se ponga toda la guard̄a custod̄ia y Vixilançia necesaria por lo que
          puede Resultar de la proion del d̄ho franzes y la alteraçion que pabra causa
          do a los Indios de su sequito y deuocion y lo firme con dos t̄ē, de mi asistençia =

   Alonso de leon   tt̄, Joseph Antones de
                                                 Leay Z Murguin
          tt̄, Joseph Gutieres

                              42

2.4 Manuscript 88-A

[folio 17r]

{LM} Auto p*ar*a la / salida a / buscar al / frances

25   ¶ En el pueblo de San Fran*ci*sco de Coauguila juri*sdiccio*n de la Nueba Es-
tremadura, en diez y ocho dias del mes de maio de mil seis*cien*tos ochenta
y ocho años, el jeneral Alonso de Leon, gober*na*dor y capitan del
presidio de esta di*c*ha probincia, digo que por quanto hauiendo llegado a este di*c*ho pueblo de vna jornada a que sali contra los yndios

30   rebelados a la Real Corona y castigado los que pudieren ser
auidos en la refriega que se tuuo con ellos ∧(hauiendo pre-
cedido el hauer emuiado vn yndio tlascalteco llamado Agustin

[folio 17v]

de la Cruz, que viue en la poblacion que llaman la Boca de los
Leones, a que juntase toda la jente amiga que pudiese para salir
con ella al castigo de los di*c*hos yndios, que no vino en tiempo para
el di*c*ho efecto∧). Por lo qual, hauiendo llegado y allado al di*c*ho Agus-

5   tin en este di*c*ho pueblo, me hizo relacion diziendo que hauia llegado de la otra banda del Rio Brauo a ber si podia conbocar algunas
naciones para lo que se le hauia enconmendado, topo con vna gran
rancheria con mucho numero de yndios donde hauia vna auitacion
echa en forma de vna sala grande techada de cueros de ciuola;

10   y que los yndios que estaban alrededor de ella, assi que llego, le
hizieron apear y lo metieron dentro y le hizieron yncar de rodillas
para que hablase a vn hombre que estaba alli dentro, lo qual hizo, y diuiso a vno de buena estatura y de color mui blanco que le parecio español, el qual estaba sentado en vn estrado vien adornado

15   de di*c*hos cueros de ciuola, de edad al parezer de cinquenta años, en-
trecano, raiado el rostro en diferentes partes, y que los yndios lo tenian en gran beneracion; por lo qual este declarante le hizo gran acatam*ien*to
y cortesia saludando*l*e en su lengua materna de di*c*ho Agustin y que no le respondio cosa alguna, por lo qual se balio de vno de los yndios que estaban

20   con el contenido y conc*c*ido suio que le siruio de ynterprete, con que el
di*c*ho hombre le correspondio, por medio de el, a la cortesia diziendole que el
hera franzes, y que de algun tiempo a esta parte estaba en aquel paraxe
agregando algunas naciones de yndios de aquella comarca para yr a
pelear con otros yndios enemigos que no se le querian agregar. Y que el

25   hera emuiado de Dios a fundar pueblos; y que a mi, di*c*ho general, me hauia
despachado yndios a llamar para que fuera con vn relixioso a berlo, y

que al dicho Agustin de la Cruz le dio seis yndios para que le acompaña-
sen asta el pueblo de la Caldera, los quales estan presentes, que me podran
seruir de guia para el dicho efecto; y que el dicho franzes le hauia quitado al
30   dicho Agustin el arcabuz que lleuaba, reteniendoselo como en prenda
        para que
boluiese; de todo lo qual el dicho Agustin me daba noticia para que yo
dispusiese lo que mas combenga. Y por mi vista su relacion, y que se recono-
ze que el dicho franzes solo aspira, con la congregacion que tiene de la dicha
jente y la demas que pretende agregar, fomentado quiza de algunos
[folio 18r]
de su nacion, para benir reconociendo toda la tierra y puestos de ella, y
buscando tiempo oportuno, hauisar a los suios para que benga alguna
tropa de ellos; y acompañandose con los yndios congregados, dar en estas
poblazones y destruirlas, que seria caso factible por las pocas fuerzas
5   con que oy se allan para la resistencia, pues solo se compone esta prob(^?)in-
cia de veinte y cinco soldados y algunos vecinos de los que an entrado para
la nueba fundacion en esta frontera de vna villa; y siendo el caso re-
(^[sig.] Alonso de Leon) pentino no se pudiera ocurrir al remedio por
la gran distancia que ai de poder benir socorro de la villa del Saltillo,
10   balle de Parras y Nuevo Reino de Leon, comarcas confinantes a esta dicha
frontera. Sobre que combiene poner el remedio mas eficaz y breue que para
euitar este peligro combenga y por la mala consequencia que se seguira
de las demas probincias de la Nueba España que fueran padeciendo la misma
ruina, y apoderandose assi los yndios enemigos como el franzes de todas ellas.
15   Por tanto mando se haga lista de diez y ocho hombres, los mas experimenta-
dos y vien armados que vbiere para salir en busca del dicho franzes y pren-
derle, quedando este puesto vien guarnecido con los demas soldados y jente
que quedare fuera de la dicha lista para que hagan la guardia y custodia
necesaria. Y assi lo probei, mande y firme con asistencia de dos ttestigos
20   por no hauer en esta probincia escribano publico ni real
{SIG} Alonso de Leon / ttestigo, {SIG} Joseph Antonio de / Ecay y Muzquiz /
ttestigo {SIG} Jose[p]h Gutierres.
[Auto 2]
        ¶ En dicho dia mes y año yo, dicho jeneral Alonso de Leon, en cumplimiento
          del au-
        to de arriba, y hauiendo prezedido la lista contenida en el, que fueron de
        todos los mas oficiales y soldados del Nueuo Reino de Leon del socorro
          que me

emuio el jeneral don Francisco Cuerbo de Baldes, gobernador y capitan
    jeneral de

25   el, y de mis hermanos, hixos y parientes que vinieron a aiudarme a las fac-
ciones de esta probincia, salimos oi dicho dia diez y ocho del corriente hazia
el rumbo del nordeste. Y a distancia de quarenta y dos leguas pasamos el Rio
Brauo y de alli, seguiendo el mismo rumbo como quinze leguas, hallamos
    cantidad
como de quinientos yncios, poco mas o menos, matando ciuolas para hazer

30   cecinas, y llegando a hablarles mediante ynterprete, les pregunte que donde
estaba vn hombre español, y me dieron por razon que estaba como en
    distancia

[folio 18v]
    de cinco o seis leguas de alli, señalando el mismo rumbo del nordeste, y
    que hera
caueza de ellos y los gobernaba y ellos le obedecian; y diziendole a vno de ellos
que me guiase adonde estaba el contenido, nos fue guiando asta donde
    tenia su
auitacion que estaba en la distancia de dichas cinco o seis leguas, y veinte
    del dicho

5   Rio Brauo. Diuisamos la poblacion que estaba en vn alto y bimos como
    los yndios ^(que
serian como trecientos^) se pusieron en forma de cuerpo de guardia;
    y hauiendo
llegado a la puerta de vna grande sala que estaba fabricada con cueros
    de ciuo-
la, estaban de posta quarenta y dos yndios con arcos y flechas. Y entrando
dentro la hallamos mui aseada, barrida y limpia, y en frente de la puerta

10   estaban tres asientos de cueros de ciuola mui vien aderezados y peinados,
y en el del medio estaba [^sentado] el franzes de que me dio relacion el
    yndio tlascal-
teco Agustin de la Cruz, reconociendo en el las mismas señas y estatura que
contiene la dicha relacion. Y en el dicho asiento tenia como forma de
    almoadas
echas de ciuola y dos yndios ^(al parecer los mas principales^) que le
    asistian

15   cada vno por su lado. Y hauiendo llegado zerca de el el padre capellan que
llebamos, fray Buenabentura Bonal, relijioso de la horden de San Francisco,
yo y el jeneral don Martin de Mendiondo, no hizo mas accion, sin salir de su

asiento, que yncarse de rodillas y besar la manga de auito del relejioso. Y a mi y
al dicho jeneral con mucha cortesia nos dio la mano y poniendola luego en

20   el pecho dixo repetidas vezes: yo franzes, afirmando en esto que hera de aquella nacion. Y en lengua castellana me pregunto que quantos heramos los que
beniamos [??], a que le dixe que muchos y que maior numero quedaba
     atrás de re-
taguardia zerca de alli; con cuias razones quedo como suspenso y confuso.
     Y en este
tiempo, por la prebencion que yo hauia lleuado de alguna ropa, naguas,
     guipiles,
25   cuchillos, zarzillos, quentas y rosarios y tabaco para repartir a los yndios
por agregarlos a mi deuocion, saque las dichas cosas y se las entregue al
     dicho fran-
zes para que por su mano lo repartiese a los yndios, como lo hizo;
     hauiendo pre-
cedido a esto el adbertir a los soldados estuuiesen a cauallo porque
     dentro de
la dicha sala no entramos mas que el dicho relijioso, yo y dicho jeneral
     don Martin
30   [^de Mendiondo]. Y a lo que reconoci, el dicho franzes saue mui vien la
     lengua materna de los
yndios con quien estaba congregado. Y le exsamine por medio de ynterprete,
que lo fue vn yndio en lengua mexicana, y a quien le adberti le dixese que
lo hauia de llebar conmigo asta el Rio Brauo, donde hauia dexado vn franzes que le hablaria en su lengua, y consultariamos lo que combinie-
35   se, y que de alli bolueria a su hauitacion. A lo qual se resistio mucho y
[folio 19r]
     lo resistieron los yndios que tenia asistentes, por lo qual viendo estta
     resistencia y que aunque el empeño hera graue y peligroso el traerlo por
     fuerza, y que arresgaba en el tod[a] la compañía, y que hauia mas de
          mil yndi-
     os de arco y flecha que nos podian acometer, por modos suaues y cortesias
5   le hize ynstancia a que viniese conmigo. Y, siempre resistiendose, lo
     sacamos con arte y yndustria de la auitacion en que estaba, poniendonos a co-
     nocido riesgo, pues los dichos yndios le asistian con tanta hobediencia,
          respec-
     to y beneracion que se yncaban de rodillas delante de el, y en la auitacion
     le hazian aire con abanicos de pluma y le limpiaban el sudor, zaumaban la

10 auitacion con seuo de tenado y otras cosas no conocidas, teniendola mui
    enrrama-
    da. Y notamos la forma y disposicion que tenian los dichos yndios en
    modo de
    milicia con sus capitanes y todo con mucha vixilancia. Vimos en la dicha aui-
    tacion vn arcabuz que aunque quebrado se reconocia hauer sido largo co-
    mo mosquete y vn frasco de poluora de baqueta negra y balas. Y
    preguntando-
15 le como se llamaba, dixo que Francisco y que es cristiano, pero que en su
    lengua
    se llama el capitan monsiur Yan Jarri, y que andaba juntando muchas nacio-
    nes de yndios para hazerlos sus amigos. Y que a los que por vien no se le agre-
    gaban los destruia y asolaba con aiuda de los yndios que tenia en su sequito,
    con lo qual aunque con resistencia suia y de los yndios, como queda dicho, lo
20 suuimos a cauallo con mucho sentimiento suio y de los dichos yndios a los
    quales
    bolui a acontentar repartiendoles algunos rezagos que me hauian quedado; y
    dandoles a entender que el llebarlo no era para hazerle ninguna bexacion ni
    agrauio, pues el ni ellos no lo hauian echo a ningunos españoles, sino porque
    el propio me hauia emuiado a llamar y tamuien porque lo queria ber el
25 excelentisimo señor virrei y el señor obispo para hablarle, bestirle y
    regalarle porque
    ya tenia noticia de su persona. Con lo qual, quedando sosegados, prosegui-
    mos la buelta de nuestro camino con el dicho prisionero asta este dicho
    puesto de
    San Francisco de Coauguila, y para que conste y proseguir las demas dilixen-
    cias que combengan en este casso, lo firme con dos ttestigos de mi asistencia
{SIG} Alonso de Leon / ttestigo {SIG} Joseph Antonio de / Ecay y Muzquiz /
ttestigo {SIG} Jose[p]h Gutierres.
[Auto 3]
{LM} declaracion del / prisionero fran- / zes
30   ¶ En el pueblo de San Francisco de Coauguila en siete dias del mes de junio
    de mil seiscientos ochenta y ocho años, el general Alonso de Leon, gobernador
[folio 19v]
    y capitan del presidio de esta dicha probincia, en conformidad del auto
    anteze-
    dente, hauiendo llegado a este dicho puesto oy dicho dia con el prisionero
    franzes

contenido en el y ser necesario para maior claridad y berificacion de lo contenido en el y aberiguar con yndiuidualidad si es cierta la poblacion de los
5   franzeses que se dize esta en la Baia del Espiritu Santo o en vno de los rios
que entran en la Mar del Norte, mande parezer ante mi a vn yndio llamado
Ygnacio, ladino en lengua mexicana y castellana, natural del pueblo de la
Caldera de esta gobernacion para que sirba de ynterprete para exsaminar
a Francisco, prisionero franzes que esta presente, por hablar en la lengua de los
10   yndios de la nacion en cuia compa[ñ]ia estaba, que entiende dicho ynterprete.
Para lo qual le receui juramiento que hizo por Dios Nuestro Señor y por
      la señal
de la cruz en forma de derecho, so cargo del qual prometio de decir verdad
de todo lo que supiere y le fuere preguntado en cuia conformidad receui
      su con-
fesion y el la hizo en la manera siguiente:
15   ¶ Preguntado como se llama, de donde es natural, que oficio tiene y de quien
es basallo, y que causa o motiuo tubo para benir a congregarse con los yndios
con quienes fue allado, por que rumbo vino y por cuio mandato y el tiempo que ha que asiste con ellos y que edad y estado tiene, dixo llamarse
Francisco, nombre que le pusieron en el bautismo, pero que sus paisanos le
20   llaman el capitan monsiur Yan Jarri y que lo es de vna compañía de las de
su nacion y es natural de San Juan de Orliens en el Reino de Francia.
Y que por mandado de monsiur Phelipe, gobernador de vna poblacion que
tienen echa orilla de vn rio grande, hauiendo este conferante aprendido la
lengua de los yndios, vino a la parte donde fue allado teniendo agregadas
25   ya otras naciones de yndios que estan en mas zercania de la dicha poblacion.
Y que el motiuo es yr reduciendo todas aquellas naciones a la hobediencia
del rei de Francia, y que es casado en dicha poblacion y tiene vna niña pequeña, y que habra tiempo de tres años que ha que se agrego con los dichos
yndios; no supo decir su edad, pareze por su aspecto de mas de cinquen-
30   ta años y esto responde.
      ¶ Preguntado que que tanto tiempo habra que los franzeses sus paisanos
      vinieron
a poblar el dicho rio y con quantas familias y en que embarcaciones y
quantas y con que pretesto, sauiendo que esta tierra es de la monarquia
[folio 20r]
del rei de España. A que responde ^(aunque lo mas dio a entender por de-
mostraciones y zeñas^) que habra tiempo de quinze años que vinieron a
dicha poblacion los franzeses ^(y no supo dar razon de quantas familias vinieron ni en quantas embarcaciones^); y que tienen dos castillos en vn rio

5   enfrente el vno del otro y el mas abentaxado y grande es del franzes. Y
tiene veinte piezas de artilleria cinco por cada lienzo y que el otro castillo es de flamencos. Y que ambos se comunican con canoas pasando el
rio de vna banda a otra por estar cada vno de la suia; y que por esta
parte del sur esta el del franzes; y que el de los flamencos no tiene piezas

10   de artilleria sino mosqueteria y es pequeño. Y la poblacion de los franzeses
esta mui vien resguardada con su castillo, pues este guarda y defiende
las cuatro calles que tiene la dicha poblacion; y que ai seis compañias
de soldados para su defensa, vna yglesia y combento de relejiosos ca-
puchinos con seis sazerdotes la yglesia mui buena y vien formada

15   y con vn canpanario con diez campanas y que de ordinario ay
tres nauios de comercio en la dicha poblacion que ban y vienen a Francia y les traen lo necesario y esto reponde.
     ¶ Preguntado si en la dicha poblacion y alrededor de ella tienen algunos
labores, estancias de ganados maiores y menores y cauallada, y que semi-

20   llas son las que siembran para su sustento, y si tienen yndios agrega-
dos que les aiudan a sembrar y coxer sus sementeras. Dixo que tiene
la dicha poblacion en su circuito labores donde siembran maiz y trigo
bastante para sustentarse, y cria de bacas y obexas, cauallada y mulas, y ataonas en que muelen el trigo para el gasto de la dicha poblaci-

25   on; y que assimismo siembran mucho tabaco, caña dulce, todo lo
qual hazen con la aiuda de muchos yndios que ya tienen reducidos
a su debocion. Y que para nabegar desde la poblacion para la costa del
mar tienen tamuien siete barcos de remo y bela, y que lo nabegan en
vn dia; y tamuien andan esta distancia por tierra a cauallo en tres

30   dias. Y preguntandole de que materia son formados los castillos,
dixo que de piedra y mezcla y que la piedra la traen de la costa y
esto responde.
     ¶ Preguntado si en algunas ocasiones los franzeses de la dicha poblacion
an benido a visitar a este conferante durante el tiempo que a estado

[folio 20v]
    con los yndios donde le allamos o si el a ydo a la dicha poblacion a berlos,
       y en
las ocasiones que le vinieron a ber, diga y declare lo que le comunicaban y
consultaban y a que yntento venian. A que responde que desde que bino y se
agrego con los yndios donde le hallamos no a ido a la dicha poblacion, pero

5   que los de ella si le an benido a ber como lo hizieron a tiempo de vn año que
vinieron diez y seis franzeses con el capitan Monsiur Jarri a visitarle, y que
aora dos meses poco mas vinieron otros al mismo efecto con solo ocasión de

comunicar con el contenido el estado que tenia en la agregacion de los yndios,
y que no comunicaban otra cosa ninguna y esto responde.

10 ¶ Preguntado si el puesto y sitio de la dicha poblacion y su circuito es tierra llana o ai

sierras o algunas lomas, cienegas o lagunas que ympidan llegar a ella. Dixo que

toda es tierra llana sin ningun ympedimiento para poder llegar a ella, y que es mui

a proposito para sus sementeras. Y aunque se le pregunto si hauia oxos de agua

o arroios con que regaban las simenteras no supo dar razon de ello y esto respon-

15 de. Fueronle fechas otras preguntas y repreguntas al caso tocantes y pertenecien-

tes por medio del dicho ynterprete y dijo que no saue otra cossa y que es la verdad so

cargo del juramiento que fecho tiene, en que leiendole su confesion se afirmo y ratifico; y

diziendole que firmase y haciendole ynstancia para ello, se escuso con decir que no

sauia. Ni lo firmo el ynterprete porque dixo no sauia, (ni lo firmo el ynterprete

20 porque dijo no sauia). Firmelo yo dicho gobernador con dos ttestigos, de mi asistencia.

{SIG} Alonso de Leon / ttestigo, {SIG} Joseph Anttonio de Ecai y Muzquiz / ttestigo {SIG} Jose[p]h Gutierres.

{LM} Autto [4]

¶ En el pueblo de San Francisco de Coauguila en siete dias del mes de junio de mil seiscientos ochenta

y ocho años, el jeneral Alonso de Leon, gobernador y capitan del presidio de esta probincia, ha-

uiendo visto la declaracion y confesion fecha por Francisco de nacion franzes y por otro nombre

monsiur Yan Jarri, prisionero, y los demas autos de esta causa y que de ellos resulta

25 la zertidumbre de la poblacion de los franzeses en el Rio o Baia del Espiritu Santo

mando que estos autos y el dicho preso se remitan al excelentisimo señor conde de la Moncloua

virrei y capitan jeneral de la Nueba España y presidente de la Real Audiendia de

ella para que Su Excelencia, con vista de ellos, disponga lo que fuese
    seruido y en estas

fronteras se ponga toda la guardia custodia y vixilancia necesaria por lo que
30   puede resultar de la prision del dicho franzes y la alteracion que habra causa-
    do a los yndios de su sequito y debocion, y lo firme con dos ttestigos de mi
    asistencia

{SIG} Alonso de Leon / ttestigo {SIG} Joseph Antonio de Ecay y Muzquiz / ttestigo {SIG} Jose[p]h Gutierres.

[folio 21r]

[Diario]

    ¶ En el pueblo de San Francisco de Coaguila en diez y och[o dias del mes de]
maio de mil seiscientos y ochenta y ocho años, el jeneral Alonso de Leon [go-]
bernador y capitan del presidio de esta probincia digo que por quanto
es necesario salir en busca del franzes por las noticias que se me han
5   dado de que esta en vna rancheria de la otra banda del Rio Brauo hazia
el rumbo del nordeste. Por tanto y ser necesario para este efecto hazer lista de los mexores soldados y mas vien armados que se alla-
ren en este puesto por ser jornada de mucho riesgo, mande hazer
y hize la lista siguientte

10   Yo, dicho jeneral Alonso de Leon
    el padre predicador frai Buenabentura Bonal, relejioso de la hor-
    den de San Francisco, nuestro capellan
    el jeneral don Martin de Mendiondo, cauo y comisario de los
    soldados del Reino de Leon
15   el capitan Carlos Cantu
    el capitan Nicolas de Medina, capitan viuo
    el capitan Christobal de Villa Real
    el alferez Thomas de la Garza
    el alferez Alonso de Leon
20   el alferez Lorenzo de la Garza
    el alferez Geronimo Cantu
    el sarxento Juan Cantu
    Francisco de Villa Real
    Juan de la Garza
25   Los contenidos arriba son del socorro del dicho Reino de Leon
    el capitan Diego Ramon
    Thomas Sanchez
    Juan Domingo Flores
    Joseph de Baeza

30   Antonio de Montes de Oca

Joseph Ximenez

tres arrieros para conducir los bastimentos

ochenta cauallos de armas

[folio 21v]

¶ Derrotero y diario de la jornada que yo, dicho jeneral Alonso
de Leon, hize con la compa[ñ]ia de soldados contenidos en la
lista de atras para yr a prender el franzes.

¶ Miércoles diez y nuebe de maio de mil seiscientos ochenta y ocho
5   años salimos del pueblo de San Francisco de Coauguila y fuimos
a dormir a la junta de los rios llamados de Nadadores y
Coauguila; es buen camino y llano, vbo distancia de seis leguas.

¶ Jueues veinte salimos con el real y pasamos por vn puesto
que llaman los Baluartes; fuimos el rio abaxo de Nada-
10   dores distancia de siete leguas, tierra comoda y llana.

¶ Viernes veinte y vno pasamos el dicho rio, fuimos a dormir al Rio
de las Sauinas; ai distancia de diez leguas, no faltan agua-
xes y la tierra mui comoda y llana.

¶ Sauado veinte y dos nos fue forzoso parar con el real
15   para que se reformase algo la cauallada.

¶ Domingo veinte y tres fuimos a dormir a vna lagunilla, distancia de siete leguas de buen camino y llano.

¶ Lunes veinte y quatro fuimos a dormir a las faldas de vna
loma grande en vn arroio que esta zerca de ella; andu-
20   uimos distancia de ocho leguas y es la tierra abundante
de agua y llana.

¶ Martes veinte y cinco salimos en demanda del Rio Grande, llegamos a el, estaba como en distancia de quatro leguas
de donde salimos.

25   ¶ Miércoles veinte y seis dexando el real en el rio con cinco
soldados y con los treze restantes y el capellan pasamos el Rio
Grande. Es el passo mui bueno y ancho, nos dio el agua asta
arriba del estriuo; tendra de ancho como dos tiros de arcabuz; no tiene ningun peligro el dicho passo, puede tra-
30   xinarse con recua. Fuimos a dormir este dia a vn arroyo
donde estan vnos charcos, distancia del dicho rio ocho
leguas; es tierra llana con pastos y agua.

¶ Juebes veinte y siete, dia de la Asencion del Señor.

[folio 22r]

Fuimos a dormir a otro arroio que esta en vna cañada
montuosa; anduvimos este dia onze leguas de tierra llana con agua.

¶ Viernes veinte y ocho. No hallandonos con noticias del fran-
5 zes, despache a los yndios que lleuaba a que buscasen la
rancheria donde viuia, y este dia paro el real.

¶ Sauado veinte y nuebe boluio vno de los yndios que
despachamos dando por razon que no hauian allado
la rancheria y que nos boluieramos al rio y alli espe-
10 rasemos nuebo auiso; con que desandando el camino del
dia antes, paramos en el dicho rio, y en el camino topamos
mas de quinientos yndios matando ganado que llaman ciuolas
que se semejan al ganado bacuno; y preguntandoles por vn
español que estaba con ellos, nos dixeron que estaba en
15 su ranchería vien zerca de alli, y que el contenido hera
su amo de ellos. Les aiudamos a matar algunas de las
dichas ciuolas y vno de ellos nos guio y lleuo a dormir asta
estar zerca de la rancheria de dichos yndios. Anduuimos
como distancia de tres leguas; y es de adbertir que el
20 rumbo que llebamos en dichas jornadas todo lo mas
fue hazia el nordestte.

¶ Domingo trenta pasamos cinco arroios de algunos
malos passos por benir crecidos y pasados diuisamos
la poblacion de la rancheria que esta en vn alto como
25 distancia de tres leguas de donde dormimos; llegamos
a ella y mediante las dilixencias que hicimos ∧(que
con yndiuidualidad constan en vn auto que esta fecho
en esta razon a que me remito∧), prendimos el franzes
y nos boluimos este dia siguiendo el mismo derrotero y
30 rumbo por donde hauiamos benido asta llegar a este
dicho pueblo de San Francisco de Coauguila, llegando a
el a seis del corriente mes de junio.

¶ Con que por lo que pareze de las jornadas ai de distancia
desde este dicho pueblo a la dicha rancheria sesenta y
[folio 22v]
siete leguas que rebajadas las cinco del dia viernes que reboluimos
quedan sesenta y dos leguas liquidas; y para que en todo tiempo
conste lo firme con dos testigos
{SIG} Alonso de Leon / ttestigo {SIG} Joseph Antonio de / Ecay y Muzquiz /
ttestigo {SIG} Jose[p]h Gutieres.

Martes 9 del dicho salio el real de dicho paraxe llamado S.n Gregorio Naçi-
anzeno, el rūbo del norte, por lomas y
cañadas, y algunos pedasos de monte en-
çino, robles, morales y parras, que fue
neçessario desmontar como cosa de vna legua y auiendo passado 6 arroyos secos
y llegado a otro arroyo, paro el real en
vna colina, que se le puso por nōbre
Jesus Maria y joseph de buena uista auiendo marchado este dia ——————— 07 —

Dicho dia alatarde llego el Gouernador al dicho real, y luego salio con
8 hombres entre ellos el cap.n D. Gregorio Salinas barona, embusca de
vn francesito, que estaua en vna rancheria de jndios, el rūbo del sureste, y auiendo marchado como cosa
de doze leguas por ser ya noche ya-
çieron, a orilla de vna colina ——— 012 —

Miercoles 10 del dicho salieron antes
de amanejer prosiguiendo el mismo
rūbo de sureste como cosa de 9 leguas
asta vna loma alta que haze antes de
entrar en vn mōte de alli siguieron el
rūbo del poniente por vn monte muy
espesso de robles, ençinos, muchas parras
y morales, y algunas plaçetas a la salida del como cosa de 9 leguas y ala
dicha salida del mōte dieron con
vn francesito, llamado Pedro Talon
que venia marchando con vna rancheria de jndios, de alli se boluieron
siguiendo el mesmo camino que auian
lleuado asta serca de la mesma colina, donde durmieron la noche antes
auiendo marchado este dia 27 ——— 027 —

2.5 Manuscript 89-B

[folio 37v]

Diario y derrotero y demarcazion de la tierra
de la jornada que por orden del excelentisimo señor
15   Conde de la Moncloua, virrey y capitan general
que fue de la Nueba España, que despuez confirmo
el excelentisimo señor Conde de Galue, actual virrey y
capitan general de dicha Nueba España, hizo
el general Alonzo de Leon, gouernador de la
20   probinsia de Coahuila y cauo principal de los
cien hombres que fueron a ella al descubrimiento
de la vaia del Espiritu Santto y poblazion

[folio 38r]

de los franzeses, es como se sigue.
¶ Mill seiscientos y ochentta y nuebe,
mar[ç]o, miercoles veintte y tres de mar[ç]o, se dispuso que saliese el real de la jentte y soldados que se
5   hallauan en Cuaguila y con efecto salio vna legua
el rio abaxo de distancia. Jueues veintte
y quatro del dicho salio el general y hallando
el real que estaua para salir el rio abaxo, camino
de la otra banda hasta la junta del de Nadadores.
10   Andubo este dia siete leguas al rrumbo del
nordeste, toda tierra llana ynabitable. Viernes
veinte y sinco del dicho caminamos el rio abaxo
de Nadadores por la uarda del sur, pasando por
medio de dos serros que llaman los Baluartes, pasa-
15   mos orillas de dicho rio donde esta vn alamo
grande, que en mucha distançia no ay otro.
Andubimos siete leguas al mismo rumbo (de)
del nordeste, toda tierra llana de buenos pastos.
¶ Sauado veinte y seis del dicho caminamos
20   el rio abaxo como el dia anttes hasta donde
se juntta con el de las Salinas; paramos distansia de vna legua de la juntta, camino llano

[folio 38v]

de buenos pastos. Andubimos este dia seis leguas
al rumbo del leste.

¶ Domingo veintte y siete del dicho caminamos
el dicho rio auaxo y lo pasamos asi[a] el nortte
5 y prosiguiendo el camino a su orilla, diuisamos
los soldados que venian del Nuebo Reyno
de Leon, que se uenian a juntar en conformidad
de hauer señalado el puertto [*sic*]. Nos juntamos ha-
siendo la salua de una y otra parte, andu-
10 bimos tres leguas al leste.
 ¶ Aqui se hizo reseña general de todos los soldados,
harrieros y otros mosos de seruiçio con el baga-
je, como todo consta con toda yndiuidualidad de la dicha reseña que esta apartte.
15 ¶ Lunes veinte y ocho del dicho caminamos al
rumbo del nordeste, distancias de seis leguas
atrauesando vnos llanos sin agua, tierra bien
penosa aunque llana. Paramos en un charco
largo de agua llouedisa.
20 ¶ Martes veinte y nuebe del dicho salimos al rumbo
del nordeste, quarta al nortte, andubimos sinco
leguas, tierra llana aunque con algunas lomitas bajas.
[folio 39r]
 ¶ Miercoles treintta del dicho caminamos
al rumbo del nortte quatro leguas. Presedio
que antes que amanesiera, embio el prisionero franses
vn yndio de los que lleuauamos de su deuosion
5 a avisar a los yndios sus conosidos de como
pasauamos por su auitazion. Con que vna legua antes
de llegar a ella, nos salieron a reseuir mas de
sesenta yndios, vnos con sus armas otros sin
ellas, y nos acompa[ñ]aron hasta su auitazion.
10 Tenian preuenida una casilla cubiertta de cueros
de sibola en donde metieron al dicho franzes,
a quien hizieron muchos cariños. Enfrente de ella
estaua clauado vn palo de altura de quatro
baras y en el colgadas diez y seis cauesas de jndios
15 que auian muerto de los enemigos. Estauan juntas
sinco nasiones segun la relazion ^(que dio el franzes^)
yntituladas Hapes, Jumenes, Xiaba, Mexcale y otra,
contamos ochenta y sinco casillas; se les repar-

tieron algunos guipiles, fresadillas, quenttas, rosa-
20 rios, cuchillos y harina, de que quedaron muy
gustosos y se les mataron sinco reses para que
comieran. Contadas todas las personas de todas
hedades, hallamos cuatrosientas y nobentta.
[folio 39v]
Paramos en un arroyo sercano a la orazion.
¶ Juebes treintta y uno del dicho fue forsoso parar
en este puesto por lo mal que lo auia pasado la
cauallada de agua.
5   ¶ Abril, viernes primero de abril salimos en
demanda del Rio Brabo; caminamos sinco
leguas atrauesando algunas lomitas baxas,
no faltaron aguages en esta distançia, lo mas del
rumbo de esta[s] sinco leguas fue al nortte (^del sur).
10 Paramos con el real enfrentte del paso de esta banda
del sur. Se badeo el rrio y se hallo estar bueno
para poder pasar el dia siguientte, tiene de ancho
el paso un tiro de mosquete. Ya lleuauamos en
nuestra compa[ñ]ia un yndio fiel por guia, el qual
15 nos aseguro que sauia toda la tierra y nos llebaria
a donde estauan vnos hombres como nosotros
poblados con seis o siete casas, y que tenian mu-
xeres y hijos y estauan en distancia como de
seis jornadas del dicho Rio Brabo. Este yndio
20 es bosal, pero por otro yndio, mal ynterpretto,
sacabamos alguna luz de lo que dezia.
¶ Sauado dos del dicho pasamos el rio y andubimos
como vna legua al nortte por descauesar vnas
barrancas y lomitas; despuez fuimos al rumbo
[folio 40r]
del nordeste lo mas, hasta llegar a vnos charcos
que estauan sinco leguas distantes del rio, que le
pusimos el paraxe de los Cuerbos, porque al anocheser
se aparesieron mas de tres mill; el camino fue
5   llano y sin montte.
¶ Domingo de Ramos, tres del dicho, salimos al rumbo del nordeste por tierra llana distancia de tres
leguas y despuez huuo otras dos de algunos montesi-

llos de mesquites; pasamos vnos arroyuelos secos y
10   luego topamos vno con agua en cuia orilla paramos,
con que este dia andubimos sinco leguas largas.
Pusimos a este arroyo el de Ramos *por* auerlo hallado
este dia. Aqui obseruamos la altura del sol
con astrolauio ^(aunque defectuoso[^]), y nos allamos en
15   veinte y seis grados y treinta y un minutos de eleuasion de polo. Es de aduertir que las tablas de esta
obserua*zi*on fueron *fe*chas anttes de la corresion grego-
riana q*ue* llaman, q*ue* fue el año de mil quinienttos y
oc[h]yentta y dos, en el qual fue el equinosio a diez
20   de março y siguiendonos *por* las Ephemerides de An-
dre[a] A[r]goli, romano, q*ue* pone este año el equinosio a
veintte *de* marzo, hallamos *por* estas tablas le
corresponden a este dia tres de abril los veinte
y quatro *de* março de este año q*ue* es primero
[folio 40v]
despuez de uisiesto y estas tablas refiere el
auttor las saco del Artte de Nauegar q*ue* hizo el
m*aest*ro Medina. A sido forsoso satizfacer con estas
razones *por* si paresiere hauer algun hierro por
5   hallarnos sin tablas modernas.
¶ Lunes Santto, quatro del *di*cho, caminamos al rumbo
del nordeste lo mas del dia, y algunos ratos quarta
al nortte distan*ç*ia de ocho leguas. Al prinsipio fue
tierra llana y despuez huuo vn monte de mesqui-
10   tes pequeños, y hauiendo salido del, nos metimos
en otro m*ayo*r de tres leguas. Fuimos a dar a un rio
q*ue* aunque traia poca agua se reconosio en el
q*ue* en tiempo de yubia sale de madre casi media
leguas. Le yntitulamos el Rio de las Nuezes
15   *por* tener muchos nogales; es algo pedregoso y todas
sus piedras son de fuego y muy finas.
¶ Martes Santto, sinco del dicho, pasamos *di*cho
rio, fue nesess*ari*o andar media legua en su orilla
y entramos *por* vna cañada y se ofresio vn
20   monte muy espeso q*ue* fue nesesario desmontar
en su entrada con alfanges y achas casi vna

legua por los muchos nopales y mesquites que
ympedian el caminar. Seguimos el rumbo

[folio 41r]

de el leste, entramos despuez en vn mesquital en que
a trechos nos obligo a desmontar y andubimos distansia
de siette leguas; topamos con vn rio a quien pusimos el
Rio Sarco por serlo el agua del; andubimos, como digo,
5   siette leguas con muchos rodeos.

¶ Miercoles Santto, seis del dicho, caminamos como tres
leguas al rrumbo del nordeste y dos al leste por tierra
llana y de famoso pasto y por vnas cañadas muy ame-
nas, y a trechos huuo vnos bosquesillos de ensinos.
10   Llegamos a un rrio a quien pusimos el Rio Hondo,
respecto a que tiene por cada lado la baxada mas
de seis o siete estados. Estan serca del, assi de la vna
banda como de la otra, algunas lomas pequeñas,
montuosas algunas de ellas. El agua fue estramada
15   y con facilidad uebio la cauallada. Al baxar al rio
allamos unas piedras grandes blandas [sic] y en algunas
de ellas vimos algunas cruses grabadas y otras figuras
hechas a mano con mucha perfecsion y al pareser
son de mucho tiempo.
20   ¶ Juebes Santto, siette del dicho caminamos al rumbo del leste el dicho rio abaxo sin hauerlo
pasado como cuatro leguas, unas veses al rumbo
del leste y otras al sueste. y paramos en su orilla de esta vanca que ba de la misma calidad

[folio 41v]

que en el paraxe anttesedentte. Tierra llana
la mas, aunque tambien huuo algun montte
de mesquite, y aunque en todas las jornadas desde
que pasamos la auitazion de las sinco naziones
5   de yndios, que fue a treintta del pasado, fuimos
atrauesando algunas ueredas de yndio, eran de
mucho tiempo, y no paresio ninguno. La tierra
en lo mas fue llana.

¶ Viernes Santto, ocho del dicho, pasamos de la otra
10   vanda del Rio Hondo y seguimos el rrumbo del

leste, quartta al nordeste, lo mas de este dia. Serca
del rio topamos con dos cañadas, la una sercana
a la otra y a lo que parese, en tiempo de aguas cresen
tantto que sube mas de vn estado de altura. A que se

15   sig[u]io vn arroyuelo en vn montte q*ue* fue ness*esari*o desmontar vn trecho p*ara* poder pasar las mulas cargadas
q*ue* fue con artto trauaxo, atascandose algunas. Pass*ad*o
este arroyo, topamos con tierra muy llana y luego
vn montte de mesquites grandes, en cuio medio

20   estauan unos charcos de agua donde paramos,
hauiendo caminado este dia ocho leguas largas
al leste, como ba referido.

    ❡ Sauado Santto, nuebe del d*ich*o, salimos al rumbo
del nordeste y p*or* algunos montes q*ue* se ofrezieron

[folio 42r]

    fue ness*esari*o hazer algunos rodeos, vnas vezes al nortte
quartta al nordeste y otras quartta al leste. La tierra
fue muy comoda, este dia pasamos un arroio seco
y a distançia de una legua [^hallamos otro con agua] mui buena y mucho

5   pasto; sacaronse del muchos robalos; le pusimos a este
Arroyo del Uino p*or* auerse auierto este dia vn barril
que se repartio entre toda la jentte. Andubimos este dia
sinco leguas; hallamos nueses debaxo de los arboles
muy cresidas, tantto como las de España, si bien difiçi-

10   les en abrirlas. Vimos muchas parras siluestres, q*ue* nos
afirmaron los yndios que lleuauamos, que a su tiempo
era el frutto muy cresido y sabroso. En este paraje
como a las nuebe de la noche nos dio la cauallada
estampida, no obstantte a que auia quinse soldados

15   de posta, no la pudieron reparar toda; se fue vna puntta
de sientto y dos cauallos, que se rreconosio por la q*uent*a el
dia siguientte.

    ❡ Domingo de Pasqua, diez del d*ich*o, salieron soldados
p*or* diferenttes rumbos a buscar los cauallos, los quales

20   se hallaron en diferenttes atajos, q*ue* los detubo asta
la oracion, y assi p*or* esta causa paro el r*e*al este dia. Y
rreconosimos la altura de polo y nos hallamos en veinte
y sinco grados y sinquentta y sinco minuttos.

    ❡ Lunes de Pasqua, onse del d*ich*o, salimos al rumbo del

25   leste atrauesando a poca distancia del paraxe dos
      arroyos de buena agua, y luego se nos ofresio vna
[folio 42v]
      selua grande ce nopales [sic] y ensinos de mas de sinco
      leguas, toda tierra amena y fertil. Fue nessesario caminar
      este dia do(^r d)sse leguas para tener agua. Topamos con
      un rio bien grande, aunque no con mucha agua, y con
5   buen uado para pasarle; le pusimos por nombre el Rio de
      Medina; tiene la baxada de nuebe a diez estados.
      El rrumbo deste dia fue la mitad al leste y mitad al
      nordeste, todo lo mas del camino fue de ensinos y nogales.
      ¶ Martes de Pasqua, dose del dicho, pasamos el rio,
10   fue el paso mui acomodado, seguimos el rrumbo del
      leste sinco leguas de unas lomitas baxas, sin ningun
      montte. Atrauesamos unas barrancas de tierra colo-
      rada y amarilla. Entramos en un mesquital y allamos
      agua en un arroyo que, aunque en los principios estu-
15   bo seco y estubimos con desconfiansa de que la guia auia
      errado el aguaxe, a trecho como de una legua yba
      bien corrientte; la tierra fue muy fertil de pastos y
      a causa de hauer hallado serca de este arroyo vn
      leon uien disforme muerto, le pusimos el Arroyo del Leon.
20   ¶ Miercoles trese de abril salimos al rumbo del
      leste y a uezes al lest nordeste distancia de seis leguas
      como media legua [^larga] del parexe, pasamos por la puntta
      de una lomita, en la qual remata vna arboleda
      de enzinos que quedo a man[o] derecha, estaban en ella
25   unos montonsillos de piedras puestas a mano; se-
      guimos vnas lomitas vajas, huuo como dos leguas
[folio 43r]
      de montte de ensinos que en parttes fue nesesario
      desmontar y despuez hasta que llegamos a vn arroyu-
      elo, toda fue tierra llana.
      ¶ Juebes catorse de abril salimos para el rumbo del leste
5   quartta al nordeste en demanda de un rrio grande
      que nos dixo la guia hallariamos. Llegamos a las dos de
      la tarde, andubimos seis leguas, caminamos las tres
      por vnas lomas y despuez por otras montuosas y con
      algunas barrancas, que fue nesesario en parttes desmontar

10   p*ara* poder pasar, la tierra fue de la mas amena que a-
        biamos andado. El rrio no es mui caudaloso, tubo
        buen passo, esta p*or* sus orillas lleno de arboleda; mata-
        ronse en el camino seis sibolos, que fueron los primeros
        que uimos en distancia de mas de cien leguas; le pusi-
15   mos a este rrio N*uest*ra *Señora* de Guadalupe, que desde Coagu-
        ila lleuauamos p*or* nuestra protectora y auogada,
        y la lleuamos pintada en el estandartte r*eal*.
        ¶ Viernes quinse del d*ich*o amanesio el dia llubioso mas
        no obstantte, salimos con el r*eal* al paso del rio que
20   estaua como una legua y le pasamos, y apretando el
        agua, paramos en un arroyuelo que estaua sercano.
        No anduuimos este dia mas q*ue* dos leguas; este dia se
        hizo consulta de guerra p*or* dezir la guia que ya
        estauamos sercanos de la poblazion, y salio determina-
25   do el que se saliese el dia siguientte con sesentta
[folio 43v]
        soldados a reconoserla y quedando el r*eal* en
        otro mas adelantte y con vastante guarda.
        ¶ Sabado diez y seis del d*ich*o, en conformidad de lo
        consultado el dia antesedentte, salio el gou*ernado*r con los
5   sesentta soldados bien apersebidos, despuez de hauer
        cantado vna misa a N*uest*ra *Señora* de Guadalupe, con toda
        solemnidad. Assimismo salio el r*eal* a vn mismo ti-
        empo y auiendo caminado como tres leguas con los
        sesentta hombres, la retaguardia diuiso vn yndio
10   en el montte y lleuadolo al gouernador y exsamina-
        do, aunque con mal interprete, resulto el decla-
        rar que su rrancheria estaua serca y q*ue* en ella
        estauan quatro franseses. Hauiuamos el passo guian-
        donos d*ich*o yndio y hauiendo embiado a que el r*eal*
15   se detubiera en la partte donde traxeron d*ich*o jndio
        p*or* hauer agua. Anttes de llegar a la rrancheria se
        hausentto toda la gentte, la qual diuisamos q*ue* se
        yba metiendo en vn montte y tras ellos yuan
        cargados ocho o diez perros cargados con cueros
20   de sibolas. Los embiamos a llamar con el mismo yndio
        q*ue* nos guio y se consiguio el que viniesen los mas.
        Se aberiguo no estar alli los quatro franceses, sino q*ue*

hauia quatro dias que hauian pasado asia los
Texas. En esta rrancheria hallamos dos yndios

[folio 44r]

que nos dixeron que dos dias de camino hallaria-
mos a los contenidos en una ranchería; les
hisimos agasaxo a estos yndios con algun tauaco,
cuchillos y otras cossas para que nos guiasen, como lo
5   hizieron, enderesandonos al rumbo del nortte
hasta puestas del sol. Y en vn montte hallamos
vna poblasion de mas de dosienttas y sinquenta perssonas.
Aqui procuramos sauer de dichos franceses, sirbiendonos
siempre de ynterprette nuestro prisionero frances, y
10   respondieron que hauia quatro dias que hauian
pasado asia los yndios Texas, y que los demas que
estauan poblados en el mar pequeño ^(que es la baia^)
murieron todos a manos de los jndios de la costta,
que los dichos franceses tenian seis cassas donde bibian,
15   y que hauia tres lunas ^(son tres meses^) que el casso
hauia susedido, y que anttes de esto, les hauia dado
vna enfermedad de viruelas, de que hauian muerto
los mas. Este dia anduuo el real al leste tres leguas
y paro en donde le señalo el gouernador, quien con los
20   sesentta hombres anduuo este dia ocho leguas
asial nortte.
    ¶ Domingo diez y siette del dicho hauiendonos que-
dado a dormir juntto a la poblazon de los yndios,
bolbimos a salir al rrumbo del nortte y hauiendo

[folio 44v]

andado sinco leguas, hallamos vnos ranchos de
yndios conosidos de nuestro prisionero frances, con quienes aberiguamos vastarttementte la derrota de los quatro
franceses que caminaban para los Texas y que hauia
5   quatro dias que hauian pasado a cauallo. Aqui se
entro en consulta de lo que se podia determinar,
por estar ya el real mui distantte y en tierra no conosi-
da, y salio determinado el que se les escribiese vna
cartta a dichos franceses y se le remitiese con vn
10   jndio. Se executo asi, escribiendola el alferez
real Francisco Martinez en lengua francesa, que en substansia

contenia de que hauiendo tenido razon de que en la
costa los yndios de ella hauian muerto vnos xpistia-
nos, y que ellos se hauian escapado, que podian venir-
15   se con nosotros, que los esperariamos tres o quatro dias
en las cassas de la poblazion de donde ellos hauian
salido. Firmo esta cartta el gouernador, y el padre fray Damian
Masanet, religioso de Nuestro Padre San Francisco, nuestro capellan, a[ñ]adio debaxo de la cartta unos renglo-
20   nes en lengua latina, por si fuese religioso alguno
de los quatro, exsortandoles a que se viniesen; y despachamos con esta cartta vn yndio y metimos en ella
papel, para si respondiesen; y nos aseguro el correo
que los alcansaria. Cerca de la orazion llego de la
[folio 45r]
partte del norte vn yndio ha uer el frances que
deuio tener notisia del, y exsaminado por su medio,
si hauia mucha distansia de alli a los Texas, respondio
que hauia muchas jornadas y dixo que hauia tres dias
5   que hauian pasado de su rancheria los quatro franceses.
¶ Lunes, diez y ocho del dicho, considerando el detremento
que podia padeser el real, no obstante hauer quedado
el real uien guarnesido, salimos en demanda del. En
el camino tuuo cartta (de) [el] gouernador de que la noche
10   anttes hauia dado estampida la cauallada y se auian
perdido cientto y tanttos cauallos de los quales se yban
hallando algunos, aunque todavia faltauan treinta
y seis. Con que auiuamos el passo al real, en donde hallamos asimismo por nobedad de que se auia perdido
15   vn soldado buscando la cauallada, con cuia nueba
se hizieron diferenttes escuadras de soldados en su
busca y no paresio este dia.
¶ Martes diez y nuebe del dicho, por no hauer paresido
el soldado ni los cauallos, salieron en su busca dos
20   esquadras de soldados por diferentes rumbos, y en perssona
salio el mismo gouernador, y aunque se hizieron
muchas deligençias, no paresieron este dia y se quedaron a dormir en el campo para proseguir en su busca.
Este dia vinieron al real yndios de diferentes ranche-
25   rias a quienes agasajamos con tauaco y otras cosas

    y se les encargo q*ue* corriesen la tierra en busca del
soldado y cauallada que faltaban prometiendoles por
ello la corespondençia.

    ¶ Miercoles ueintte (^y quatro) del d*i*cho no salio el r*e*al
5   respecto a que no paresio el soldado ni cauallos con
que se rrepitio este dia la deligençia con otras esquadras
de soldados, y acabadas de salir llego el que se hauia
perdido guiado de vnos yndios y dixo hauer dormido aquella noche en vna rrancheria de yndios en
10   donde aporto, y que reselandose que lo auian de matar
estubo yndeterminable el quedarse alli y que resibio
mucho agasaxo, que no fue poca suertte el escaparsse
del peligro p*or* esta jentte tan barbara. Este dia aunque
el astrolauio se hauia quebrado, (^??) lo mexor que se
15   pudo, se adereso y obseruamos el sol y nos hallamos
en ueinte y ocho grados y quarenta y vn minutos
de eleuasion de polo.

    ¶ Juebes ueintte y vno del d*i*cho salimos con el r*e*al al
rumbo del leste y a veses quarta al norte y nordeste
20   quarta al norte caminando p*or* vnos llanos grandes
sin hauer en mucha distançia arboleda; andubimos
ocho leguas hasta vn arrcyo de buena agua y aqui
nos dixo la guia q*ue* la poblasion de los franceses estaua
orillas de este arroyo, y en sercania. La tierra fue toda
25   muy amena y topamos con muchas sibolas.

    ¶ Viernes veintte y dos del d*i*cho, no obstante hauer
amanesido el dia llubioso, p*or* hallarnos cerca

    de la poblasion, salimos con el r*e*al y a distancia de
tres leguas, el arroyo abaxo, la hallamos. Y hauiendo
parado con el r*e*al como vn tiro de arcabuz de ella, la
fuimos ha uer y hallamos todas las cassas saqueadas,
5   quebradas las caxas, frasqueras y todas las demas alajas
que tenian sus pobladores. Mas de dosientos libros ^(a lo que
paresio^) despedasados y podridas ya las ojas y tiradas
p*or* los patios y todos en legua francesa. En que discurrimos
que los agresores de estas muertes sacaron todo lo que
10   tenian afuera de las cassas y se lo repartieron, y lo que

no les seruia lo despedasaron y haziendo vn orrendo
saco de todo quanto tenian, porque demas de la ebidensia
del hecho en hauerlo hallado todo en esta forma,
lo yndicaron el que en las rancherias por donde pasa-
15   mos antes de llegar a la poblasion, hallamos algunos
libros que tenian los yndios en lengua fransesa muy
bien acondisionados con otras alajillas de mui poco
valor, cuios libros se rescataron y pusieron sus titulos
por memoria. Y no solo hisieron los yndios el estrago
20   en las alahajas sino en las armas, pues hallamos mas
de sien cauesas de arcabuses de rrastrillo sin llaues
ni cañones, que se los deuieron de lleuar, que se berifico
por vn cañon que se hallo en alguna distansia de las casas.
Hallamos tres difuntos tirados en el campo que el vno
25   paresio hauer sido muxer por el traxe que todovia tenia
pagado a los guesos, que se recoxieron todos y
[folio 46v]
se les dio sepultura con misa cantada de cuerpo pressente.
La casa principal de esta poblazion es de madera de
nauio fecha en forma de fuerte y el techo de tablason
y otro techo con corriente para el reparo de las aguas
5   y tambien de tablason y junto de ella sin dibision esta
otro aposentto aunque no tan fuertte que deuia de seruir
de capilla en que selebraban misa. Las otras sinco
cassas son de palisada y aforradas con lodo por de dentro y fuera y los techos de cueros de sibolas bien ynu-
10   tiles todas para qualquier defensa. Estauan junto al
fuertte y casas ocho piesas de artilleria de hierro de
mediano porte de a quatro y seis libras de bala, tres pedre-
ros muy biejos que les faltan las recamaras. Se hallaron
algunos vergajones de hierro, pernos de nauio, que todo
15   se reputto por veintte arrobas. Las piesas estaban vnas
en el suelo tiradas y otras en sus cureñas, aunque
quebradas dichas cureñas; hubo algunos barriles des-
fondados y como todo estaua tirado en la calle no auia
cosa de probecho; assimismo se hallo alrededor de las
20   cassas alguna jarçia maltratada. Buscamos los demas
difuntos y no pudieron descubrirse que discurrimos los he-
charon en el arroyo y se los comieron los caimanes, por

hauer muchos. La poblazion estaua en famosa parte y llana
para poderse defender vastantemente de qualquier acometimiento.
25   En el marco de la puertta principal del fuerte estaua
puesto el año que poblaron que fue el de mill seiscientos y ochenta
y quatro, con otras particularidades que se pusieron

[folio 47r]

en la descripsion que se hizo separada del puesto.
Este dia anduuo el real tres leguas al leste,
en lo qual, por lo que parese por la suma, ay de distancia desde el presidio de Coahuila hasta esta
5   poblasion sientto y treinta y seis leguas.
    ¶ Descubrimiento de la Baia del Espiritu Santo y su puerto.
    ¶ Sauado veinte y tres del dicho salimos con treintta
hombres a reconoser la baia por la parte del sur, procuran-
do seguir el arroyo abaxo de la poblazion, lleuandose
10   por guia el prisionero frances, por hauernos dicho la subia [sic]
y hauia andado toda en barco, con cuia seguridad
nos dexamos guiar y no lo hizo por el arroyo abajo
respecto a que dixo no hauia passo; andubimos sinco
leguas al sudueste y descabesados dos arroyos, andubimos
15   asia el leste otras tres leguas hasta dar con la orilla
de la baia en donde dormimos por hauer llegado a ella
al anocheser.
    ¶ Domingo veintte y quatro del dicho salimos muy
de mañana por la orilla de la baia que a la sason estaua
20   de baxa mar. Ay en sus sercanias muchas lagunas de
agua salada que nos ympedian en partes el passar a
cauallo por los muchos atascaderos, con que anduuimos
muchos trechos a pie estrando los cauallos. El vn
braso de mar que nos parezio el mayor ba encaminado
25   hasia el nortte, otro menor al sur y en el mas
pequeño asia la poblazion referida en este diario.

[folio 47v]

Anduuimos ocho leguas largas por la orilla hastta que
fue Dios seruido descubriesemos la uoca por donde
se entra en la vaia, que de donde podimos llegar
con los cauallos de ella, aora como dos leguas de que
5   resibimos mucho regosijo y en señal del hizimos
la salua con la arcabuseria, afirmandonos el prisionero

frances ser la uoca y puertto y hauer entrado
por el quando vino aquellas parttes con monsiur
Phelipe de Tal. Tiene la boca del puertto a lo que se
10   discurrio dos leguas corttas; ay en ella un mogotte
de tierra baxa q*ue* esta mas arrimado asia la costa
de la Ueracruz que no a la de la Florida y p*or* la uoca
mas pequeña, dize el frances, que entran las embar-
cazions. Entra en esta baia por la p*ar*te del sur el rio
15   que pusimos p*or* nombre N*uest*ra Se*ñor*a de Guadalupe q*ue* aunq*ue*
por la ymposibilidad de pasar no (^so)lo divisamos, lo discurrimos asi p*or* la zercania en que le uimos quando
le pasamos y tambien porque nos lo afirmo el franses.
El braso de mar que enderesa al nortte de la vaia
20   tiene tantta distançia, que no pudimos diuisar
la tierra de la otra banda. En la orilla q*ue* costeamos
esta baia que fue de ocho leguas [vimos] vn mastelerio de nauio
grande(s), otro peque[ñ]o de juanette, vn cabrestantte
y alguna tablason de duelas de pipas y de barriles
25   y otras maderas, q*ue* todo deuio de ser de algun
nauio q*ue* se perdio dentro de la vaia o en la costa
[folio 48r]
cuio cerco no diuisamos. Vista y reconosida la
voca de la uaia, nos bolbimos p*or* el mismo rumbo
por donde hauiamos ydo y dormimos orillas de vn
arroyo juntto a un montesillo, en donde huuo
5   poblasion de jndios q*ue* de algun tiempo la auian
desamparado, en la qual hallamos vn libro en lengua
francesa, vna frasquera quebrada y otras cosas q*ue*
nos dieron yndisio de hauerse hallado los yndios
de esta abitasion en las muertes de los franceses.
10   En este arroyuelo ^(que era el agua algo salobre^) hallamos quatro canoas.
⁋ El dia ueintte y sinco de abril salimos de
aqui y nos venimos al r*e*al en donde hallamos res-
puesta de la cartta q*ue* se auia escrito a los franceses
15   q*ue* se yban a la nasion de los Texas, q*ue* leida por el
alferez r*e*al contenia en sustançia q*ue* dentro de dos
dias llegarian a donde estabamos, que ya estaban
cansados de andar entre barbaros. Firmo la carta

vno solo cuia firma dezia Juan Larcheberque
20 de Baionne, estaba escrita con almagre. Con que
en yda y buelta al descubrimientto de la vaia
huuo de distançia treintta y dos leguas. Este dia,
lunes, veintte y sinco del dicho paro el real.
¶ Descubrimientto del Rio de San Marcos
25 ¶ Martes ueintte y seis de abril se determino
[folio 48v]
saliese el real por el mismo rumbo que auiamos
ydo respecto a que el agua del arroyo es salobre como
se a dicho y se maltrataba la cauallada que bebia de
ella. Con efecto salimos tres leguas el arroyo arriba.
5 Paramos en el mismo puesto donde hauiamos parado
a la yda y con ueintte hombres salimos a reconoser un rrio muy grande que dixo el prisionero frances estaua asial nortte y entraua en la baia,
y a distancia como de tres leguas le hallamos. Segui-
10 mos su orilla hasta donde hubo ympedimiento de algunas lagunas. Es este rio mui grande y nos parezio mayor
que el Rio Brabo. Con serlo tantto parese que con
vasso peque[ñ]o se puede nauegar por el. Determinamos
auunque fuese con dificultad ber su entrada en la
15 baya, como finalmentte lo conseguimos desde
vna lomitta que esta como en distançia de tres
quarttos de legua de la boca del dicho rio, y otro
tantto nos paresio que hauia desde ella a la boca del
arroyo donde viuian los franceses, y de dicha voca a la
20 poblasion ay como legua y media. Andubimos este dia
quinse (^di)leguas. Obseruamos en la orilla de la vaia
esta dia la altura de polo y nos hallamos ^(saluo
todo yerro por el defecto del astrolauio^) en veinte
y nuebe grados y tres minuttos, poco mas o menos. Pusimos
25 a este rio San Marcos por hauerlo descubiertto vn
dia despuez de su festibidad.
[folio 49r]
¶ Prosigue el diario de nuestra buelta con la
nueba entrada que se hizo asi[a] el nortte en busca
de los franceses.
¶ Miercoles veintte y siete de abril salimos con el real

5   y venimos a parar a unos charcos serca de vn montesillo
que esta juntto a el camino.

    ❡ Juebes veintte y ocho del dicho salimos por nuestra
derota y al mismo tiempo el gouernador con treinta
compa[ñ]eros asia a la banda del nortte a buscar los

10   franceses que hauian escrito. Paro el real en el rio de
Nuestra Señora de Guadalupe de la otra uanda. Viernes ueintte y nuebe paro el real.

    ❡ Sauado treintta del dicho asimismo paro el real.

    ❡ Domingo primero de maio serca de la orasion llego el

15   gouernador con los compa[ñ]eros y truxeron dos fransesez.
rrayados a vsansa de los yndios, los quales allo
en distancia de ueintte y sinco leguas y mas de donde
salimos con el real. El vno de ello[s] fue el que
escribio la carta llamado Juan y el otro llamado Xa-

20   come, natural de la Rrochela; estos dieron razon de
la muerte de los suios, diziendo lo primero que de vn
achaque de uiruelas hauian muertto mas de cien
personas y que las que quedaron, estando en buena
amistad con los jndios de toda aquella comarca,

25   nunca se reselauan de ellos, y que auia poco mas
de un mes que hauian llegado a la poblazion

[folio 49v]

    sinco jndios con pretexto de benderles algunas
cosas, y pararon estos en la casa mas apartada
de la poblazion, y luego fueron llegando otros con
el mismo pretexto, y como los franceses no sospecha-

5   ban nada, los fueron todos ha uer a la casa y sin
armas. Estando dentro fueron llegando otros jndios
y abrasandose con ellos y al mismo tiempo salieron
una esquadra de jndios, que estaua oculta en el
arroyo, y los mataron todos a puñaladas y palos y

10   entre ellos mataron dos religiosos y vn clerigo y
hauian saqueado todas las casas. Y que ellos no se hallaron presentes por hauerse ydo a los Texas,
y que hauiendo tenido nuebas de este suseso, se vinieron quatro de ellos, y hauiendo hallado muertos

15   sus compañeros, enterraron hasta catorse perssonas
que hallaron y quemaron cassi cien barriles de

poluora, por que los yndios no se la lleuaran; y que la
poblasion estaua mui peltrechada de todas armas
de fuego, espadas y alfanges, ornamentos, tres
20   calises y mucha libreria con enquadernadura
muy curiosa. Los dichos dos franseses estan rrayados
en el rrostro a usansa de los jndios, tapados con
gamusas y sibolas; los hallamos en una rrancheria
del capitan de los Texas, que los tenia con mucho
25   cuydado sustentandolos, al qual trujimos al real
[folio 50r]

y se hagasajo; aunque bosal, jndio en quien
se reconosio capacidad, y tenia vn oratorio con algunas
ymagenes, se agasajo vastanttementte por el gouernador
con los resagos que hauian quedado de guipiles,
5   fresadillas y cuchillos, cuentas y demas jeneros y a otros
jndios que con el vinieron, con que se fue muy gustoso,
prometiendo venir con algunos jndios de su nasion
a la prouinçia de Coaguila. A los dos franseses les
resibio el gouernador las declaraziones separadamente
10   de todo lo que ymportto y convino para remitir-
las a su excelencia y proseguimos nuestro viaje hasta
el Rio de las Nueces. Y martes, diez de mayo,
se adelanto el gouernador con algunos compa[ñ]eros
para haser despacho a su excelencia, dandole la razon de
15   este descubrimientto; y llegamos al presidio de Coahuila
oy trese del dicho mes de maio al anocheser, con que
se da fin al diario y para que conste lo firmo dicho gouernador,
Alonzo de Leon

á buscar con un Indio, y al memo tiempo der
pacharon dos Soldados al Real para que fuesen quatro Soldados con bastimento por si no
viniese el Frances para ir á buscarlo, y á ese
tiempo fueron á pasar el Rio de San Marcos
por haver llovido esta tarde, y no crecierse el
Rio; haviendo marchado este dia . . . . 26.

Viernes 12. por la mañana lle-
gó el Frances llamado Pedro Molinero con
tres Indios y los Soldados del Real con que
prosiguieron su viage hasta alcanzarle, que
los alcanzaron 6. leguas del rio, el rumbo del
Norte . . . . " 06.

Miercoles 10. prosiguió con el
Real el Capitan Juan.co Martinez el rumbo del Norte por lomas y Cañadas á pasar
el Rio de San Marcos, donde le pasó, y proseguimos nuestro viage el memo rumbo hasta
una Colina donde encontramos los Compañeros que el Governador havia dexado, donde
paramos, haviendo caminado este dia 8 leg. y
se le puso por nombre S.n Yldefonso - - - - - - 08.

Jueves 11. del dho. se mejoró
el Real á otro parage mas aventajado, como
cosa de tres leguas el rumbo del Nordeste,
donde paró en una Colina, q.e se le puso por
nombre S.n Jose . . . . - 03.

Sabado 13. del dho. Salió

2.6 Manuscript 90-B

[folio 4v]

20   ¶ Diario, derrotero y demarcazion de la tierra de
la jornada que por horden de el excelentissimo señor conde de Galue, virrey y cappitan
general de la Nueua España hizo el general
Alonso de Leon, gouernador de la prouinzia de

[folio 5r]

Cuahuila y capitan de el presidio que por quenta de
su magestad esta puesto en ella, y cauo superior de
los soldados que fueron a ella al reconozimiento de
los francesses que huuiere en la Bayia del Espiritu

5   Santo y prouincia de los Tejas, es como se sigue.
¶ Domingo veinte y seis dias del mes de marzo año
de mill seiscientos y nouenta salieron las requas
y vagaje de la villa de Santiago de la Moncloua
vna legua fuera de el pueblo de los yndios, legua y

10   media de dicha villa el rumbo de el norte.
¶ Lunes veinte y siete de el dicho se leuanto el real
y fuimos a parar abaxo de las lomitas orilla del Rio
de Cuaguila, el rumbo de el nordeste quarta al norte,
anduuimos tres leguas.

15   ¶ Martes veinte y ocho de el dicho salimos por el rumbo de el nordeste rio abajo y passando por el puerto
de Baluartes dimos vna guiñada al rumbo del
norte. Paramos orilla de el rio hauiendo marchado ocho leguas.

20   ¶ Miercoles veinte y nueue de el dicho salio el real
rio abaxo el rumbo de el leste quarta al nordeste,
y pasando el alamo paro el real orilla del rio
marchando este dia cinco leguas. Toda es tierra
llana, aunque ay algunos chaparros y lechuguilla.

25   ¶ Jueues treinta de el dicho salimos el rumbo del leste

[folio 5v]

quarta al nordeste rio abajo hasta las juntas de el
Rio de las Sauinas, hauiendo marchado este dia
quatro leguas y media. Y aquella tarde se junto la
compañia de el Reyno de Leon y los padres missione-

5   ros que venian en ellas.

¶ Viernes treinta y vno de el dicho marchamos rio a-
bajo y atravezando vna loma al rumbo del leste
pasamos el Rio de las Sauinas. Paro el real orillas
de el rio, anduvimos dos leguas.

10   ¶ Sabado primero de abril caminamos el rumbo del
nordeste; paramos en vn charco de agua llouediza;
anduuo el real este dia seis leguas.

¶ Domingo dos de abril despues de missa salimos el
rumbo de el nordeste quarta al norte, llegando a

15   vnos charcos de agua llouediza, donde paro el real,
hauiendo marchado cinco leguas. Toda es tierra
llana, aunque ay algunos chaparros.

¶ Lunes tres de el dicho salimos el rumbo del norte
por tierra llana orilla de vn arroyo. Hallamos los

20   yndios de el frances, a los quales les dimos tauaco
y ropa; anduuimos este dia quatro leguas.

¶ Martes quatro de el dicho mes salimos el rumbo
de el norte en demanda de el Rio Grande; paro el real orilla de el y se hallaron algunas

[folio 6r]

siuolas, hauiendo marchado este dia cinco leguas.

¶ Miercoles cinco de el dicho estuvimos parados porque se
confessaran todos y cumplieran con la iglessia antes
de passar el rio.

5   ¶ Jueues seis de el dicho passamos el rio y caminamos
el rumbo de el norte quarta al nordeste y
paramos orilla de vn arroyo seco, auiendo marchado ocho leguas. Dormimos esta noche sin agua.

¶ Viernes siete de el dicho marchamos el rumbo del

10   nordeste por tierra llana, donde paro el real en
el Arroyo de Ramos, hauiendo andado este dia
tres leguas.

¶ Sabado ocho de el dicho salio el real el rumbo de
el nordeste quarta al norte por tierra llana,

15   aunque en partes ay algunos mesquites, y paramos
orilla de vn arroyo, que le pusimos por nombre Caramanchel y por estar malo el passo gastamos

lo mas de el dia en passar las requas. Marchamos
este dia tres leguas.

20   ¶ Domingo nueue de el dicho despues de missa salimos el rumbo de el norueste quarta al norte
por tierra llana, y passando dos cañadas de arboles
entramos en vn mesquital y dimos en el passo
de el Rio de las Nuesses y paramos en vn

[folio 6v]

potrero orilla de el rio, hauiendo marchado cinco leguas.
    ¶ Lunes diez de el dicho mes salimos el rumbo del leste
hauiendo passado el rio por vn hailadero de arboles
como dos leguas y luego seguimos el rumbo de el

5   norte como otras dos, y dando vna guiñada al
leste por tierra llana, aunque con algunos mesquites,
passamos el Rio Zarco y paro el real hauiendo
marchado este dia siete leguas.
    ¶ Martes onze de el dicho salimos al rumbo de el

10   norte por vnas llanadas atrauezando algunas lomitas. Paramos en el Rio Hondo, hauiendo andado seis leguas.
    ¶ Miercoles doze de el dicho estuuimos parados con el
real por buscar dos compañeros que se perdieron

15   con vna tempestad el dia antes marchando.
    ¶ Jueues trece de el dicho a medio dia llegaron los dos
compañeros y a este tiempo tuuimos noticia de vnos
yndios que seis leguas de este paraxe estaua vna
junta de yndios donde auia venido a dar vn

20   frances. Sali este dia con veinte soldados el rumbo
de el poniente por orilla de el rio de la vanda del
norte como cinco leguas, pare esta noche.
    ¶ Viernes catorze de el dicho al amanezer prosegui
el rumbo y dando vna guiñada al norte

[folio 7r]

por vna llanada, llegue a la orilla de vn rio donde
estaua la rancheria de yndios, saliendonos a reconozer mucha cantidad de ellos, chicos y grandes,
y dandoles tauaco y vizcocho, nos dieron razon

5   que dos franceses estauan de la otra vanda del Rio

de Guadalupe. Y vn yndio tenia vn mosquete franzes.
Y hauiendo tomado esta razon nos voluimos al real,
acompañandonos mucha cantidad de yndios hasta
el real, donde los agasajamos con ropa, arina y taua-
10   co y otras chucherias, hauiendo andado nosotros siete leguas.
    ¶ Sabado quince de el dicho salio el real el rumbo del
leste, rio abaxo hasta llegar al passo, hauiendo marchado seis leguas.
    ¶ Domingo diez y seis de el dicho despues de missa pas-
15   samos el rio de el rumbo de el leste quarta al nordeste
por tierra llana, llegamos al Arroyo de Chapa donde hizimos vna puente para passarlo, y prosiguiendo hasta llegar a vnos charcos paro el real orilla de ellos,
hauiendo marchado ocho leguas.
20   ¶ Lunes diez y siete de el dicho salimos el rumbo del
nordeste y por algunos montes que se ofrecie-
ron dimos algunas guiñadas al norte nordeste
y leste hasta llegar al Arroyo de los Robalos, donde
paro el real hauiendo marchado este dia cinco leguas.
25   ¶ Martes diez y ocho del dicho salimos por differentes
[folio 7v]
    rumbos a buscar ciento y veinte y seis cauallos que
dieron estampida, y hauiendo parecido este dia despues de mediodia, salio el real y a poca distanzia
perdio el tino la guia y nos fue forzoso seguir el
5   rumbo de el norte por yr en busca de el Rio de
Medina, y por ser ya tarde, paro el real en vna
lomita a quien le pussimos el real de el Rosario,
aunque hauia poca agua, vasto para la compañía.
Anduuimos este dia quatro leguas.
10   ¶ Miercoles diez y nueue de el dicho salimos al rumbo
de el norte hauiendo llegado al Rio de Medina,
arriba de el passo paramos en vn baxio, hauiendo
andado siete leguas.
    ¶ Jueues veinte de el dicho caminamos al rumbo de
15   el leste y a distancia de dos leguas llegamos
al passo de el rio, donde paro el real por ser ne-
cessario aliñar el passo de el.
    ¶ Viernes veinte y vno de el dicho caminamos el rum-

bo de el leste y llegamos al Arroyo del Leon, mar-
20   chamos este dia cinco leguas.

    ¶ Sabado veinte y dos de el dicho caminamos el rum-
bo de el leste y a vezes al nordeste y paramos en
vn arroyo de agua salobre, anduuimos seis leguas.

    ¶ Domingo veinte y tres de el dicho despues de missa
25   salio el real el rumbo de el leste quarta a el
[folio 8r]

nordeste por algunos enzinales y paramos junto
al Rio de Guadalupe donde haze vn arroyo pe-
gado al rio, anduuimos cinco leguas.

    ¶ Lunes veinte y quatro de el dicho salio el real rio a-
5   baxo y auiendo passado el rio con algun trabajo por
lleuar mucho agua, paramos de la otra vanda hauiendo marchado dos leguas.

    ¶ Martes veinte y cinco de el dicho sali con veinte sol-
dados dexando el real en dicho paraxe y fui
10   a reconozer la Vahia de el Spiritu Santo al rumbo del leste. Anduuimos este dia catorze leguas y pasamos a orillas de vnos charquitos de agua.

    ¶ Miercoles veinte y seis de el dicho llegamos a la pobla-
zon de los franceses que vimos el año pasado y ha-
15   uiendola reconozido de la forma que estaua de antes
y adonde esta la artilleria enterrada, quemamos
el fuerte de madera y pasando dos leguas adelante
reconozimos en la vahia al parezer dos boias, vna
a la punta de la voca de el Rio de San Marcos
20   y la otra a vn lado señalando la misma canal.
No se obseruo el sol por estar el dia nublado. De
alli dimos la vuelta el arroyo arriba de la poblazon de los francesses, por ver si topauamos algunos
yndios por tomar razon y no hauiendo hallado
25   ningunos, paramos orilla de el dicho arroyo, hauiendo
[folio 8v]

marchado este dia de yda y vuelta catorze leguas.

    ¶ Jueves veinte y siette de el dicho dimos vuelta a el
real hauiendo caminado el arroyo arriba de los
franceses en busca de algunos yndios de quien
5   tomar razon; dando algunas guiñadas, llegamos

al real; anduuimos este dia veinte leguas.

¶ Viernes veinte y ocho de el dicho sali con ocho soldados
rio arriba de Guadalupe, dando algunos humazos
por ver si topaua con algunos yndios de quien tomar
10 razon, y hauiendo andado seis leguas, nos voluimos al real, andando este dia doze leguas de
yda y vuelta.

¶ Sabado veinte y nueue del dicho salio el real el rumbo de el leste como tres leguas y luego seguimos el
15 de el nordeste como otras tres leguas por tierra llana y llegando a vnos charcos de agua llouediza
pusimos por nombre San Pedro Martir. Anduuimos
este dia seis leguas.

¶ Domingo treinta de el dicho despues de missa
20 hauiendo llegado dos soldados de los presidios de
la Vizcaya, y dando razon que venian atrás sus
compañeros en mi alcanze, por la horden de el
excelentissimo señor Conde de Galue, virrey y
capitan general de la Nueua España, para venir
25 a esta jornada, los embie a topar con bestias y vastimento y dexe el real en aquel paraxe para esperarlos.

[folio 9r]

Sali con diez y seis soldados a que demostrassen vnos
ayladeros y buscar algunos yndios que nos guiassen
y diessen razon de si hauia algunos francesses en estos
paraxes. Pare esta noche en vnos charcos de agua lloue-
5 diza, hauiendo marchado nueue leguas.

¶ Lunes primero de mayo prosegui mi viaxe passando
algunos arroyos y rancherias despobladas sin encontrar con ningun yndio. Dormimos en vna lomita
hauiendo andado doze leguas.

10 ¶ Martes dos de el dicho prosegui mi viaxe y llegue
a vn potrero cerca del Rio de San Marcos, donde dormimos, hauiendo andado este dia por algunas guiñadas, hauiendo andado este dia catorze leguas.

¶ Miercoles tres de el dicho hauiendo puesto en vn arbol
15 vna cruz, llegue al Rio de San Marcos y hauiendo-
lo passado prosegui mi viaxe, y como cinco leguas
de el rio, orilla de vn montezillo, diuissamos vna

yndia y vn muchacho, y llamandolos con vn
pañuelo, no quisieron salir, antes si se metieron den-
20   tro de el monte. Paramos esta noche en vna loma
llana a vna vista, dejandoles en su rancheria vn
pañuelo, vizcocho, tauaco, nauaxas y cuchillos. Anduuimos este dia siete leguas.

     ¶ Jueues quatro de el dicho nos vino a ver vn yndio y
25   hauiendo hablado con el por señas nos dixo que era
de los Texas y que este dia llegariamos a vna rancheria

[folio 9v]

     y que el nos guiaria con su muger y vn cuñadito su-
yo que viuian alli. Le di vn cauallo en que cargara
sus trastes y a tres leguas de distancia resoluimos
despacharlo, y voluiendonos al paraxe donde haua-
5   mos dormido diziendo le aguardasemos alli que yria
a llamar al gouernador de los Texas, donde se hallauan algunos franceses entre ellos. Anduuimos este
dia seis leguas.

     ¶ Viernes cinco de el dicho por la mañana despache
10   al capitan Francisco de Venauides con tres soldados
al real para que viniesse marchando. Y como a
las cinco de la tarde voluio el yndio que despache
al capitan de los Texas, que por hauersele juido
el cauallo, me venia a auisar.

15   ¶ Sabado seis de el dicho envie a quatro soldados por
el rastro para que reconocieran si se hauia juntado con algunos yndios, y hauiendo encontrado
con otro yndio, lo truxeron al real al qual le
ofrecimos ropa porque fuera a los Texas a auisar
20   al gouernador para que nos viniesse a ver, con
que el yndio primero, codicioso de la offerta me dixo que
le volviesse a dar otro cauallo, que el yria a llamar
al gouernador de los Texas, y que nos dexaria a su
muger y vn cuñado suyo para que nos guiaran hasta
25   toparnos, con que lo despache este dia.

     ¶ Domingo siete de el dicho y lunes ocho estuuimos

[folio 10r]

     parados donde nos dixo el yndio le esperasemos, y assi
mesmo, a uer si diuisamos algunas humaredas para

salir a topar el real que era la seña que les dimos

¶ Martes nueue de el dicho hauiendo diuisado vn humo

5   sali con quatro soldados a encontrar el real; y pasado el Rio de San Marcos, cerca de el mediodia, encon-
tre dos yndios y a poca distancia al capitan Francisco
de Venavides con tres soldados con vn yndio ladino
en la lengua mexicana, de quienes tome razon que

10   vn franzesito estaua en vna rancheria, como dos dias
de camino al poniente, y otro en otra rancheria
al oriente. Despache al dicho capitan Venauides
con dos soldados a donde dexe los compañeros que me
esperassen y passe al real, que lo halle en vn arroyo

15   que acauaua de parar. Y dandoles horden que fueran marchando otro dia y me esperassen a donde
estauan los compañeros, y hauiendo coxido a tres cauallos, ocho soldados y vastimento, guiandonos el
yndio ladino, anduuimos esta tarde doze leguas.

20   ¶ Miercoles diez de el dicho prosiguiendo al poniente
como cossa de nueve leguas, seguimos el rumbo
por vn monte de enzinos y parras, como otras
cinco leguas y a la salida de el monte encontramos vnos yndios y a un francesito llamado Pedro

25   Talon, y dandonos razon no hauia otro por aquella
parte, nos voluimos a dormir cerca de el paraxe

[folio 10v]

de aquella noche, hauiendo andado aquel dia de yda
y vuelta veinte y siete leguas.

¶ Jueues onze de el dicho proseguimos nuestro viaje al
rumbo de el nordeste como cossa de doze leguas

5   hasta vna loma alta que tiene vna mota de arboles
muy altos, donde hallamos vnos yndios rancheados que nos dieron noticia de otro frances que estaua
zerca de alli en vna rancheria. Embie a llamarlo
con vn yndio. Y otro yndio despues nos dio razon

10   que hauian llegado otros franceses a la voca de la
Bahia de el Espiritu Santo. Y al mismo tiempo despache dos soldados a el real para que viniessen
quatro con vastimento y bestias de remuda por
si no viniera el frances yrle a buscar. Esta tarde

15 pasamos el Rio de San Marcos por hauer llouido
   mucho y que no creciera y atajarnos vnos de vna
   parte y otros de otra. Anduuimos este dia diez y
   seis leguas.
      ¶ Viernes doze de el dicho por la mañana llego el
20 frances con tres yndios y dixo llamarse Pedro Muñi
   y al mismo tiempo los soldados que embie a llamar
   de el real, con que proseguimos nuestro viaje
   hasta alcanzarle al rumbo de el nordeste, anduuimos seis leguas.
25   ¶ Sabado treze de el dicho salio el real del paraxe
   de San Joseph al rumbo de el leste cossa de tres

[folio 11r]

   leguas y otras tres al nordeste, atrauezando algunas
   cañadas y arroyos de poca agua, y parando orilla
   de vn arroyo le pusimos por nombre San Francisco de
   Asis; anduvimos seis leguas.
5   ¶ Domingo catorçe de el dicho salio el real atrauezando
   algunas cañadas al rumbo de el nordeste en busca del Rio Colorado, y parando orillas de el le pusimos
   por nombre el Rio de el Spiritu Santo, hauiendo
   marchado seis leguas.
10   ¶ Lunes quinçe de el dicho salio el real rio auajo y a
   distancia de media legua se paso el rio, y atrauezando vn monte muy espesso al rumbo del nordeste
   con algunas guiñadas al norte, paramos en vn
   arroyo que le pusimos por nombre San Juan.
15 Anduuimos este dia cinco leguas.
      ¶ Martes diez y seis de el dicho salio el real el rum-
   bo de el nordeste como cossa de dos leguas atrauezando dos arroyos por el mismo rumbo y paro
   el real en vnos charcos, hauiendo marchado
20 quatro leguas, y le pusimos por nombre el Beato
   Saluador de Horta.
      ¶ Miercoles diez y siete de el dicho salio el real
   el rumbo de el nordeste quarta al norte y
   paramos en vn arroyo que le pussimos San Diego
25 de Alcala; anduuimos este dia seis leguas.

¶ Jueues diez y ocho de el dicho salio el real el rumbo
de el nordeste quarta al leste, atruezando algunos arroyos. En vno de ellos encontramos al yndio que
inviamos con el gouernador de los Texas acompañado
5   de catorze yndios de los principales de ellos, a quienes
les reparti ropa y otras alhajas de las que lleuaba,
mostrando el dicho gouernador y los suyos mucho
regozijo de auernos visto y que nos esperaua toda
su gente con mucha alegria. Voluiendo hasta vn
10   valle muy ameno, donde paro el real en vn arroyo,
y le pusimos por nombre el Valle de Santa Eluira,
hauiendo marchado este dia ocho leguas.

¶ Viernes diez y nueue de el dicho marchamos el
rumbo de el norte quarta al nordeste y a poca
15   distancia salimos a otro valle muy grande y ameno
que le pussimos por nombre el de Galue, y por la
orilla de el passa vn rio grande que le pussimos
por nombre el de la Santissima Trinidad; y
aunque se aliño el passo, se passo lo mas de el dia
20   en passar los bastimentos; y pasado el rio
hallamos otro valle muy ameno que se le pusso
por nombre el de la Moncloua, hauiendo
andado este dia legua y media.

¶ Sabado veinte de el dicho marchamos el rumbo
25   de el nordeste quarta al leste por vnos enzinales

y arroyos distancia de quatro leguas y a la salida del
monte hallamos vn valle grande que se le puso
por nombre San Seuastian; y a un lado del dicho
valle, hallamos quatro viuiendas (que) [de] yndios que
5   tenian maiz y frixoles sembrados, sus cassas con
mucho aseo y camas altas en que dormir. Los aga-
zajamos y proseguimos el rumbo de el nordeste
por vnos enzinales y arroyos hasta vnos charcos
de agua llouediza, que le pussimos por nombre
10   San Bernardino; hauiendo andado siete leguas.

¶ Domingo veinte y vno del dicho despues de missa
salimos al rumbo de el nordeste quarta al leste

por vnos enzinales y pinos atrauezando quatro arroyos sin agua. Y hauiendo llegado a vn arroyo de
15   agua, paro el real en vna plazeta que le pussimos
por nombre San Carlos, hauiendo marchado
seis leguas.

    ¶ Lunes veinte y dos de el dicho salimos el rumbo
de el nordeste quarta al este por vnos enzinales
20   atrauezando cinco arroyos secos y algunas lomitas
donde ay algunas betas de piedra negra y colorada
hasta llegar a vn valle poblado de muchas cassas
de yndios Texas, y alrededor de ellas muchos
sembrados de maiz, frixoles, calauazas y sandias;
25   y le pussimos por nombre San Francisco Xauier;

[folio 12v]

    y dando vna guiñada al norte por vna loma de en-
zinos a cossa de vn quarto de legua, dimos con otro
valle de yndios Texas con sus cassas; y diziendonos
el gouernador de ellos que estaua [^muy] cerca su cassa, pa-
5   ramos el real orilla de vn arroyo, y a esta poblazon
le pussimos San Francisco de los Texas, hauiendo
marchado este dia cinco leguas. Y esta tarde fui con
el gouernador de dichos Texas a dexarlo a su casa
donde me salio a receuir su madre, su muger y
10   vna hija suya y mucha gente que lo estauan
aguardando, sacando vn banco en que sentarme
dandome de merendar tamales de maiz y atole
con mucha limpieza.

    ¶ Martes veinte y tres de el dicho sali con los religiossos
15   padres missioneros como cossa de media legua que
ay de el real hasta la cassa del gouernador en
procession con officiales y soldados a quienes seguian
mucha cantidad de yndios con dicho yndio
gouernador, y llegado a su cassa cantaron el Te
20   Deum Laudamus los missioneros. Y hauiendo estado
vn rato en su cassa sentados en vnos bancos que
mando sacar dicho gouernador, sacaron de merendar en vnas ollas y cazuelas frixoles cozidos

[folio 13r]

    (cozidos), atole de maiz y pinole que merendaron dichos

padres y soldados y voluimos al *real*.

¶ Miercoles veinte y quatro de el dicho se dispusso vna
capilla en que celebrar la fiesta del Corpus Christi,
5 hauiendo este dia agazajado a los yndios con ropa
y los demas generos. Y este dia auisse al gouernador
citasse a toda su gente viniesse a la festiuidad del
Corpus Christi.

¶ Jueues veinte y cinco de el dicho se celebro la fiesta
10 de el Santisisimo Sacramento con toda solemnidad
y procession, acompañando todos los offiziales y soldados y el yndio gouernador y mucha gente
suya toda la proçession, y assistiendo a la missa
cantada, y despues de acauada la missa, se hizo
15 la ceremonia de leuantar el estandarte en nombre
de su magestad ^(que Dios guarde^). Y yo dicho general Alonso de Leon, como cauo superior de todas
las compañias que por horden de el excelentissimo señor Conde de Galue, virrey de esta Nueua
20 España han venido a esta jornada, en nombre de
su magestad, acepte dicha obediencia que dan a su
magestad, y en su *real* nombre les prometi de
fauorecerles y ayudarles, y le entregue vn vaston
con vna cruz, dandole titulo de gouernador de
25 todos sus pueblos para que los rija y gouierne,
dandole a entender por medio de ynterprete

[folio 13v]

lo que deuia obseruar y guardar, y el respecto y obediencia que el y toda su gente deuian tener a los
sacerdotes; y que hiziesse acudieran a la doctrina
a todas sus familias para que se yndustriaran en
5 las cossas de nuestra santa fee catholica para q*ue*
despues de baptizassen y fuessen christianos. El qual
vaston açepto con mucho gusto, prometiendo hazer
todo lo que se le dezia. Y se hizo salua real
por tres vezes y assi mesmo se le dio pocession a el
10 *reveren*do padre comissario fray Damian Massanet
que lo es de estas conuersiones en esta mission para que los ynstruyan en los mysterios de nuestra
santa fee catholica. Y hauernos pedido el d*i*cho

gouernador y los suyos _es dexasemos religiosos
15   para que le enseñassen la doctrina christiana,
y en fee de la amistad, le pedimos al dicho gouernador
que nos diesse tres yndios de los principales de
esta prouincia, entre ellos vn hermano suyo y
vn sobrino suyo y otro primo de el dicho gouer-
20   nador, que con mucho gusto prometieron yr con
nosotros a ver al excelentissimo señor Conde de
Galue, virrey y capitan general de la Nueua España. Este dia se obseruo el sol y nos hallamos
en treinta y quatro grados y siete minutos.
25   ¶ Viernes veinte y seis de el dicho sali con los padres
missioneros y algunos soldados y officiales con el

[folio 14r]

dicho yndio gouernador el rumbo de el nordeste
a uer el paraxe mas a proposito para poner la mision.
Y hauiendo visto tres valles pequeños hasta donde
nos dixeron hauian muerto dos franceses donde
5   querian poblarse, que alli vimos las sepulturas
de ellos, les pusimos vna cruz en vn arbol. Y llegando a un rio que no le hallamos passo, sino es por vn
arbol que tienen los yndios atrauezado y vna
maroma por donde se van teniendo, que al rio
10   le pusimos San Miguel Arcangel, y de alli nos
voluimos al real, hauiendo andado seis leguas.
¶ Sabado veinte y siete, domingo veinte y ocho, lunes veinte y nueve, martes treinta, miercoles
treinta y uno se trabaxo en hazer la yglessia y
15   viuienda de los padres apostolicos en medio de la
poblazon principal de los Texas.
¶ Jueues primero de junio di pocession de dicha mission, hauiendo cantado la missa el reverendo padre
comissario fray Damian Masanet en dicha ygle-
20   sia, assistiendo el dicho yndio gouernador y su
gente a la missa y bendicion de la yglessia. Este
dia en la tarde despache el real en prossecuzion de
la vuelta a la prouincia de Cuahuila por el mesmo
camino que lleuamos. Pero esta noche en el real
25   de San Carlos, hauiendo marchado cinco leguas.

¶ Viernes dos de el dicho sali con el *reveren*do padre comissario fray Damian Massanet y seis soldados
en seguimiento de el r*eal* de el pueblo de San
Francisco de los Texas. Viniendo en nuestra compa-
5   ñia vn hermano de el gouernador de ellos, vn
sobrino suyo y vn primo suyo con otro yndio de
el dicho pueblo, y llegando al r*eal* proseguimos
hasta el r*eal* de San Bernardino poco mas de
media legua, marchando este dia seis leguas y
10   media el r*eal*.

¶ Sabado tres de el dicho proseguimos nuestra marcha;
atrauesando el valle de San Seuastian y el de la
Moncloua, llegamos al Rio de la Santissima Trinidad y por estar demaciado crecido, no pudimos
15   passar. Paramos junto al rio, hauiendo marchado este dia seis leguas y media.

¶ Domingo quatro, lunes cinco, martes seis, miercoles
siete, jueues ocho, viernes nueue, sabado diez.
Este dia se hizo balsa y se comenzo a pasar el rio.

20   ¶ Domingo onze se acauo de passar el rio; como a
cossa de las dos de la tarde salio el real por
el valle de Galue hasta llegar al de Santa Eluira, donde paro en vnos charcos de agua llouediza, hauiendo marchado tres leguas.

25   ¶ Lunes doze de el dicho salio el real de dicho

quartel y passando por el de San Diego de Alcala,
como cossa de dos leguas paro el r*eal* en vnos charcos de agua llouediza, hauiendo marchado nueue leguas.

5   ¶ Martes trece del dicho salio el r*eal* del dicho paraje
y passando por el del Beato Saluador de Horta
llegamos al Arroyo de San Juan, hauiendo andado este dia ocho leguas.

¶ Miercoles catorze de el dicho salio el r*eal* del d*i*cho
10   paraxe y pasando por el Rio de el Espiritu Santo
llegamos a vnas lomitas tendidas donde (donde)
haze vn arroyo de agua, donde paro el real,

hauiendo andado este dia ocho leguas.

¶ Jueues quince del dicho salio el real del dicho
15 paraxe y pasando por el real de San Francisco
de Asis, llegamos a vnos arroyos de agua de
donde despache al yndic a llamar al gouernador
de los Texas, hauiendo andado este dia siete
leguas.

20 ¶ Viernes diez y seis de el dicho salio el real
de el dicho paraxe y passando por el real
de San Joseph, llegamos a vn arroyo de
agua donde paro el real, hauiendo
andado este dia seis leguas.

25 ¶ Sabado diez y siete del dicho salio el real del
[folio 15v]

dicho paraxe y passando por el Rio de San Marcos
llegamos a vn arroyo de agua, donde paro el
real, hauiendo andado este dia cinco leguas
y se le pusso por nombre Jesus, Maria y Joseph
5 de Buena Vista.

¶ Domingo diez y ocho de el dicho salio el real
prosiguiendo su viaje, y yo el general Alonso
de Leon, con diez y seis soldados, el rumbo de
el nordeste en busca de los francesitos y
10 vna francessa que me dieron noticia vnos yndios que estauan rancheados en dicho paraje
por vnos llanos como cossa de quatro leguas
hasta llegar a vn montezillo, el qual passamos y despues seguimos el rumbo de el
15 leste como cossa de tres leguas por otra llanada
donde dimos en vn monteçillo con vna rancheria de yndios. De alli proseguimos por otros
llanos muy grandes que hauia mucha cantidad de siuola, hasta orilla de vn riachuelo,
20 que al principio de el haze vn manchon de
arboles, donde paramos por ser ya muy noche,
hauiendo andado este dia diez y siete leguas.
¶ Lunes diez y nueue de el dicho proseguimos
nuestro viaxe por orillas del dicho riachuelo

[folio 16r]

que tiene de vna parte y otra alboreda y hauiendole passado y caminado como dos leguas, dimos
con vna rancheria de yndios a los quales
agazaje y quedaron muy nuestros amigos.

5   De alli proseguimos nuestro viaxe el rumbo
del sur por vnos llanos; y como cossa de vna
legua dimos con otra rancheria de yndios
a los quales tambien agazaxamos. De alli
proseguimos por dichos llanos el mismo rumbo

10   como cossa de quatro leguas, hasta entrar en
vn monteçillo, el qual passamos y proseguimos nuestro viaxe el rumbo del poniente. Y pasando vn arroyo grande en vn monte
dimos con vna nacion de yndios muy grande

15   a los quales agazage y quedaron muy nuestros
amigos y nos dieron yndios que nos guiassen
hasta otra rancheria. De alli salimos por
vnos llanos y ya muy noche paramos a orilla
de vn arroyo, hauiendo andado este dia quin-

20   ce leguas.
    ¶ Martes veinte de el dicho proseguimos nuestro
viaxe el rumbo de el leste donde dimos
con vna rancheria de yndios, a los quales
agazaje y nos dieron quatro yndios que

[folio 16v]

nos guiassen a donde estauan los francesitos, de
donde salimos por vnos llanos que estauan cu-
biertos de siuola el mesmo rumbo a pasar el
Arroyo de los Franceses, y hauiendole pasado

5   seguimos a la poblacion vieja de ellos, y de alli
proseguimos el rumbo de el sur hasta llegar al
arroyo que llaman los yndios de las Canoas,
y hauiendole passado dimos con otro arroyuelo
donde paramos, hauiendo (^para) marchado este

10   dia catorze leguas.
    ¶ Miercoles veinte y vno de el dicho salimos el
rumbo de el sueste; y como cossa de vna legua dimos con dos yndios que venian a cauallo

de la nacion que tenian los francesitos, los
15 quales nos lleuaron a su rancheria que estaua
en vna punta de vna ensenada donde estauan
Roberto y Madalena Talon, de los quales trate
el rescate. Y hauiendoles agazajado y dado
el rescate que pedian, anduuieron con nosotros
20 con mill desuerguenzas, pidiendonos todos los
cauallos, hasta la ropa que trayamos a cuestas,
entre tanto que yban a traer el otro francessito
que estaua dos leguas de alli en la misma
nacion. Y hauiendole traydo, prosiguieron

[folio 17r]

mas con sus desuerguenzas, trayendo arcos y flechas,
viniendo mucha cantidad de yndios con adargas
pidiendo cossas exorbitantes y que si no se las
dauamos, nos hauian de flechar y matar a
5 todos, y diziendo esto y comenzando a flechar
fue todo vno, con que nosotros dimos sobre ellos
y hauiendoles muerto quatro y herido otros, se re-
tiraron, hauiendonos herido dos cauallos. Nos fuimos saliendo con mucha horden a dormir
10 como cossa de quatro leguas, donde hauiamos
dormido la noche antes, hauiendo andado este
dia doze leguas.
     ¶ Jueues veinte y dos de el dicho salimos al ama-
necer el mismo rumbo de el norte por vnos
15 llanos muy grandes orilla de el rio de Guadalupe y como a cossa de las diez de la noche paramos
cerca de vn montezillo, hauiendo marchado
este dia catorze leguas.
     ¶ Viernes veinte y tres de el dicho salimos el rum-
20 bo de el norte como cossa de dos leguas, donde
dimos con el rastro de el real que hauia pasado, y como a cossa de tres leguas dimos con el
en el passo de el Rio de Guadalupe, donde
paramos, hauiendo andado cinco leguas.

[folio 17v]

     ¶ Sabado veinte y quatro de el dicho, dia de el señor San Juan,
salio el real de el dicho paraxe y passando el Rio de

Guadalupe, proseguimos nuestro viaje hasta vn arroyo
que esta antes de el real del Agua Salada a donde paro,
5   hauiendo andado este dia siete leguas.
¶ Domingo veinte y cinco del dicho salio el real del dicho
paraxe y passando por el real de la Salada llegamos
al Arroyo de el Leon donde paro el real; hauiendo
andado este dia siete leguas.
10   ¶ Lunes veinte y seis de el dicho salio el real de
el dicho paraxe y llegamos al Rio de Medina donde
paro el real, hauiendo andado este dia cinco leguas.
¶ Martes veinte y siete de el dicho. Salio el real de el
dicho paraxe y llegamos a vn arroyo de agua donde
15   paro el real, hauiendo andado este dia ocho leguas.
¶ Miercoles veinte y ocho del dicho salio el real de el
dicho paraxe y por auer perdido el tino la guia,
paramos en vn arroyo de agua, arriua de el passo
de el Arroyo de los Robalos, hauiendo andado este
20   dia cinco leguas.
¶ Jueves veinte y nueve del dicho salio el real del
dicho paraxe y pasando por el real del Ayre, llegamos
a vnos charcos de agua, donde paro el real, hauiendo andado cinco leguas.
25   ¶ Viernes treintta de el dicho salio el real de el dicho
paraxe y passando por el Rio Hondo llegamos a las
Cruzes, como tres leguas arriua de el passo de el
[folio 18r]
Rio Hondo, hauiendo andado este dia ocho leguas.
¶ Sabado primero de jullio salio el real del dicho paraxe y llegamos al Rio Zarco, hauiendo andado
este dia cinco leguas.
5   ¶ Domingo dos de el dicho salio el real del dicho paraxe
y passando por el Rio de las Nuezes llegamos a vnos
charcos de agua donde paro el real, hauiendo andado este dia ocho leguas.
¶ Lunes tres del dicho salio el real del dicho paraxe
10   y pasando por el Arroyo de Ramos llegamos a vnos
charcos de agua, donde paro el real, hauiendo
andado este dia diez leguas.

¶ Martes quatro de el dicho salio el real de el dicho paraxe y llegamos al Rio Grande y por estar muy
15   crecido no se pudo passar, donde paro el real,
hauiendo andado este dia ocho leguas.
¶ Miercoles cinco, jueues seis, viernes siete, sabado ocho,
domingo nueue, lunes diez y martes onze es-
tuuimos parados orilla de el Rio Grande por no
20   poder passar, por estar todavia muy crezido, de donde despache correo a su excelencia remitiendole vn françes
llamado Pedro Muñi, los autos, ma[p]a y este derrotero, dandole razon a su excelencia de toda la jornada.
Alonso de Leon

montes, con algunas llanadas cortas con pozeros zerra dos
de enzinos y robres, y dos arroyos secos, luego siguimos el Rum
bo de siguiente que eres a lnorte, hallando los mesmos mon
tes y chaparros de enzinos que se encitaron de montar y al
gunas llanadas y 4 arroyos secos que llevan muy poca agua
donde paro el R.l la zorilla denuo que les dio por nombre
la aparision de los Mys arcanseles, auiendo marchado estedia. 0g

Lunes 8 de d.ho salio el R.l del sobre d.ho quartel
el Rumbo de lnorte por unas lomas y cañadas bazando
8 arroyos secos y algunos manchones de enzinos y robres,
donde llego el R.l aun arroyo que lleva muy poca agua don
de paro en una placeta que hace forma de media luna que
ba da a esta del Rumbre de lnordeste, y siguiendo por
nombre Ag.l de S.n Gregorio nazianzeno auiendo marchado
este dia y leg. 0g

Martes 9 del d.ho salio el Real del d.ho quartel nom
brado San Gregorio Nazianzeno el Rumbo del
norte por lomas y cañadas y algunos pedazos de
monte enzino, Robles morales y Piñas que fue
nezesario demontar como cosa de 3 legua y hauie
endo parado seis arroyos secos y llegado a otro
arroyo paso el Real en una colina que se le puso
por nombre Jesus Maria y Josep de buena vista —
hauiendo marchado este dia 5 legua — — 7=
d.ho dia 9 ala tarde lle que al d.ho Real donde sali
con ocho hombres entre ellos el Capitan Don Grego
rio Salinas Varona en busca de un franzes lo que
estaba en (the Pancheria de gn.dios el Rumbo
del sudueste y hauiendo marchado como cosa de
12 legua por ser la noche pare a orilla del the

Folio 5v of manuscript 90-D showing two distinct hands and hand A's unique hybrid letter, a z with cedilla tail (Yale Collection of American Literature, Beinecke Rare Book and Manuscript Library)

2.7 Manuscript 90-D

[folio 1r]

Biaje que hizo el gouer*na*dor Alonsso de Leon de horden
del ex*celentisi*mo se*ñ*or Conde de Galues, virrey de esta Nueba
Spa*ñ*a en compa*ñ*ia del capi*tan* don Gregorio de Salinas Varona
desde la Prou*inci*a de Cuaohuila a la Baia del Spiritu

5   Santo y Prou*inci*a de los Tejas en 26 de marzo de
1690.

    ¶ Domingo d*i*cho dia 26 salieron las requas y vagaje de la
villa de Santiago de la Monclova a parar vna legua
fuera del pueblo de los indios que hubo desde

10   d*i*cha villa luega [*sic*] y m*edi*a el rumbo del norte.

    ¶ Lunes 27 del d*i*cho se leuanto el r*e*al y fuimos
a parar abajo de las lomas orilla del Rio de Cuaohuila el rumbo del nordeste quarta al leste 3 leg*ua*s.

    ¶ Martes 28 del d*i*cho [^salimos del dicho paraje] al lesnordeste rio
      abajo y de-

15   jando el rio entramos por el puerto de Baluartes
y del d*i*cho puerto dimos vna guiñada de una legua
por parar a orilla del rio, donde se paro el r*e*al, auiendo marchado este dia 3 leg*ua*s.

    ¶ Miercoles 29 del d*i*cho salio el r*e*al rio abajo

20   el rumbo de leste quarta al nordeste y pasando el alamo poco mas de una legua, paro el r*e*al
orilla del rio por tierra llana con algunos
chaparros y lechuguilla, auiendo marchado este dia 5 [leguas].

    ¶ Juebes 30 del d*i*cho salio el r*e*al el rumbo

25   del leste quarta al nordeste rio abajo asta las
ajuntas de las Sabinas donde paro a orilla del,
auiendo marchado este dia por tierra llana con

[folio 1v]

    (con) algunos mezquitales y lechuguilla donde
se junto la compa*ñ*ia del Reyno de Leon y los padres mi-
sioneros; este dia andubimos 4 leg*ua*s.

    ¶ Viernes 31 del d*i*cho salio el r*e*al rio abajo y atra-

5   uesando la loma que esta enfrente el rumbo de leste
llegamos al Rio de las Salinas, auiendo caminado como dos leguas passamos el rio donde paro
el r*e*al.

¶ Sauado primero de abrill caminamos el run-
10 bo del nordeste distanzia de 6 leguas atrauesando
vnos llanos sin agua, tierra bien penossa por los
muchos mezquites aunque llana, donde dimos
en un charco de agua dulze, donde paro el real.
¶ Domingo 2 del dicho salimos el rumbo
15 del nordeste quarta al norte pasando algunas lomitas de chaparros y tierra llana. [L]lega-
mos a unos charcos de agua llouediza donde
paro el real, auiendo marchado este dia 5 leguas.
¶ Lunes 3 del dicho salimos el rumbo del
20 norte por tierra llana con muy pocos chaparros asta orilla de un arroyo donde allamos los indios del franzes a los quales les dimos tauaco
y rropa, donde paro el real auiendo marchado 4 [leguas].
¶ Martes 4 del dicho salimos el rumbo del
25 norte en demanda del Rio Grande por tierra llana con algunos mezquites, y auiendo dado
con el passo, paro el real en la orilla del rio don-

[folio 2r]

de se hallaron algunas sibolas, auiendo marchado
este dia 5 leguas.
¶ Miercoles 5 del dicho estubimos parados para que
se confesaran todos y cumplieran con la iglesia
5   antes de pasar el rio.
¶ Juebes 6 del dicho pasamos el rio y caminamos el rumbo del norte quarta al nordeste
y paramos orilla de un arroyo seco, auiendo andado este dia ocho leguas; durmio el real sin
10 agua, auiendo passado algunas lomas y chaparros
de mezquites, 8 [leguas].
¶ Viernes 7 del dicho salio el real el rumbo del
nordeste por tierra llana, donde paro el real en el
Arroyo de Ramos, donde haze un enzino grande
15 y algunos chaparros de mezquites, auiendo andado este dia 3 leguas.
¶ Sauado 8 del dicho salio el real el rumbo
del nordeste quarta al norte por tierra llana
en partes muchos mezquites, donde llegamos a un

20   arroyo que por tener mal passo se gasto todo
      lo mas del dia en acomodarle y pasar las re-
      quas, donde paro el real, auiendo marchado
      3 leguas y se le puso por nombre el de Caraman-
      chel.
25   ¶ Domingo 9 del dicho salio el real el rumbo
      del nordeste quarta al norte por unos llanos y pa-
      sando dos cañadas de arboles entramos
      en un mezquital y a cossa de media legua di-
[folio 2v]
      mos con el Rio de las Nuezes donde hay muchos
      pedernales a orilla del rio, paro el real en un potre-
      ro grande que haze, auiendo caminado este dia 5 [leguas].
      ¶ Lunes 10 del dicho pasamos el rio y caminamos
5   el rumbo del leste por una cañada que tiene muchos
      nogales y mezquites muy espesos asta llegar a una lo-
      ma como cosa de 2 leguas, y luego siguimos el rumbo del
      norte como otras 2 leguas y despues dimos otra guiñada
      al leste por tierra llana, llena de mezquites, donde
10   dimos con el Rio Çarco. y auiendole passado paro el
      real de la otra vanda, auiendo marchado este dia 7 [leguas].
      ¶ Martes 11 del dicho salio el real el rumbo del
      norte por unas llañadas en partes mezquites, lo-
      mitas y cañadas donde dimos con el Rio Hon-
15   do, donde paro el real auiendo marchado 6 leguas.
      ¶ Miercoles 12 del dicho se detubo el real en el dicho
      paraje para buscar dos compañeros que se perdieron
      en la marcha el dia antes.
      ¶ Juebes 13 del dicho tubimos noticia que 6 leguas del
20   real estaua una junta de indios donde auia beni-
      do a dar un franzes, donde sali este dia a la tarde
      con 20 hombres y entre ellos el capitan don Gregorio Sali-
      nas Varona el rumbo del poniente por orilla del
      rio de la otra vanda como 5 leguas, donde pare es-
25   ta noche.
      ¶ Viernes 14 del dicho al amanezer prosegui mi via-
      je dicho rumbo como cosa de media legua y luego se-
      gui el rumbo del norte por una llañada que ti-
      ene muchos robres asta la orilla de un rio

donde dimos con la rancheria como cosa de media
legua y donde nos salieron a rrezeuir nuchos jndios
jndias y ni[ñ]os, a los quales agasajamos con tabaco
y nos dieron razon que los dos franzeses estaban
5   de la otra vanda del Rio de Guadalupe y un jndio
tenia un mozquete franzes. De alli nos boluimos derechos
al real viniendo muchos jndios acompañandonos
asta el real donde los regalamos con ropa, arina y tauaco. Este dia llegaron los dos soldados a el, auiendo
10   marchado nosotros este dia 7 leguas.
    ¶ Sauado 15 del dicho salio el real el rumbo del les-
te rio abajo por unas cañadas con algunos mezquites donde dimos con el passo del rio donde paro el real por acomodar el paso del rio, auiendo
15   marchado este dia 6 [leguas].
    ¶ Domingo 16 del dicho passamos de la otra vanda
del Rio Hondo siguiendo el rumbo del este quarta
al nordeste por tierra llana, donde dimos con vn
arroyo que fue neçessario acomodar el passo y des-
20   montar alrrededor del, donde fuimos prosiguiendo nuestro viaje asta unos charcos de agua llouediza
donde paro el real, auiendo marchado este dia 8 [leguas]
    ¶ Lunes 17 del dicho salio el real el rumbo del nordeste
y por algunos montes que se ofrezieron pasar fue neçessa-
25   rio el hazer algunos rodeos vnas vezes al norte
quarta al nordeste y leste, donde dimos con el Arroyo de los Robalos donde paro el real, auiendo
marchado este dia 5 leguas.

[folio 3v]

    ¶ Martes 18 del dicho salimos los soldados por dife-
rentes rumbos a buscar 126 cauallos que dieron estanpida
asta que parezieron, este dia a la tarde salio el real
y a poca distanzia perdio el tino la guia y nos fue forzosso seguir
5   el rumbo del norte por ir en busca del Rio de Medina,
y por ser ya tarde paro el real en una lomita que se le puso
el real del Rosario, auiendo marchado (^?)4 leguas por tierra
llana en partes robres y mezquites.
    ¶ Miercoles 19 del dicho salio el real el rumbo del

10   norte en busca del dicho Rio de Medina por entre montes
de robres, enzinos y mezquitales asta llegar al cajon del
rio, donde paro el real a la parte de arriba del rio,
auiendo marchado 7 leguas este dia.

    ¶ Juebes 20 del dicho salimos el rumbo del leste
15   y a distanzia de 2 leguas dimos con el passo del rio donde paro el real por ser neçessario aliñar el passo.

    ¶ Viernes 21 del dicho pasamos el rio y caminamos
el rumbo del leste por tierra llana con algunos robres, enzinos, mezquitales, sauzes donde dimos con
20   el Arroyo del Leon donde paro el real, auiendo
marchado este dia 5 leguas.

    ¶ Sauado 22 del dicho salio el real el rumbo de
leste y a uezes al nordeste por tierra llana con enzinos y robres asta que dimos con vn arroyo de agua
25   salada, donde paro el real auiendo marchado 6 [leguas].

    ¶ Domingo 23 del dicho salio el real el rumbo de
leste quarta al nordeste por tierra llana y lomas
con manchones de enzinos y robres, donde llegamos junto al Rio de Guadalupe, donde paro el
30   real çerca de un arroyo, auiendo marchado 5 [leguas].
[folio 4r]

    ¶ Lunes 24 del dicho salio el real rio abajo asta llegar al
passo del que estaua jondable y se passo lo mas del dia
en pasarlo, donde paro el real de la otra vanda, a-
uiendo marchado este dia 2 leguas.
5   ¶ Martes 25 del dicho sali con el capitan don Gregorio
de Salinas Varona y 20 soldados camino del hueste para rreconozer la Baia del Spiritu Santo. Andubimos como cossa de 14 leguas este dia por tierra llana y
fertil en partes algunos enzinos y robres, y auiendo lle-
10   gado a un charco de agua llouediza paramos.

    ¶ Miercoles 26 del dicho proseguimos nuestro viaje a la
poblazion vieja de los franzeses y como a cossa
de 5 leguas dimos con ella, dicho camino al hueste a
onde hizimos alto para quemar el fuerte y despues
15   de quemado passamos a reconozer la baia como
cossa de 2 leguas, donde se rreconozio hauer dos
boias, vna a la punta del Rio de San Marcos y la

otra a un lado que mira el Rio de Guadalupe
señalando canal. No se obseruo el sol por estar
20   nublado. De alli dimos la buelta rio arriba de
los franzeses por uer si allauamos algunos jndios
en sus rancherias viejas y no podimos conseguir el
dar con ninguno, y por ser ya tarde paramos orilla
del rio, auiendo marchado este dia en yda y buel-
25   ta 14 leg*uas*.

¶ Juebes 27 del *dic*ho dimos buelta al *rea*l hauiendo caminado este dia 20 leg*uas* rio arriba por uer si
dauamos con jndios, y no se dio con ninguno.

[folio 4v]

¶ Viernes 28 del *dic*ho sali con 8 soldados rio arriba de
Guadalupe dando humazos por uer si daua con jndios
como cossa de 6 leg*uas*, y por no auerme rrespondido di la buelta al *rea*l, auiendo marchado este dia de yda y buelta 12 [leg*uas*].
5   ¶ Sauado 29 del *dic*ho salio el *rea*l el rumbo del leste como
cossa de 3 leg*uas* y luego seguimos el del nordeste como otras
leguas por tierra llana, algunas cañadas y manchones
de enzinos y robres, y auiendo llegado a unos charcos
de agua llouediza paro el *rea*l en la falda de una loma
10   que se le pusso por nombre S*a*n P*edr*o Martir, 6 [leg*uas*].
¶ Domingo 30 del *dic*ho despues de missa auiendo llegado
dos soldados de los presidios del Parral que benian siguiendo sus compañeros, sali con 16 soldados a desmontar algunos pedazos de monte y ber si topaua al-
15   gunos yndios que nos guiasen a la prou*inc*ia de los Tejas,
y llegando a unas rancherias viejas pare esta noche,
auiendo marchado este dia 9 leg*uas*.
¶ Lunes 1º de mayo prosegui mi viaje y llegue a una loma alta donde pare por ser ya tarde, andubimos este dia 12 leg*uas*.
20   ¶ Martes 2 del *dic*ho prosegui mi viaje y llegue a un
potrero orilla del Rio de S*a*n Marcos que por estar el
rio hondo no pude pasar a la otra vanda, andubimos este dia 14 leg*uas*.
¶ Miercoles 3 del *dic*ho prosegui mi viaje rio arriba asta
25   el passo que halle muy bueno, donde le passe y fui prosiguiendo mi viaje, y como 5 leg*uas* mas alla del rio
orilla de un monte diuisamos dos jndios y llamando-

los no quisieron venir antes si se metieron en el monte
donde pare esta noche por uer si querian venir,
30 auiendo marchado este dia 7 leguas.
[folio 5r]
¶ Juebes 4 del dicho por la mañana nos vino a ber el jndio
y auiendo hablado con el por señas nos dijo que hera de los
Tejas y que este dia llegariamos a una rancheria y prosiguiendo ha andar guiandonos como cossa de 3 leguas nos dijo que
5 estaua muy lejos y que le diera un cauallo que el yria a llamar al capitan de los Tejas. Con que le despache y me bol-
ui al paraje de la noche antes por auerme dicho que lo aguar-
dasse alli, auiendo marchado este dia de yda y buelta
6 leguas. Este dia llego a juntarse con el real en el quartel de San Pedro Mar-
10 tir los 20 soldados de los presidios del Parral.
¶ Viernes 5 del dicho por la mañana despache a 4 soldados
al real para que viniesse marchando, y como a cossa de las
5 de la tarde boluio el jndio que despache al capitan de los
Tejas que por auersele huido el cauallo no proseguia que
15 me venia avisar.
¶ Sauado 6 del dicho enbie a 4 compañeros por el rras-
tro para que bieran si se auia junto con algunos de los
jndios, y toparon con otro jndio el qual me trujeron
y hauiendole ofrezido darle ropa por que fuera a los Tejas
20 ha auisar al gouernador como esteua alli. Con que el jndio primero, codizioso de la oferta me dijo que le boluiesse
a dar otro cauallo que el yria a los Tejas, con que
lo despache luego. Este dia llegaron los 4 soldados
al real.
25 ¶ Domingo 7 del dicho salio el real del dicho quartel
nombrado San Pedro Martir siguiendo el rumbo como
cossa de 3 leguas quarta al nordeste por entre montes espesos de rrobres y enzinos, que en partes fue neçessario des-
[folio 5v]
montar, con algunas llanadas cortas con potreros zerrados
de enzinos y robres y dos arroyos secos. Luego siguimos el run-
bo del poniente y auezes al norte, hallando los mesmos montes y chaparros de enzinos que nezesitaron desmontar y al-
5 gunas llanadas y 4 arroyos secos que lleuan muy poca agua,
donde paro el real a la orilla de uno que se le pusso por nombre

la Aparizion de San Miguel Arcanjel, auiendo marchado este dia 9 [leguas].

¶ Lunes 8 del dicho salio el real del sobre dicho quartel
el rumbo del norte por unas lomas y cañadas pasando
10   8 arroyos secos y algunos manchones de enzinos y robres,
donde llego el real a un arroyo que lleua muy poca agua, donde paro en una plazeta que haze forma de media luna que
la dicha esta el rumbo del nordeste, se le pusso por
nombre el quartel de San Gregorio Nazianzeno, auiendo marchado
15   este dia 9 leguas.

¶ Martes 9 del dicho salio el real del dicho quartel nombrado San Gregorio Nazianzeno el rumbo del
norte por lomas y cañadas y algunos pedazos de
monte, enzino, robles, morales y parras, que fue
20   nezesario desmontar como cossa de 1 legua y hauiendo passado seis arroios secos y llegado a otro
arroio pa[^r]o el real en vna colina que se le pusso
por nombre Jessus, Maria y Joseph de Buena Vista,
hauiendo marchado este dia 7 leguas.
25   Dicho dia 9 a la tarde llegue al dicho real donde sali
con ocho hombres, entre ellos el capitan don Gregorio Salinas Varona, en busca de vn franzesito que
estaba en vna rancheria de yndios el rumbo
del sudueste, y hauiendo marchado como cosa de
30   12 leguas por ser ya noche pare a orilla de vna
[folio 6r]
colina.

¶ Miercoles 10 del dicho salimos antes de amanezer
prosiguiendo el mismo rumbo del sudueste como cosa
de 9 leguas asta vna loma alta que haze antes de
5   entrar en el monte. De alli seguimos el rumbo del
poniente por vn monte mui espesso de robles, enzinos,
muchas parras y morales y algunas plazetas a la
salida de el como cosa de 5 leguas y a la dicha salida
del monte dimos con el franzesito llamado Pedro Ta-
10   lon que benia marchando con vna rancheria de yndios.
De alli nos voluimos siguiendo por el mismo camino
asta zerca de la misma colina donde dormi la noche
antes, hauiendo marchado este dia 27 leguas de
yda y buelta.

15   ¶ Juebes 11 del dicho vinimos prosiguiendo nuestro viaje
      desde antes de amanezer el rumbo del nordeste como cosa
      de 12 leguas asta vna loma alta que haze vna mota
      de nogales mui altos, donde di con vna rancheria de
      yndios que nos dieron noticia de otro franzes que esta-
20   ba alli zerca con otra rancheria de yndios, el qual
      embie a buscar con vn yndio, y al mismo tiempo despache
      2 soldados al real para que viniesen 4 con bastimen-
      to por si no viniese el franzes para yr a buscarle, y
      a este tiempo fuimos a pasar el Rio de San Marcos
25   por hauer llouido mucho esta tarde y no creziese el
      rio, hauiendo marchado este dia 16 leguas.
           ¶ El dia siguiente, viernes por la mañana 12, llego
      el franzes con 3 yndios y los soldados del real, con que
      proseguimos nuestro viaxe asta alcanzarle, que
30   le alcanze 6 leguas del rio el rumbo del norte.
[folio 6v]
           ¶ Miercoles 10 prosiguio con el real el capitan Francisco
      Martinez el rumbo del norte por lomas y cañadas
      a pasar el Rio de San Marcos, donde le passo, y
      prosiguio su viaje el mismo rumbo asta vna colina
5   donde hauia encontrado los compañeros que yo ha-
      uia dexado, donde paro hauiendo caminado este dia
      8 leguas y se le puso por nombre San Elifonso.
           ¶ Juebes 11 del dicho se mexoro el quartel a otro pasa-
      xe mas abentaxado como cossa de 3 leguas el
10   rumbo del nordeste donde paro en vna colina que
      se le pusso por nombre San Joseph.
           ¶ Viernes 12 paro el real por esperarnos que llega-
      semos con los franzes.
           ¶ Sabado 13 del dicho salio el real del dicho quar-
15   tel nombrado San Joseph el rumbo del leste
      como cossa de 3 leguas y como cossa de otras 3 al nor-
      deste por colinas y cañadas y 3 arroios que lleban
      alguna poca de agua, donde paro el real a la
      orilla de otro riachuelo en la falda de vn montezi-
20   llo que se le pusso por nombre San Francisco de Asis, 6 [leguas].
           ¶ Domingo 14 del dicho, salio el real del quartel
      nombrado San Francisco de Asis por vnas colinas y

cañadas el rumbo del nordeste en demanda del
Rio Colorado con mucho monte por las orillas de

25   el, donde paro el real y se le puso por nombre el Rio
del Espiritu Santo, hauiendo marchado este dia 6 leg*uas*.
     ¶ Lunes 15 del dicho salio el real del *di*cho quartel del
Rio del Espiritu Santo el rumbo del leste como
cossa de 3 leg*uas* por vn monte mui espesso que se

30   desmonto para pasar las requas, y despues el rumbo
[folio 7r]

    del nordeste como cosa de 1 legua por vnas plazetillas
y algunos montesillos a trechos, y despues el rumbo del
norte como cosa de otra legua, donde paro el real en vn
arroio que hallamos q*ue* se le puso por nombre San Juan, 5 [leguas].

5   ¶ Martes 16 del *di*cho salio el real del *di*cho quartel nombrado San Juan el rumbo del nordeste como cosa de 2 leg*uas*
asta vn arroio atascador y luego se siguio otro arro-
iuelo de buen passo donde siguimos el rumbo del nordeste quarta al norte como otras 2 leg*uas*, donde hallamos

10   vnos charcos de agua, paro el real y se le puso por nombre el Beato Saluador de Horta, hauiendo march*a*do 4 [leguas].
    ¶ Miercoles 17 del *di*cho salio el real del quartel nom-
brado el Beato Saluador de Horta el rumbo del nordeste quarta al norte por tierra llana, donde paro el

15   real en vn arroio que se le puso por nombre San Diego de Alcala, hauiendo marchado este dia 6 leg*uas*.
    ¶ Juebes 18 del *di*cho salio el real del sobre *di*cho quar-
tel el rumbo del nordeste quarta al leste por tierra llana aunque en partes fue nezesario acomodar

20   (algunos) (^p)el passo de algunos arroios y desmontar
algunos palos que embarazaban el passo. Este dia
dimos con el capitan de los Tejas a la orilla de vn riachuelo con 14 yndios que le acompañaban a los quales
les di ropa y otros jeneros. De alli proseguimos el

25   viaxe asta entrar en vn valle mui ameno que se le
puso por nombre el de Santa Eluira, donde dimos con
vn arroio donde paro el real a orilla de el, que se
le puso por nombre al quartel el de Santa Elvira
hauiendo marchado este dia 8 leguas.
[folio 7v]

¶ Viernes 19 del dicho salio el real del dicho quartel Santa
Eluira el rumbo del norte quarta al nordeste por vn
montezillo donde dimos con otro valle mui grande y
[^ que se le puso por nombre el de Galaue]
5   ameno, y a la salida de el dimos con vna arboleda grande donde se dio con vn rio grande y hondo que se le
puso por nombre al Rio de la Santissima Trenidad que
fue nezesario acomodar para pasarle, donde se gasto
lo mas del dia para pasar las requas. Y al otro lado
10   hallamos otro valle mui ameno que se le puso por nombre el de la Moncloua, donde paro el real a orilla del
rio y se le puso por nombre al quartel el de San Sebastian,
hauiendo marchado como cossa de legua y media este dia.
¶ Sauado 20 del dicho salio el real del dicho valle de la
15   Moncloua y (^valle) y quartel de San Sebastian el rumbo
del nordeste quarta al leste por vn monte de robles,
de nogales y parras distancia de 4 leguas, y a la salida del monte se dio con otro valle que se le puso por nombre el de San Sebastian, y en vn monte que esta el
20   rumbo del leste en frente del camino dimos con 4 casas
de yndios que se le puso por nombre San Bernardino.
Estos tienen sembrad[o] maiz y mucho aseo en sus casas,
a estos se les agasaxo y de alli proseguimos nuestro viaje
el rumbo del nordeste por otro monte de robles. Los ar-
25   boles mui claros y grandes y 2 arroios que lleban
mui poca agua y algunas plazetas a donde dimos
con vnos charcos de agua dulze, donde paro el real
a orillas de ellos y se le puso por nombre el quartel de
San Bernardino, habiendo marchado este dia 7 [leguas].
[folio 8r]
¶ Domingo 21 del dicho salio el real del dicho (del dicho) quartel de
San Bernardino el rumbo del nordeste quarta al leste por
vn monte de robles, enzinos y algunos pinos y sarmientos
con razimos de vbas a vn lado y otro del camino, donde pa-
5   samos 4 arroios hondos del mal paso sin agua y algunos
zerritos de tierra muerta, llenos de robles, todo el monte es
mui claro, y hauiendo llegado a vn arroio de agua, paro el real
en el mismo monte donde haze vna plazeta que se le puso por
nombre el quartel de San Carlos, hauiendo marchado este dia 6 [leguas].

10   ¶ Lunes 22 del dicho salio (^?)el real del dicho quartel San Car-
        los el rumbo del nordeste quarta al leste por el sobre dicho
        monte de robles y algunos pinos y en partes sepas a lo lar-
        go del camino por vn lado y otro, y hauiendo pasado cinco
        arroios secos y (^??) lomitas las dos de ellas con betas de
15   metal, chaparros de enzino y robles grandes y luego dimos
        con vn balle con muchas casas de yndios de los Tejas y
        alrededor de ellos sus sembrados de maiz y frixoles y
        calabazas y sandias. De alli dimos otro guiñada al norte
        por vna loma alta de los mismos chaparros y caimos en
20   otro valle de las mesmas cassas de yndios y sembrados donde
        dijo el gouernador de los yndios que estaba mui zerca de su cassa
        que hiziesemos alto a la orilla del valle zerca de vn ria-
        chuelo donde paro el real que se le puso por nombre el valle
        y quartel de la Madre Jessus Maria de Agreda, hauiendo
25   marchado este dia 5 leguas.
[folio 8v]
[blank]
[folio 9r]
        El primero se nonbro San Antonio de Padua, el segundo
        Santa Juana, el terzero Santa Margarita, el quarto
        San Carlos, de los quatro valles son estos los nombres.
        ¶ El dia 25 se obseruo la altura de la poblazion de los
5   Tejas que esta en 34 grados 7 minutos.
        ¶ El dia 27, 28, 29, 30 y 31 se trauajo en hazer la yglesia,
        y viuienda de los misioneros apostolicos, y tomaron posesion
        de la cassa de biuienda y yglesia dicho dia 31.
        ¶ Juebes 1º de junio se vendijo la yglesia y el reverendo padre comisario
10   fray Damian Manzanet canto la missa y despues de la vendizion
        de la yglesia que se hizo con prozesion. Este dia a la tarde salio
        el real del dicho quartel de San Francisco de los Tejas en persecuzion
        de la buelta a la provinzia de Cuaohuila por el mesmo camino
        que lleuamos. Paro este noche en el quartel de San Carlos auiendo
15   marchado 5 leguas.
        ¶ Viernes 2º del dicho salio el gouernador Alonso de Leon y los capitanes
            don Gre-
        gorio de Salinas Varona y Francisco Martinez y el reverendo padre
            comissario fray

Damian Manzanet y 4 soldados en seguimiento del real del dicho quartel de
San Francisco de los Tejas donde dimos con el en el sobre dicho quartel
  (^don)
20 y de alli proseguimos nuestro viaje con el real asta [^el] valle que esta d'esta
    vanda del quartel de San Bernardino como media legua donde paro
[folio 9v]
    el real auiendo marchado este dia 6 [leguas].
    ¶ Sauado 3 del dicho salio el real del quartel de San Bernardino
    y pasando el valle de San Seuastian y el valle de la Monclova lle-
    gamos al Rio de la Santissima Trinidad y por estar demasia-
5   do crezido que no se pudo vadiar, hizimos alto a orilla del
    en el dicho valle de la Monclova, auiendo marchado este dia 7 [leguas].
    ¶ Domingo 4, lunes 5, martes 6, miercoles 7, juebes 8, viernes 9,
    sauado 10, este dia se hizo valssa para pasar el rio y se
    comenzo a pasar.
10 ¶ Domingo 11 se acauo de pasar como a cosa de las dos de la
    tarde y salio el real por el valle de Galues asta dar
    con el de Santa Elvira, donde paro çerca de unos charcos
    de agua dulze, auiendo marchado 3 [leguas].
    ¶ Lunes 12 del dicho salio el real del dicho quartel y auiendo pa-
15 ssado por el quartel nombrado San Diego de Alcala como
    cossa de 2 leguas paro el real acerca de unos charcos de
    agua llouediza, auiendo marchado este dia 9 [leguas].
    ¶ Martes 13 del dicho salio el real del dicho quartel y auiendo
    passado el quartel del Beato Saluador de Orta y llegando
20 a el de San Juan, paro el real auiendo marchado este
    dia ocho leguas.
    ¶ Miercoles 14 del dicho salio el real del sobre dicho quartel
    y pasando el Rio del Spiritu Santo llegamos a una lomita
    arrimado a un enzino que salen quatro del que esta solo,
25 donde paro el real en un charco de agua llouediza auien-
    do marchado este dia 9 [leguas].
    ¶ Juebes 15 del dicho salio el real del sobre dicho quartel y pasan-
    do por el de San Francisco de Asis llego a un arroyo de agua en la
    falda de una colina donde paro arrimado a una motita de
30 (de) arboles, auiendo marchado este dia 7 [leguas].
[folio 10r]
    ¶ Viernes 16 del dicho salio el real del sobre dicho

quartel y pasando por el de San Joseph y San Ildifonsso
llego zerca de un arroyo de agua llouediza en la falda
de una lomita que tiene algunos robles y enzinos pequeños por la parte de leuante y al poniente el arroyo adonde paro, auiendo marchado este dia 7 [leguas].

5

¶ Sauado 17 del dicho salio el real del sobre dicho paraje
a pasar el Rio de San Marcos asta llegar al paraje
y quartel de Jesus Maria y Joseph de Buena Vista, donde paro auiendo marchado este dia 5 [leguas].

10

¶ En este quartel auia muchas naziones de jndios como
son los Cantona, los Thoaga, los Chana y Cabas.
¶ Domingo 18 del dicho salio el real prosiguiendo su biaje y el gouernador Alonso de Leon, el capitan don Gregorio de Salinas
Varona y 16 soldados el rumbo del nordeste en busca de

15

2 franzesitos y una franzesa por unos llanos como cosa
de 4 leguas (^??) asta llegar a u[n] montezillo el qual passamos y
despues (^p) seguimos el rumbo de leste como cosa de otras
3 leguas donde dimos con otra rancheria de jndios en un
montezillo que se llaman los Tho-o. De alli proseguimos asta

20

las ocho de la noche el rumbo del sueste por unos llanos que auia enfinidad de sibola, asta orilla de un riachuelo que al principio haze un manchon de arboles, donde
paramos, auiendo marchado este dia como 16 leguas.

25

¶ Lunes 19 del dicho al amanezer se prosiguio nuestro biaje
por orilla del riachuelo que tiene de una parte y otra
arboleda, y auiendole pasado y caminado como cossa de 2

[folio 10v]

leguas dimos con otra nacion de jndios que se llaman
los Co-oc, a los quales agasajamos y quedaron por
nuestros amigos. De alli proseguimos nuestro biaje el rumbo
del surr por unas llanadas y como a cosa de una legua

5

dimos con otra nazion de jndios que se llaman Tho-o.
De alli proseguimos el rumbo del sur por una llanada que auia sinnumero de sibola como cosa de 4 leguas
asta entrar en un montezillo, que fuimos prosiguiendo
nuestra jornada el rumbo del poniente, y pasando un

10

arroyo grande en un monte dimos con una nazion de
jndios muy grande que tenia mas de tres mil personas
que se llaman los (^Ta) na-aman, a los quales agasajamos y que-

daron nuestros amigos y nos dieron jndios que nos guiasen
asta otra rancheria, y de alli salimos por unos llanos
15 y ya muy noche paramos orilla de un arroyo, auiendo
marchado este dia como quinze leguas.
¶ Martes 20 del dicho prosiguimos nuestro biaje el rumbo
de leste donde dimos con una nazion de jndios que se lla[ma]n
Caisquetebana, a los quales agasajamos y nos dieron 4 jndios
20 para que nos guiassen aonde esteban los franzesitos donde
salimos el mesmo rumbo a pasar el arro[yo] de los franzeses y auiendole pasado seguimos [a] la poblazion de los
franzeses y de alli proseguimos el rumbo del sur asta
el Arroyo de las Canoas y aviendole pasado dimos con un
25 arroyuelo donde paramos, auiendo marchado este dia 14 [leguas].
¶ Miercoles 21 del dicho salimos el rumbo del sueste
y como a cosa de 1 legua dimos con dos jndios a cauallo de la nazion que tenian los franzesitos, los quales
[folio 11r]
nos guiaron a su rancheria que estaua en la punta
de una ensenada que se llama la nazion los Cascossi,
donde esteuan los (los) franzesitos Roberto y Madalena Talon, de los quales tratamos el resca-
5 te, y auiendolos agasajado y dado el rescate de los
dos, andubieron con mil desberguenzas, pidiendo que
les diesemos todos los cauallos y asta la rropa que
lleuauamos a cuestas. Entre tanto que yban a buscar
el otro franzesito que esteua 2 leguas de alli en la mesma
10 nazion, y auiendole traido prosiguieron mas con sus desberguenzas traiendo arcos y flechas, biniendo mucha cantidad de jndios preuenidos con adargas,
pediendo cosas sorbitantes y que si no se las dauamos
que nos auian de flechar y matar a todos, y diziendo
15 esto y comenzar a flechar todo fue vno, con que
nosotros dimos sobre ellos, y auiendoles muerto
quatro y herido dos se rretiraron, auiendonos herido
2 cauallos. Nos fuimos saliendo a dormir como
cossa de 4 leguas, donde auiamos dormido la noche
20 antes, auiendo marchado este dia [^12 leguas el rumbo]
del norte donde paramos en un llano a orilla de un
arroyo.

¶ Juebes 22 del dicho al amanezer salimos el
rumbo del norte por unas llanadas a orilla
25   del Rio de Guadalupe donde allamos algunos
manchones de palo de Brasalil, y como a cosa de
las 10 de la noche paramos zerca de un mon-
tizillo auiendo marchado este dia 14 [leguas].
¶ Viernes 23 del dicho salimos el rumbo del
30   norte como dos leguas don[de] dimos con el rastro

[folio 11v]

del real que auia passado, y como a cosa de 3 leguas
dimos con el en el passo de Guadalupe, donde
paramos auiendo marchado este dia 5 [leguas].
¶ Sauado 24 del dicho salio el real del dicho
5   passo a pasar el Rio de Guadalupe y auiendole pasado, prosiguimos nuestro viaje asta un arroyo
que esta antes del quartel del Agua Salada, donde
paro auiendo marchado este dia 7 [leguas].
¶ Domingo 25 del dicho salio el real prosiguien-
10   do su viaje y pasando el quartel del Agua Salada llegamos al Arroyo del Leon, auiendo
marchado este dia 7 leguas paro el real.
¶ Lunes 26 del dicho salio el real prosiguiendo su viaje asta pasar el Rio de Medina, don-
15   de paro auiendo marchado este dia 6 [leguas].
¶ Martes 27 del dicho salio el real del dicho paraje
del rio por entre montes de rrobles y mezquitales
el rumbo del sueste y sur asta llegar a un arroyo,
donde paro el real auiendo marchado este dia 7 [leguas].
20   ¶ Miercoles 28 del dicho salio el real del sobre dicho
paraje el rumbo del hueste por entre montes
de rrobres y llanadas como cosa de 4 leguas, y luego siguimos el rumbo del sur como cosa de
una legua donde dimos con unos charcos de
25   agua llouediza y alrrededor mezquitales y tuna-
les, donde auia una rancheria de jndios que se
llaman los Tho-o-e, donde paro el real auiendo
marchado este dia 5 [leguas].

[folio 12r]

¶ Juebes 29 del dicho dia del Apostol San Pedro salio el

real del dicho paraje y pasando los charcos del
Ayre en una cañada paro el real en unos charcos
de agua llouediza. Este dia se apartaron los cauallos

5   cansados que fueron 207 con 25 hombres para que
los traigan poco a poco. Este dia se marcharian
como 4 leguas.

¶ Viernes 30 del dicho salio el real del sobre dicho
paraje a pasar el Rio Hondo y auiendole

10   passado (^paro) fuimos caminanado como cossa
de 3 leguas asta el passo de las Cruzes, donde
paro orilla del rio auiendo marchado este dia 9 [leguas].

¶ Sauado 1º de jullio salio el real del dicho

15   passo de las Cruzes a pasar el Rio Frio
y auiendo dado con el, paro el real auiendo
marchado este dia.

¶ Domingo 2 del dicho passamos el rio y prosiguio el real su biaje a pasar el Rio de las

20   Nuezes (^donde paro en el mesmo protrero
auiendo marchado este dia)
y llegado al rio le passamos y prosiguimos
nuestro viaje asta unos charcos de agua que e-
sta antes de llegar al Arroyo de Caraman-

25   chel, donde paramos auiendo marchado
este dia 8 [leguas].

[folio 12v]

¶ Lunes 3 del dicho salio el real del dicho quartel
y pasando el arroyo y quartel de Caramanchel llegamos a los charcos de (^??) [^Ramos], donde prosiguimos
nuestro viaje asta el quartel de donde dormimos sin

5   agua, donde paro el real teniendo agua los
charcos, auiendo marchado este dia 8 [leguas].

¶ Martes 4 del dicho salio (^??) el real del
sobre dicho paraje a pasar el Rio Grande
y auiendo llegado a el por allarle muy cre-

10   zido fue neçesario parar de la otra vanda
del a la orilla, auiendo marchado este dia 8 [leguas].

¶ Desde el dia quatro asta el dia miercoles
12 estube detenido, y este dicho dia a la tarde aun-

que estaua muy crezido, no atreuiendose nayde a badi-
15   arle, me arroje a pasarle nadando el cauallo, y dandome el agua abajo de los pechos, le passe para
notiçias a su *excelenci*a de n*uest*ra jornada y luego me siguio
el p*adre* comis*ario* fray Damian Manzete y quatro
sold*ados* y un franzesito llamado P*edro* Moñe.
20   ¶ Juebes 13 del d*icho* mes marche asta los
charcos del agua be[^r]de que ay desde d*icho* rio 14 [leguas].
¶ Viernes 14 del d*icho* antes de amanezer sali-
mos prosiguiendo n*uest*ro viaje a pasar el Rio de
las Sauinas donde llegamos mas arri-
25   ua de las ajuntas, donde paramos auiendo marchado este dia 17 [leguas].
¶ Sauado 15 del d*icho* salimos prosiguiendo n*uest*ro
viaje asta la Villa de Santiago de la Monclova.
auiendo marchado este dia 12 [leguas] .
[folio 13r]
Cantona, To-aja-eslana, Cabas, Tho-o, Co-oc, Na-aman, Caisquetebana, Ca-co-ossi, Mojoman

3.

The English Translations

3.1 Translation Methodology

No prior study or publication contains full-length English translations of all five De León expedition diaries. As stated elsewhere, only three publications (West 1905; Bolton [1908] 1916; Chapa 1997) offer unabridged English translations of some, but not all, of the diaries. Foster's edition of Chapa (1997) includes Ned Brierley's translation of Chapa's *Historia*, which comprises the only known copy of the 1686 diary (86-A) and the only contemporary narrative summary of the 1687 expedition (87-A). Foster's edition also contains the first English translation of a revised copy of the 1690 diary (90-D). The 1688 *autos* and expedition diary (88-A), however, have never been translated into English in their entirety. Ximenes (1963) and Weddle (1999) offer only narrative summaries based on the AGI manuscript copies (88-B and 88-C), not on the signed *autos* and diary (88-A). The only full-length English translation of the important 1689 diary is to this day West's flawed rendition (1905), which was republished in Bolton ([1908] 1916). As shown elsewhere in this book, this problematic translation based on *Historia 27* (89-D), a faulty copy of the original manuscript, presents numerous mistranslations and factual errors. Bolton ([1908] 1916) also includes an English translation of the 1690 expedition diary; however, it is a version coalesced from three different manuscripts (90-A, 90-B, and 90-D) and also contains several inaccuracies.

A philological analysis of the Spanish manuscripts preceded the translation process. A comparison of the linguistic features of the different extant copies made it possible to identify the oldest manuscripts. The unabridged annotated English translations presented in this chapter are based on the signed document (88-A), the only known contemporary manuscript copies (86-A, 87-A), archetypes of the original diaries (89-B, 90-B), and an ostensibly revised diary (90-D). For the 1690 expedition, two of the extant versions of the diary (90-B and 90-D) were chosen for translation because they differ considerably and provide a great deal of divergent information, as discussed by McLain (2005). Manuscript 90-B was identified as the archetype and basis for the English translation instead of the somewhat older 90-A, because 90-A is missing the first fourteen entries and therefore must be considered an incomplete document.

In fashioning these translations, it was decided to stay as close to the Spanish text as possible. The renditions are often very literal and at times include long, run-on sentences and comma splices with numerous relative clauses and gerund phrases that do not conform to English syntax. Some of the terms (e.g., *auto, ranchería*) have been deliberately left in Spanish, either because they are common parlance or because there is no true equivalent in English. In these instances, footnotes provide further explanation. Discrepancies with prior translations are also documented in the notes. The names of rivers, towns, and other geographical locations are kept in Spanish. However, Spanish spelling is modernized and accent marks are used where needed, for example in proper names as well as in common words left in Spanish. Foliation is indicated to allow for easier access to the texts and to facilitate comparison between the Spanish transcription and English translation. Spanish paragraphing is mostly but not strictly observed.

3.2 English Translation of Manuscript 86-A

[**folio 46r**] Route, diary, and demarcation of the journey that I, General Alonso de León, lieutenant governor and *capitán general* of this Nuevo Reino de León, made in the discovery of the coast of the Mar del Norte [Gulf of Mexico] and the mouth of the Río Bravo; [**folio 46v**] the foundations and motives that existed for it [the journey], with all that happened on it, the number of people, horses and supplies, etc.

The Señor Marqués de San Miguel de Aguayo, governor and *capitán general* of this Nuevo Reino de León, received a dispatch on the 8th day of the month of June from the Most Excellent Señor Viceroy of New Spain, this year of 1686, in which he charges him, based on the news given to him by the royal officials of the city of Veracruz, that the French were settled at the Bahía del Espíritu Santo, which was six or seven days' journey from this kingdom, to make a discovery from this direction and to find out the truth with all the details, in order to reach the most suitable solution. Ordering that a council be convened on the 11th day of said month in the city of Monterrey, capital of said kingdom, with prior notifications sent to all jurisdictions, he [the governor] was pleased to call me to said council meeting, during which, once it was held, it was resolved that said journey would be made on the 25th day of July [*sic*].[1] Leaving on this

---

1. This is an obvious scribal transcription error. The expedition was planned to start June 25, 1686.

day from the city of Monterrey, a company of thirty soldiers was to be led by Captain Nicolás Ochoa to the town of Cadereyta; and another [company] was to be enlisted in the jurisdiction of said town [Cadereyta] to be led by Captain Antonio Leal. And His Lordship would descend from the city [Monterrey] to it [Cadereyta] on said day, where the soldiers would pass muster and submit to the captains that he would name; and both companies would be under my charge, bestowing hereby an honor upon me, more due to his greatness than my merits. And having organized everything as described, His Lordship was pleased to descend from the city of Monterrey with said company on June 26, [**folio 47r**] arriving on this day later than planned due to the heavy rains that occurred. On this same day, I arrived to said town with the company of the twenty soldiers from said jurisdiction [Cadereyta], who joined the company from Monterrey near said town so that on the next day, the 27th, they could pass muster. Having gathered on that day in said city in full military order, in marching formation, the Señor Marqués held[2] the titles [of commission] made for the captains, *alférez*,[3] and sergeants to present them by his own hand to those chosen, and he ordered said muster to pass in his presence, which was done as follows:

The company that Captain Nicolás Ochoa had led from Monterrey passed, with the soldiers from it and its jurisdiction, in the following manner: First, when the above-mentioned passed, His Lordship took the title of captain made for Carlos Cantú, which he ordered to be read aloud, and then presented it to him. The soldiers passed in their rows on horseback in this manner:

Said Captain Carlos Cantú; *Alférez* Diego Rodríguez; Sergeant Nicolás Ochoa; *Sargento Mayor* Lucas Caballero; Captain Nicolás García; Sergeant Lorenzo de Ayala; Sergeant Gaspar de Lerma; Gonzalo de Treviño; Sergeant Juan de la Garza; Jacinto de la Garza; [**folio 47v**] Joseph de Treviño; Francisco de la Garza; Joseph de la Garza; Alonso García de Quintanilla; Marcos Flores; Alonso de Olivares; Andrés Fernández Tijerina; Nicolás de Montalvo; Juan Pérez de la Garza; Francisco de la Garza; Juan de la Garza; Diego Martín; Joseph Pérez; Antonio Pérez; Joseph González; Francisco González; Mateo de Peña; Santiago de León; Nicolás Cantú.

---

2. Brierley's translation "and when the marquis had presented the titles of the captains, alférez, and sergeants so as to turn them over from his hand" (Chapa 1997, 105) is inexact. The marquis presented those documents later, during the muster, and had them read out loud. The Spanish manuscript indicates that he was carrying those documents with him but did not present them to the officers at that time: "y teniendo dicho señor marques los titulos / echos de los capitanes, alferez y sargentos para / entregarlos por su mano a los electos" (86-A 47r8–10).

3. *Alférez* is a military rank equivalent to ensign or second lieutenant.

And subsequently, our company from the town of Cadereyta passed muster, led by Captain Antonio Leal, who turned it over to Captain Nicolás de Medina, its elected captain, whose title was read and presented to him. They passed in this formation:

Said Captain Nicolás de Medina; *Alférez* Thomás de la Garza; Sergeant Miguel de León;[4] Alonso de León, the younger;[5] Sergeant Lorenzo de la Garza; [**folio 48r**] Sergeant Juan Cantú; Sergeant Agustín García; Sergeant Thomás Cantú; Joseph Gutiérrez; Sebastián de Villegas; Francisco Falcón; Lucas de Betancourt; Francisco de Escamilla; Luis Pérez; Nicolás de Lira; Miguel González; Matías de Herrera; Santiago de la Garza.

After the muster had passed in this manner, His Lordship presented the titles of *alférez* and sergeant to the selected persons from the Monterrey company: *Alférez* Diego Rodríguez and Sergeant Nicolás Ochoa, the younger; from the company of the town of Cadereyta: *Alférez* Thomás de la Garza and Sergeant Miguel de León.

Likewise, the baggage of the two companies passed in this formation: forty loads of provisions, including flour, biscuit, meat, and chocolate; four hundred and sixty-eight horses. Muleteers, servant boys and pages of these companies: Diego Monita, Pascual de Gumendio, Mateo Esteban, [**folio 48v**] Juan Rodríguez, Juan de Olivares, Juan de Villagrán, Juan Rendón, Thomás de Torres, Nicolás de Losa, Matías de Munguía, Juan Cavazos, Cristóbal de Ávila, Juan de Ochoa, Bernabé de la Garza, Miguel, Juan, José, Juan; Alonso, an Indian captain from the Zacatil *ranchería*, our guide; Bernabe, an Indian; Mateo, an Indian.[6]

After this, His Lordship ordered my title to be read, in which he was pleased to name me commander-in-chief of these companies with full commission and instruction, and he named as chaplain Fray Diego de Orozco, the presiding padre of this town; and His Lordship added Don Pedro Fermín de Echeverz, his brother; *Alférez* Francisco de Benavides; and Juan Bautista Chapa.

On this same day, Thursday, June 27, after the muster, I set out with the combined royal company[7] to sleep at a post they call San Diego, which is four

4. This is General Alonso de León's brother.

5. This is General Alonso de León's son.

6. Brierley gives the translation as "Alonso, an Indian captain of the Zacatil village, our guide called Bernabé, and another Indian called Mateo" (Chapa 1997, 106). In Manuscript 86-A 48v14–15, the punctuation clearly shows that the Zacatil chief Alonso is the guide, not Bernabé: "Alonso, yndio capitan de la rancheria Zacatil, nues- / tro guia; Bernabe, yndio; Matheo, yndio."

7. See note 16, sec. 1.

leagues[8] in distance from said town, close to the river, flat land, in an easterly direction.

Friday, June 28. I set out with the company to sleep on this side of the Río de San Juan, by some pools; the road [**folio 49r**] was level although there was about one league of small hills. The company marched this day eight leagues in an easterly direction.

Saturday, June 29. I set out with the company in a northeasterly direction, keeping in sight a little pointy hill, which is about half a league on this side of the Río de San Juan; the way was somewhat wooded but penetrable. We arrived at the river crossing, which was very good; we marched two more leagues after crossing it. We traveled on this day four leagues toward the northeast.

Sunday, June 30. I set out with the company, being necessary to march in a southeasterly direction for about a league and a half, for we were unable to cross a large thicket; we traveled five leagues mostly east by north. We stopped on this day by some pools of water near the *ranchería* of my Indians.[9] The river straightened toward the north in this area.

Monday, July 1. We set out from said post and followed the course east by north, flat land; we traveled a distance of six leagues; we stopped at some pools on flat land; their water is rainwater as is the one of the others mentioned.

Tuesday, July 2, the Day of the Visitation of Our Lady. We left with forty-four Indians of the Caurame nation[10] who had joined us the day before; and said night they had spied a *ranchería* of enemies of theirs, and to see if I could capture two Indians as guides, I went ahead with twenty men. They must have been warned because they had abandoned it [the *ranchería*]. On this day, we marched mostly in a northerly and northeasterly direction for eight leagues. The Indian Alonso told us that the Río Grande was near. The company could not penetrate a large wooded area with the loads and the horses, so we stopped by a small marsh. I penetrated said wooded area through a narrow path, which was very arduous; at no more than two leagues[11] [**folio 49v**] to the river, which runs at this point very wide and the water [is] very muddy. As it appears, it is navigable by small vessel; there was no way of sounding it, it is the width of a harquebus shot[12] and it runs in this part, toward the north.

8. One Spanish league corresponded to a fixed distance of five thousand varas, which is approximately 2.6 miles.

9. "Mis yndios" refers to the Indians of de León's *encomienda*, the Caurame (Chapa 1997, 206)

10. See note 9 above.

11. Brierley translates "a no mas de dos leguas" as "more than two leagues" (Chapa 1997, 107).

12. The range of a harquebus was between 150 and 200 yards.

Wednesday, June 3. Not finding a ford, it was necessary (although with much labor) to march with the company through the dense brush. We traveled no more than two leagues on this day because I decided to set out swiftly to reconnoiter the route through which we were going to go the next day. In fact, I left with twelve[13] members of the company, and traveling downriver, we unexpectedly came upon a *ranchería* devoid of people, who, having heard us, had abandoned it and left all their belongings, which I ordered not to be touched. We continued to follow the river downstream and saw how some Indian men and women were swimming across, and in fact crossed it. Although I called to them in peace, I could not get anyone to come, on the contrary, one came to the narrowest part to shoot arrows at us, from less than harquebus range, from which we concluded that they had not seen Spaniards [before] because he did not fear the harquebus shot. The course was toward the east.

Thursday, July 4. I set out with the company in a northeasterly direction for a distance of four leagues; we stopped at a lagoon and a ravine about a league away from the river because the river has mostly very dense thickets along its banks. I went swiftly with twelve men to reconnoiter said river, for which, because of the dense woods, it was necessary to travel three leagues to reconnoiter it. In this part the river runs very wide and appears to be navigable; it has a strong current, and there was no way to see an appropriate place for the horses to go down to drink.

Friday, July 5. We marched four leagues toward the east, passing a narrow path of half a league opened by hand by the Indians. We stopped next to the river and some long hills. The horses drank with difficulty. It is navigable by small vessel. I left swiftly with ten men [**folio 50r**] to discover the land; I followed a footpath that led to such dense thicket that we were unable to penetrate it.

Saturday, July 6. I set out with the company in the direction discovered the previous day; we took a narrow path a on a little hill, very short and dense. We traveled four leagues across a plain until we reached a dry marsh, which, had it contained water, would have been impossible [to cross], full of holes and inconveniences. We did not find a passage through a wood we encountered; we followed a ravine until it divided into two and then we followed the one going north until we reached the river with difficulty because of the many thorny thickets there. There was an excellent watering place. It appears less

13. Brierley's translation "I set out with two members of the company" (Chapa 1997, 107) is incorrect, as manuscript 86-A 49v9–10 clearly reads "Sali con efecto con doze compañeros." Twelve soldiers, not two, accompanied de León.

navigable and with less water than seen before. I left with a few men to find a way out for the next day and to see if I could find an Indian as guide. There are many footpaths, but not well worn. We traveled on this day in a northeasterly direction.

Sunday, [July] 7. We set out in a northeasterly direction in view of the river; there were some thickets to avoid. We came upon the river which appears navigable and continued along its bank for about one league to some tall trees which are on a plain, where we found a small watering hole that seemed to be a spring. From here I left with twelve men to find a crossing for the next day. We saw some long hills, we climbed the highest one; we saw wide plains and the river at a distance of about two leagues. I remained on this hill with seven men, with the intention of sleeping on it that night, and, before the sun set, about forty Indians started appearing; and as soon as we saw them, we mounted our horses, and they fled. I left them a white cloth, biscuit, tobacco and other things and returned to the main camp. We traveled six leagues this day, toward east-northeast.

Monday, [July] 8. We set out in an east-northeasterly direction along the trail [**folio 50v**] of the previous day. I went ahead with twenty men [to see] if we could capture one of the Indians from the day before, and at a distance of three leagues (passing over the hill from the day before, where I had left the cloth and other things, which we found in the same place) about fifty of them came out from a nearby thicket. I made many friendly gestures, but none wanted to come. I put on a little tree a cloth and a knife from my sheath and withdrew, and indeed they came to take it, and in return they whirled a banner of feathers and placed a feather ornament for me to take, making signs that I should go and get it, which I did. I continued following the course, and they followed us always, sheltered by the brush. We traveled this day eight leagues in different directions, mostly to the east; and coming upon a dense wood and not finding water, we were forced to backtrack three leagues to look for the river, which we found with a good watering place although less navigable.

Tuesday, July 9. It was necessary to halt with the company at this stopping place on the river. I set out with twenty-five men to discover the land for the following day. It was necessary for me to travel eight leagues to reach it [the river], on whose bank there are many dense thickets which lead out to the plains three to four leagues; and not having found another watering place, I dispatched six men on the following day, Wednesday, so that the main company would set out and follow our trail.

Wednesday, [July] 10. The main company set out along the trail, guided by the soldiers I had dispatched, and shortly before starting to harness the pack animals, from the other side of the river, about thirty Indians started howling, making signs to come over or that they would get together and kill us all. They were playing two flutes, and having come out a short distance, another squadron of about sixty appeared. Although they never attacked, they followed the main company as far as a plain, where there were wide tracks, where, [**folio 51r**] it seemed, more than three hundred Indians had gathered for a dance. The company stopped on a plain with no water. We traveled about five leagues in an east-southeasterly direction on this day.

Thursday, [July] 11. The main company set out along my trail and arrived, after a distance of three leagues in an east-northeasterly direction, at the river, where I was waiting for them. It runs, in this part, very wide and [is] navigable with a small vessel, although with too much current. The land was flat, and from what we could make out, we anticipated a good route for the next day.

Friday, July 12. The main company set out from the river. I went ahead with fifteen men to look for a trail; we found an estuary formed by the river at a distance of six leagues in an east-southeasterly direction. The company having stopped, I left again with twelve men to search for a route for the next day, and at a distance of four leagues, we found two lagoons of salt, although there was not any because it had rained recently.[14] One [of them] is a league and a half long and one-half league wide; the water is very salty and could not be drunk.[15]

Saturday, July 13. The main company left the estuary where they had slept, and I directed them at the beginning in the direction of the previous day, and we traveled this day in different directions for a distance of four leagues, although mostly to the east-southeast. I stopped with the company by the river near a large trail that was left by a *ranchería* of Indians, which fifteen days prior had been abandoned. Here we found a barrel stave. Toward the afternoon, I went ahead with twenty-eight men, judging myself already very near the sea, we traveled six leagues with much caution, always looking for the river, and at six in the afternoon, we came unexpectedly upon a *ranchería* of Indians, and because they had sighted us, they had time to abandon it. So we

14. Brierley's translation "Four leagues away we found two salt lakes, although there was no [water] because it had rained so little recently" (Chapa 1997, 110) poses some problems. Manuscript 86-A 51r14–16 indicates that it had rained recently and that because of the rain what was lacking was salt, not water: "y a distancia de quatro / leguas hallamos dos lagunas de sal, aunque no la hauia / por hauer poco que hauia llouido." The antecedent of the pronoun "la" is "sal" 'salt,' and the meaning of "poco" in the phrase "por hauer poco que hauia llouido" needs to be rendered as "it had rained recently." The recent rain had dissolved the salt.

15. This statement confirms that there was water in the lagoons. See note 14 above.

captured only three Indian women,[16] who, when treated in a friendly manner and asked with signs as to [**folio 51v**] where there were Spaniards[17] and people with clothes, pointed toward the region to the north, and [indicated] that they were in two places, from which I inferred that they would not be at the mouth of the river that we were following as it led east. They named many times the two places where they [the people with clothes] were, saying that they were called Taguili, the closest one to the northwest, and the other to the north, Zaguili (they said [it] in their language, of course). They did not know [how] to give us account of the distances, although we made attempts to find out, because not even by conjecture did they understand us or we them. We found in this *ranchería* a piece of the bottom of a cask, a broken bolt from a ship, a link of chain, and a small piece of glass, and no other valuables. I stayed this night with the men to sleep on the bank of the river, and with the calm of it [the night], we heard the roar of the sea.

Sunday, [July] 14, Day of Saint Buenaventura. I dispatched four soldiers to the main company so that all would set out and come marching to the designated location. I went on with the other men to discover the sea, conquering marshes, reed beds, willow thickets, and dense woods along the river bank, and at a distance of two leagues we found it [the sea] to the northeast; and this day the main company traveled four leagues. There was no trace of either Spaniards or foreigners having arrived at this mouth of the river. I skirted along the coast for one league to reach said mouth. It enters very turbidly into the sea; about a league in distance into the sea the water is vermilion colored; the mouth is a bit wider than a musket shot.[18] I ordered a raft made to sound in five or six locations, and the deepest was seven and a half and eight *brazas*,[19] so that a seagoing vessel can enter, as it appears, about two leagues inland. This day I skirted along the coast of the sea for four leagues toward the Río de Palmas.[20] There were some fresh Indian tracks and some poles standing in various parts where they had camped, but a long time ago;[21] no

16. In *Gallant Outcasts*, the number of Indian women captured is stated as two instead of three: "Two Indian women captured at this place near Matamoros were brought before de León for questioning" (Ximenes 1963, 72). Manuscript 86-A 51r30–31reads "con que no se coxieron mas que / tres yndias."

17. The term "españoles" here is employed as a generic term meaning Europeans or white people.

18. The range of a musket is approximately two hundred yards.

19. A *braza* is the equivalent of a fathom (1.67 meters or 5.485 feet). Seven and a half to eight fathoms would correspond to 41–43 feet.

20. Río de Palmas is believed to be modern-day Soto la Marina.

21. Brierley's translation does not mention that the remnants of the Indian encampments were from a long time ago (Chapa 1997, 111).

[**folio 52r**] stone was found along this entire shore. The coast runs north to south, somewhat more to the northeast. The sea is very rough although there is no wind. On its shore there are many cypresses, pines, palms, and cane as thick as a leg, and others that have been cast by the sea. The coast is very clean, without any boulders, and the shore is easy to travel on horseback without getting bogged down. [The tide] rises and falls more than one *estado*.[22]

Monday, July 15. Being at the very mouth of the river at the point of midday, the height of the sun was taken with an astrolabe, and we found it to be 25°45' of northern elevation (except for any error, as the astrolabe, as it appears, was badly aimed and somewhat defective). Due to the limited pasturage available, I ordered the main company to set out after noon as far as they could travel on that day, and on the next [day] to stop at the estuary where they had been on Saturday. And I, with twenty-five soldiers, set out to reconnoiter the coast again, toward the Río de Palmas, for a distance of more than eight leagues, in which we found some planking from the side of ships, bowsprits, masts, pieces of keel and rudder, bottoms of casks, staves, buoys, and four small wheels from pieces of artillery, a cask with willow hoops, three broken canoes, a small round glass flask, very thick, topped with a cork, in which, when opened, I found a little wine, already spoiled. The glass is very [eye-catching] and it appears not to have been made in the kingdoms of Castile because of its form. And finally there were on this shore all sorts of planks and wreckage of ships, so that, without a doubt, a few capsized here [as can be inferred] from the variety of said debris, and some of the wood being older than the other. What amazed me the most was to see some corn stalks brought in by the undertow of the sea, apparently from the planting of this year, which were starting to grow tassels, with their roots [still on] the corn stalks, from which I inferred that there was some settlement nearby and that [**folio 52v**] flooding had carried away some of their corn fields.[23]

Tuesday, [July] 16. I set out from near the shore of the sea in search of the main company, and I could not get across some lagoons or pass through some

22. In the notes, Foster, citing Polzer, states that when measuring depth, one *estado* corresponds to approximately seven feet (Chapa 1997, 206).

23. Brierley translated this section as "I concluded that there was some settlement nearby and that corn had been brought to it by some means" (Chapa 1997, 112). Manuscript 86-A 52r32–52v1 states that a violent flood ("una avenida") had ripped the stalks from a cornfield, "sobre que discurri que ay alguna poblazon zercana y que / alguna abenida les llebo alguna milpa." The translation seems to insinuate that corn was taken to a nearby settlement by somebody, whereas the manuscript clearly shows that a current or flood tore the corn from the field.

bogs, so I was forced to return to the route along the shore of the sea and follow the trail in search of it [the company]. I did not reach it on that day.

Wednesday, July 17. I arrived at the main company early, and because the horses were worn out, we did not cross that day. I found them by the estuary where they had halted on Friday, the 12th of this present month. The estuary is at a distance of eight leagues from the sea.

Thursday, [July] 18. I set out with the company for the river, a distance of six leagues.

Friday, [July] 19. I went with the company to stop at the spring on the plain, where we had stopped on our way [to the coast] on Sunday, the 7th of the current month. We traveled that day eleven leagues, having marched them in three days on our way there. There were many Indian tracks that led to the ford of the river, where they had threatened us.

Saturday, [July] 20. We left the place above and the main company camped for the night beyond the bad watering place by the river, on a small hill without water. We traveled eight leagues.

Sunday, [July] 21. We left the small hill and camped for the night near the *ranchería* where the Indians had shot arrows at us; and seeing some of them, we attacked them; there were over fifty. *Sargento Mayor* Lucas Caballero, wanting to capture one of them, hid in a scrub oak, and [the Indian] shot an arrow at him that lodged below his nipple because he did not have a coat [of mail]. Two [Indians] were killed and two boys were captured. We traveled eight leagues.

Monday, July 22. We left this place, traveled five leagues; we set out through the densely wooded narrow path from where we had discovered the river. To avoid the long way, we wanted to take another route, but another lagoon impeded it. We slept on a plain with pools of water.

Tuesday, July 23. I set out with the main company in different directions from the one by which I had come because by then we had descended a great deal to reach [**folio 53r**] the *ranchería* of the Pajarito. We traveled seven long leagues; we stopped at the Charco de las Calaveras.

Wednesday, [July] 24. I set out with the company from said place, passing by the *ranchería* of the Caurame, who had been waiting for us on the trail. We crossed at the ford of the Río de San Juan. We traveled twelve leagues.

Thursday, July 25. We set out from that place, we arrived at the *real* de San Simon, from there we continued to the *real* de San Diego. There was a distance of fourteen leagues.

Friday, [July] 26. While we were at said *real*, orders arrived from His Lordship for the companies to go rest and be ready, should it be necessary, to move out again. After resting the horses because they were worn out, we went to the town [of Cadereyta] on this day, and later I [went] to give a report to the Señor Marqués about the journey. Done in Cadereyta on July 27 of the year 1686. Alonso de León.

3.3 English Translation of Manuscript 87-A

[**folio 53r**] Chapter 32 in which the events continue.

The Marqués de San Miguel de Aguayo was always firm in his opinion that the French were settled on the Mar del Norte, and so he ordered that the journey be repeated on the other side of the Río Bravo, passing through the town of Cerralvo, for it was known throughout this kingdom that there was a good ford at a distance of twenty leagues from it. At the beginning of the year 1687, he formed three companies: one was under the command of General Martín de Mendiondo, the other under Don Pedro Fermín de Echeverz, and the third under Captain Nicolás de Medina, and as commander-in-chief General Alonso de León. They set out from this city at the end of February, and on March 20 they reached the coast of the sea, traveling through many nations of warlike Indians, who gave them ample signs of their animosity,[24] and they even wandered in different directions. They did not find the settlement of the French or anyone who could give them any news. [**folio 53v**] Instead a large salty river[25] prevented them from crossing to the north, so the hopes of discovery were frustrated and ill feelings were had by all, and especially by the Marqués, who wished that this issue, which had caused so many worries, could have been resolved during his tenure;[26] and now his term as governor was coming to an end, inasmuch as he had sent a request of relinquishment to his majesty in order to return to Spain. In fact, having received it in said year of 1687, the Conde de la Monclova appointed as interim governor General Don Francisco Cuervo de Valdés, a gentleman from the mountain region[27]

24. Brierley misinterprets the idiomatic expression "que le dieron arto en que entender" (87-A 53r31) to mean "the leaders had a difficult time understanding the various Indian languages" (Chapa 1997, 114). However, "dar en que entender" means to make it difficult for someone or to give someone a hard time.

25. See note 20, sec. 1.

26. The expression "vna cossa" 'a thing, an issue,' which appears in the manuscript (87-A 53v5), was misread by Cavazos Garza as well as Brierley as "una costa" 'a coast.' Therefore, Brierley's English rendition is "especially that of the governor, who had wished that during his term the coast that had attracted so much effort would be fully explored" (Chapa 1997, 114).

27. The region of Asturias in northern Spain is often simply referred to as the mountain region. The oldest Spanish nobility hails from there. Hence, the statement that Francisco Cuervo de Valdés is "un cauallero montañez," implies that he is a very capable, fine nobleman.

Alonso de León and soldiers observing a buffalo hunt
(drawing by Scott Harshbarger)

of very good qualities, who took office in the month of September. During his tenure, which lasted a little over nine months, the Indians were very well controlled; this was attained through preventive measures, because in order to protect properties as well as mines and farm lands, it was necessary to use fear and punishment with these native people.

3.4 English Translation of Manuscript 88-A

[*Auto* 1]
[folio 17r]

Official declaration on the expedition to search for the Frenchman

In the village of San Francisco de Coahuila, jurisdiction of Nueva Extremadura, on the 18th day of the month of May of 1688, I, General Alonso de León, governor and captain of the presidio of this province, report that after returning to this village from an expedition on which I set out against the Indians that rebelled against the Royal Crown and punished those that could be caught in the skirmish we had with them. (Prior to this, I had sent a Tlaxcalan[28] Indian

28. Tlaxcalan or Tlaxcaltecan Indians were originally from Tlaxcala, central Mexico, and spoke Nahuatl. As allies of the Spaniards since the time of Cortés they had obtained certain privileges in return for their loyalty (e g., they were allowed to carry weapons, ride horses, own land, etc.). In an effort to advance the pacification of hostile Indians in the frontier, the Spaniards transplanted

named Agustín [**folio 17v**] de la Cruz, who lives in the settlement called Boca de los Leones, to gather all the friendly people he could in order to set out with them to punish those Indians, but he did not arrive on time to do so.) Therefore, after I returned and found said Agustín in said village, he gave me an account, telling me that he had arrived at the other side of the Río Bravo to see if he could call together some nations for the purpose he was entrusted. He came upon a large *ranchería* with a great number of Indians, where there was a dwelling made in the form of a large room with a roof of buffalo hides. And that the Indians, who were around it, as soon as he arrived, made him dismount and took him inside and made him get on his knees so that he could speak to a man who was in there, which he did. And he saw a man of good height and of very white color, who appeared to be Spanish, who was seated on a dais, well decorated with buffalo hides. He appeared to be fifty years of age, with graying hair, streaked on different parts of his face,[29] and the Indians held him in high veneration. Therefore, this informant made great reverence and courtesy, greeting him in his own mother tongue of said Agustín,[30] and that he [the man] did not reply anything. Thus he [Agustín] made use of one of the Indians[31] who was with the man and was an acquaintance of his [Agustín's] to serve as an interpreter. Then the man returned the courtesies by way of [the interpreter], telling him that he was French, and that for some time he had been at that location, gathering some nations of Indians from the region to go fight against other Indian enemies who did not want to join him, and that he was sent by God to found villages. And that he had dispatched Indians to me, the general, to call me so that I would go with a religious to see him. And to Agustín de la Cruz he gave six Indians to accompany him to the Pueblo de la Caldera; they are present and can serve as guides for said purpose; and that said Frenchman took the harquebus that Agustín was carrying and kept it as a token so that he would return. Of all this, Agustín informed me so that I could decide what would be the most appropriate thing to do. After receiving this report, I recognized that

---

entire Tlaxcalan villages and settled them in the north—for instance, San Esteban de la Nueva Tlaxcala, a town founded near Saltillo in 1591. Tlaxcalan Indians often assisted Spaniards in their frontier endeavors (Campbell 2010).

29. A literal translation of "raiado" (88-A 17v16) is 'striped' or 'with stripes' or 'streaked.' Here the word most certainly refers to facial tattoos.

30. Since he was a Tlaxcalan, Agustín de la Cruz spoke Nahuatl.

31. Manuscript 88-A (17v17–18) reads "Por lo cual se balio de vno de los yndios que estaban / con el contenido y conocido suio que le siruio de ynterprete." Weddle, relying on 88-C, translates that Agustín was aided not by one Indian, who was his acquaintance, but by all the Indians present, who volunteered as interpreters (1999, 136).

the Frenchman only aspires, with the congregation of those people he already has and the others he is trying to assemble, encouraged perhaps by some [**folio 18r**] from his nation, to start reconnoitering the entire land and the places in it. And, waiting for an opportune time, he will inform his countrymen to bring some of their troops, and accompanied by the Indians he has congregated, he will attack these settlements and destroy them, which would be a feasible thing to do, due to the limited forces that we presently have for resistance. This province is only composed of twenty-five soldiers and a few inhabitants, who have come for the new founding of a town in this frontier. And in a sudden situation, we could not get assistance due to the great distance there is for support to come from the town of Saltillo, the valley of Parras, or Nuevo Reino de León, which are the closest locations to this frontier. Therefore, it is advisable to provide the most efficient and fastest solution which is suitable to avoid this danger, also because of the bad consequences that would befall the other provinces of New Spain, which would suffer the same downfall, with the Indian enemies as well as the Frenchman seizing them all. I, therefore, order that a list be drawn of eighteen men, the most experienced and well armed there might be, to set out in search of the Frenchman, and to apprehend him, leaving this post well manned with the other soldiers and people who were left off the list to keep the necessary guard and protection. I so ordered, commanded, and signed it [this *auto*] in the presence of two witnesses because this province does not have a public or royal scribe.

[Signatures] Alonso de León; witness, Joseph Antonio de Ecay y Múzquiz;[32] witness Joseph Gutiérrez.[33]

[*Auto 2*]

On said day, month and year, I, General Alonso de León, in fulfillment of the aforementioned *auto*, and having previously completed the list contained in it, which consists mostly of officers and soldiers from Nuevo Reino de León, from the support troops sent to me by General Don Francisco Cuervo de Valdés, governor and captain general, as well as my brothers, sons, and relatives, who came to help me in their duty to this province, we set out today, the 18th day of the current month, in a northeasterly direction. And at a distance

---

32. José Antonio de Ecay y Múzquiz (?–1738) was a *criollo* who served as a soldier, governor, and commander of the presidio of San Juan Bautista on the Coahuila-Texas frontier. He witnessed the official founding of Santiago de la Monclova in 1689 and participated in various expeditions into Texas (Weddle 2010a).

33. Manuscripts 88-B and 88-C present a different second witness signature in all of the *autos*, that of Carlos Cantú. Carlos Cantú was one of the soldiers who accompanied de León on this expedition.

of forty-two leagues, we crossed the Río Bravo and from there, following the same direction for about fifteen leagues, we found about five hundred Indians[34] more or less, killing buffalo to make jerky. We approached to speak to them through an interpreter, and I asked them where there was a Spanish man,[35] and they informed me that he was at about a distance [**folio 18v**] of five or six leagues from there, pointing in the same northeasterly direction, and that he was their chief, and he governed them and they obeyed him. And telling one of them to guide me to where the aforementioned was, he guided us to where he [the Frenchman] had his dwelling, which was at a distance of five or six leagues, and twenty from said Río Bravo. We discerned the settlement, which was on an elevation, and we saw that the Indians (which were about three hundred) positioned themselves in the formation of a group of guards. And having arrived at the door of a large room which was fashioned of buffalo hides, there were forty-two Indians standing as sentries, with bows and arrows. Upon entering, we found it very tidy, swept, and clean; and facing the door were three seats of buffalo hide, very well arranged and brushed, and on the one in the middle sat the Frenchman, about whom the Tlaxcalan Indian Agustín de la Cruz had given the account; and I recognized him by the same marks and height given in said report. And on the seat there were cushions of some kind made from buffalo hide, and two Indians (they appeared [to be] the most principal ones) attended to him, one on each side. And when the chaplain we had with us, Fray Buenaventura Bonal, a padre from the order of Saint Francis, I, and General Don Martín de Mendiondo came near him, he [the Frenchman] did no other action than, without leaving his seat, fall on his knees and kiss the sleeve of the habit of the religious. And to me and to the general he gave his hand with much courtesy, and then, placing it on his chest, he said repeatedly: "I French," affirming with this that he was from that nation. And in the Castilian language he asked me how many we were who had come, to which I said that [we were] many and that a greater number remained behind as rearguard nearby, with which account he seemed somewhat baffled and confused. And at this time, because in foresight I had brought

34. Ximenes misstates the number of Indians hunting bison as fifteen hundred (1963, 84).

35. Ximenes has misinterpreted the Spanish source text (1963, 86). Thus, the English translation "A Spaniard was hunting with the Indians and through his services de León learned that the *ranchería* was nearby and that the Frenchman was their leader" is incorrect. Manuscript 88-A (18r33–35) states: "y llegando a hablarles mediante ynterprete, les pregunte que donde / estaba vn hombre español, y me dieron por razon que estaba en distancia / de cinco o seis leguas de alli." De León uses the term "hombre español," a synonym for white man or European, to refer to the Frenchman. It does not mean that there was a Spaniard hunting with the Indians. Had this been the case, de León would have questioned the man and mentioned his name.

some clothing, petticoats, cotton tunics, knives, earrings, beads, rosaries, and tobacco to distribute among the Indians in order to make them devoted to me, I took out those things and turned them over to the Frenchman so that he could distribute them from his hand to the Indians, which he did. Before this, I had instructed the soldiers to remain on horseback,[36] because only the padre, I, and General Don Martín de Mendiondo had entered the room. And I ascertained that the Frenchman knows the mother tongue of the Indians with whom he was assembled very well. And I examined him through an interpreter, who was an Indian, in the Mexican language.[37] And I instructed him to tell [the Frenchman] that I was going to take him with me to the Río Bravo, where I had left [another] Frenchman, who would speak to him in his own language, and we would consult whatever was necessary; and that from there he would return to his dwelling. This he resisted very much [**folio 19r**] as did the Indians who were attending to him. As I saw this resistance, and although the task was difficult and dangerous to bring him by force, and it put the entire company at risk because there were more than a thousand Indians with bows and arrows that could attack us, I insisted with soft and polite manners that he come with us. And always resisting, we took him with artfulness and industry from the dwelling where he was, knowing that we were putting ourselves at risk, because the Indians attended to him with so much obedience, respect, and veneration that they kneeled before him; and in the dwelling they fanned him with feather fans, and they wiped his sweat, they smudged the room with [incense made from] deer tallow and other things unknown [to us], and it [the dwelling] was adorned with branches.[38] And we noticed that the Indians were formed and organized in the manner of a militia with their captains and everything with a great deal of vigilance. In the dwelling we saw a harquebus

36. Manuscript 88-A (18v28–31) reads "hauiendo pre- / cedido a esto el adbertir a los solda-dos estuuiesen a cauallo porque dentro de / la dicha sala no entramos mas que el dicho relijioso, yo y dicho jeneral don Martin / [^de Mendiondo]. Y a lo que reconoci, el dicho franzes saue mui vien la lengua materna de los / yndios con quien estaba congregado." Weddle renders it as "Before this he had remarked about the soldiers on horseback, and I realized from his question that the Frenchman knows very well the mother tongue of the Indians who were gathered, because no one had entered the salon but the said religious, myself and General Mendiondo" (1999, 138). This rendition makes it seem as if the Frenchman had mentioned something about the Spanish soldiers being on horseback, which is not the case. It was de León who, even before entering the hut, had advised his soldiers to remain on horseback.

37. Here "lengua mexicana" means Nahuatl. The Indian translator spoke both Nahuatl and the language of the Indians with whom the Frenchman was living in addition to Spanish. Thus, neither the interpreter nor Jean Henri was communicating in his mother tongue.

38. The term "enramada" usually means 'bower' or 'arbor.' However, here it might refer to branches as well as aromatic flowers and herbs kept in the room for their scent.

which, although broken, was recognized as having been long like a musket, and a flask of powder of black ramrod and balls. Asked what his name was, he said Francisco and that he was Christian, but that in his language he was called Captain Monsieur Jean Henri,[39] and that he was gathering many nations of Indians to make them his friends; and that those who did not join him for good, he would destroy and devastate with the help of the Indians that he had as followers. And although with his resistance and that of the Indians, as has been mentioned, we put him on a horse with much emotion from him and from the Indians, whom I kept happy once more by distributing the remainders [of the items] that were left. And I explained to them that taking him was not to inflict any humiliation or harm, since neither he nor they had harmed any Spaniards, but because he himself had sent for me and also because His Most Excellent Lord Viceroy and the Lord Bishop wanted to see him in order to talk to him, dress him, and regale him because they had already received news about him. With this, they remained appeased, and we pursued the return of our journey with the prisoner as far as said post of San Francisco de Coahuila. And for the record and in order to continue with further actions that are necessary in this case, I signed below with two witnesses in my presence. [Signatures] Alonso de León; witness Joseph Antonio de Ecay y Múzquiz; witness Joseph Gutiérrez.

[*Auto 3*]

Declaration of the French prisoner

In the village of San Francisco de Coahuila on the 7th day of the month of June of 1688, General Alonso de León, governor [**folio 19v**] and captain of the presidio of this province, in agreement with the preceding *auto*, having arrived at this post today, the abovementioned day, with the French prisoner, as stated, and being necessary, for greater clarity and verification of its contents, to investigate, with details, if it is true that there is a settlement of the French, that is said to be located in the Bahía del Espíritu Santo or on one of the rivers that enter the Mar del Norte, I ordered to appear before me an Indian named Ignacio, who knows the Mexican and the Castilian languages, a native of Pueblo de la Caldera, of this jurisdiction, to serve as an interpreter in order to examine Francisco, the French prisoner, who is present, for he speaks the language of the Indians of the nation in whose company he was found, which is understood by said interpreter.[40] For this [purpose] I took his oath which he made upon God Our Lord and in the sign of the cross, as

39. See note 25, sec. 1.
40. See note 37 above.

required by law, and he promised to tell the truth about everything he knew and everything he was asked. He gave his agreement and I received his confession which he made in the following manner:

Asked what his name is, where he is from, what his profession is, whose vassal he is, and what cause or motive he had to come and congregate with the Indians, with whom he had been found, what direction he came from, and by whose command, and the length of time he has been with them, and what his age and state are, he answered that his name was Francisco, the name he was given at baptism, but that his countrymen call him Captain Monsieur Jean Henri, and that he is [captain] of a company of his nation, and he is a native of Saint Jean d'Orléans,[41] in the Kingdom of France. And that [he came] by order of Monsieur Philippe, governor of a settlement they have on the banks of a large river. Since this informant had learned the language of the Indians, he came to the region where he had been found, having already congregated other nations of Indians that are in closer proximity to the aforementioned settlement. And that the motive is to subdue all those nations to the obedience of the King of France, and that he is married in the settlement and has a small daughter, and that it has been about three years since he joined said Indians. He could not say his age; he seems, from his appearance, to be more than fifty years of age, and this is what he responds.

Asked how long ago the French, his countrymen, came to settle at said river, and with how many families, and in what vessels, and how many, and under what pretext, knowing that this land belongs to the monarchy [**folio 20r**] of the King of Spain. To which he responds (although for the most part he made himself understood through gestures and signs) that it has been about fifteen years since they came to said French settlement (and he could not give an account about how many families came or in how many vessels), and that they have two castles on a river, one facing the other, and the largest and most outstanding one belongs to the Frenchman. And that it has twenty artillery pieces, five on each wall, and that the other castle is Flemish. And that both communicate via canoes, crossing the river from one side to the other, as each is on his own side, and that on the side to the south is the Frenchman's; and that the one belonging to the Flemish does not have artillery pieces but muskets, and it is small. And the settlement of the French is very well protected by its castle, as it guards and defends the four streets that said settlement has,

---

41. The Frenchman may be referring to Saint-Jean-de-l'Île d'Orléans, which is located in Québec, Canada, not in France as assumed in other secondary sources. Québec was part of the Kingdom of France.

and that there are six companies of soldiers for its defense, a church and a Capuchin convent with six priests and a very good church, and well constructed with a bell tower with ten bells; and that ordinarily there are three merchant ships in said settlement that come and go to France and bring them all the necessities, and this he responds.

Asked if in said settlement and its surroundings they have any crops, farms to raise large and small livestock and horses, and what seeds they sow for their sustenance, and if they have Indian subjects that assist them in sowing and harvesting their fields, he answered that the settlement has in its surroundings fields where they sow corn and wheat, enough for their sustenance, and breeding of cows and sheep, horses and mules, and a flour mill in which they grind the wheat for the consumption of the settlement, and that likewise they sow much tobacco, sugarcane, all of which they do with the help of many Indians whom they have already subdued to their devotion. And that to navigate from the settlement to the coast of the sea, they also have seven ships with oars and sails, and that they navigate it in one day; and they travel this distance by land on horseback in three days. And asked of what material the castles are made, he said of stone and mortar, and that the stone they bring from the coast; and this he responds.

Asked if on some occasions the Frenchmen from the settlement have come to visit this informant during the time he has been [**folio 20v**] with the Indians where we found him, or if he has gone to said settlement to see them; and on the occasions when they came to see him, that he should say and declare what they communicated to him and consulted with him, and with what intent they came, to which he responds that since he came and he joined the Indians where we found him, he has not gone to said settlement, but that its inhabitants did come to see him, as they did about a year earlier, when sixteen Frenchmen came to Captain Monsieur Henri to visit him. And that now, a little over two months ago, some others had come to the same effect, with only the purpose of communicating with the informant about the state of his progress in the gathering of Indians, and that they did not communicate anything else; and so he responds.

Asked if the place and location of said settlement and its surroundings is flat land, or if there are some mountains or hills, marshes or lagoons, which impede passage to it, he said that all the land is flat without any impediment to reach it, and that it is very adequate for their fields. And although he was asked if there were any natural pools or arroyos with which they watered their crops, he could not give any information about this; and so he responds. He was asked other questions and cross-examined pertaining to the case in question by means of the interpreter, and he said that he does not know anything else, and that it is the truth, under the charge of the oath he took. His confession was read to him, affirmed and ratified, and when he was told to sign and insisted that he do it, he excused himself saying that he did not know how [to write]. The interpreter did not sign it either because he said he did not know how. I, the governor, signed it with two witnesses in my presence.

[Signatures] Alonso de León; witness, Joseph Antonio de Ecay y Múzquiz; witness Joseph Gutiérrez.

[*Auto 4*]

In the village of San Francisco de Coahuila, on the 7th day of the month of June of 1688, General Alonso de León, governor and captain of the presidio of this province, having seen the declaration and confession made by Francisco, of French nationality and also known as Monsieur Jean Henri, prisoner, and all the other *autos* of this case, and that from them results the certainty of the settlement of the French on the Río or Bahía del Espíritu Santo, I order that these *autos* and said prisoner be remitted to the Most Excellent Lord Conde de la Monclova, viceroy and captain general of New Spain and president of her Real Audiencia, so that His Excellency, upon viewing them, may determine what needs to be done. In this frontier we must take all the necessary precaution, guard, and vigilance owing to what may result from having imprisoned the Frenchman, and the upset this may have caused among his Indian followers and devotees. And I signed it with two witnesses in my presence.

[Signatures] Alonso de León; witness Joseph Antonio de Ecay y Múzquiz; witness Joseph Gutiérrez.

[Expedition Diary]

[**folio 21r**] In the village of San Francisco de Coahuila, on the 18th of May of 1688, General Alonso de León, governor and captain of the presidio of this province, I say that it is necessary to set out in search of the Frenchman owing to the news given to me that he is in a *ranchería* on the other side of the Río Bravo in a northeasterly direction. Because it is necessary for this purpose to make a list of the best soldiers and the most well-armed that can be found in this post because it is a journey of much risk, I ordered it and I made the following list:

I, General Alonso de León, the *padre predicador*, Fray Buenaventura Bonal, a religious from the order of Saint Francis, our chaplain; General Don Martín de Mendiondo, head and commissary of the soldiers of the Reino de León; Captain Carlos Cantú; Captain Nicolás de Medina, captain for life; Captain Cristóbal de Villarreal; *Alférez* Thomás de la Garza; *Alférez* Alonso de León; *Alférez* Lorenzo de la Garza; *Alférez* Jerónimo Cantú; Sergeant Juan Cantú;

Francisco de Villarreal; Juan de la Garza. The above mentioned are from the support troop of the Reino de León.

Captain Diego Ramón; Thomas Sánchez; Juan Domingo Flores; Joseph de Baeza; Antonio de Montes de Oca; Joseph Ximénez; three muleteers to drive the supplies; eighty military horses.

[**folio 21v**] Route and diary of the journey that I, General Alonso de León, made with the company of soldiers contained in the aforementioned list to go and capture the Frenchman.

Wednesday, May 19, 1688, we left the village of San Francisco de Coahuila and made camp for the night at the junction of the rivers named Nadadores and Coahuila. The road is good and level, it was a distance of six leagues.

Thursday, [May] 20, we set out with the company and passed by a place they call Los Baluartes. We went down the Río de Nadadores a distance of seven leagues, comfortable and flat terrain.

Friday, [May] 21, we forded said river and made camp for the night at the Río de las Sabinas. The distance is ten leagues, no lack of watering holes and the terrain [is] very comfortable and flat.

Saturday, [May] 22, we were forced to stop with the company to allow the horses to recover somewhat.

Sunday, [May] 23, we made camp for the night at a small lagoon at a distance of seven leagues, good and level road.

Monday, [May] 24, we slept at the foot of a large hill by an arroyo which is near it. We marched a distance of eight leagues, and the land is abundant in water and flat.

Tuesday, [May] 25, we set out in search of the Río Grande, we reached it; it was at a distance of four leagues from where we left.

Wednesday, [May] 26, leaving the main company by the river with five soldiers, we crossed the Río Grande with the remaining thirteen and the priest. The ford is very good and wide; the water reached to above the stirrups; it has the width of about two harquebus shots. The ford is without any danger; it can be crossed with a pack train. We slept on this day by an arroyo, where there are some pools of water, at a distance of eight leagues from said river; the land is flat with pastures and water.

Thursday, [May] 27, the Day of the Ascension of Our Lord. [**folio 22r**] We slept at another arroyo which is in a wooded ravine. We traveled that day eleven leagues on flat land with water.

Friday, [May] 28, not having had any news from the Frenchman, I dispatched the Indians I had with me to search for the *ranchería* where he lived; and this day the company halted.

Alonso de León determining latitude with his astrolabe
(drawing by Scott Harshbarger)

Saturday, [May] 29, one of the Indians we had dispatched returned and informed us that they had not found the *ranchería*, and that we should return to the river to wait for further notice. Thus, retracing the path of the day before, we stopped at said river, and on the way we came across more than five hundred Indians[42] hunting livestock which they call *cíbolas* and resemble cattle. And when we asked them about a Spaniard who stayed with them, they told us that he was in their *ranchería* very nearby, and that he was their master. We helped them kill some of said buffalo,[43] and one of them guided us and took us to camp for the night near the *ranchería* of said Indians. We marched a distance of about three leagues, and it should be mentioned that the direction we took on these journeys was mostly toward the northeast.

Sunday, [May] 30, we crossed five arroyos, some with difficult crossings because they were swollen, and after crossing them, we sighted the encampment of the *ranchería*, which is on an elevation, about three leagues from where we had slept. We arrived there and through the steps we took (which are written in detail in an *auto* drawn up specifically for this purpose, and to

42. See note 34 above.
43. Manuscript 88-A 22r16–17 reads "Les aiudamos a matar algunas de las / dichas ciuolas." Weddle translates it as "They helped us to kill some of the *cíbolas*" (1999, 137). The manuscript states that the Spaniards helped the Indians kill buffalo, not vice versa.

which I refer), we captured the Frenchman and returned on this day, following the same route on which we had come, until we reached said village of San Francisco de Coahuila, arriving on the 6th of the current month of June.

Thus, as it appears from the journeys, from said village to said *ranchería*, there is a distance of sixty-seven [**folio 22v**] leagues, which, discounting the five that we retraced on Friday, leaves sixty-two fluid leagues, and for the record for all times, I signed this with two witnesses.

[Signatures] Alonso de León; witness Joseph Antonio de Ecay y Múzquiz; witness Joseph Gutiérrez.

3.5 English Translation of Manuscript 89-B

[**folio 37v**] Diary, route, and demarcation of the land of the journey made by order of the Most Excellent Señor Conde de la Monclova, viceroy and captain general of New Spain, and later confirmed by the Most Excellent Señor Conde de Galve, current viceroy and captain general of said New Spain, and led by General Alonso de León, governor of the Province of Coahuila and commander-in-chief of the one hundred men who went on the journey to discover the Bahía del Espíritu Santo and the settlement [**folio 38r**] of the French, which is as follows:

1689, March, Wednesday, March 23, it was ordered that the entire *real* of people and soldiers, who were in Coahuila, set out, and indeed they traveled a distance of one league down the river.

Thursday, March 24, the general[44] set out, and finding the company ready to move out downriver, he marched on the other bank to the junction with the Nadadores. He marched this day seven leagues in a northeasterly[45] direction, all the land is flat and uninhabitable.

Friday, March 25, we marched down the Río de Nadadores on the south bank, passing between two hills which they call Los Baluartes. We traveled along the river where there is a tall cottonwood and no other one in a great distance. We traveled seven leagues in the same northeasterly direction, all the land is flat with good pastures.

Saturday, March 26, we marched downriver, as on the day before, to where it flows into the Sabinas. We stopped at a distance of one league from the

---

44. West translates "salio el general" (89-B 38r7) as "the whole body (*el general*) set out" (1905, 203).

45. West translates here "towards the north" (1905, 203), since she is basing her rendition on 89-D 51v1.

junction, level road [**folio 38v**] and good pastures. We traveled this day six leagues in an easterly direction.

Sunday, March 27, we marched down said river [Sabinas] and crossed it toward the north, and continuing the way along its bank, we sighted the soldiers who were coming from Nuevo Reino de León to join us according to the designated location; we came together and fired salvos on each side. We traveled three leagues to the east.

Here a general review was held of all the soldiers, mule drivers, and other servant boys with all the baggage, as is recorded with all the details of the review, which appears separately.[46]

Monday, March 28, we traveled in a northeasterly direction a distance of six leagues crossing some plains without water, very difficult terrain although flat. We stopped at a pool of rainwater.

Tuesday, March 29, we set out northeast by north.[47] We traveled five leagues, flat land, although with some small hills.[48]

[**folio 39r**] Wednesday, March 30,[49] we marched four leagues in a northerly direction. It happened that before sunrise, the French prisoner had sent one of the Indians of his devotion, whom we had with us, to inform the Indians [who were] his acquaintances that we were passing through their habitation. As a result, a league before arriving there, more than sixty[50] Indians came to receive us, some with their weapons and some without, and they accompanied us to their village. They had prepared a hut, covered with buffalo hides, where they put the Frenchman, toward whom they expressed much affection. In front [of the hut], a pole four varas[51] in height was driven into the ground and from it hung the heads of sixteen Indians, enemies whom they had killed. There

46. West omits this reference to another document that contains additional information about the members of the expedition (1905). Juan Bautista Chapa provides a detailed list with the names of all the expedition party members: eighty-eight men, including a religious and the French prisoner (here misnamed Juan Andrés); twelve muleteers; thirteen servants; 721 horses and mules; eighty-two loads of flour, biscuit, and other provisions; and three loads of clothing and other items to distribute among the Indians (Chapa [1961] 2005, 213; my translation).

47. West, following 89-D 52r7–8, translates "toward the northeast" (1905, 204), which corresponds to 45.00°. Manuscript 89-B 38v21 states "nordeste quarta al norte," which corresponds to 33.75°.

48. Relying on Manuscript 89-D, West combines the March 29 and 30 entries into one long entry for March 29 and includes no entry for March 30.

49. See note 48 above.

50. West makes a translation error when she renders "more than seventy Indians" (1905, 204). Manuscript 89-D 52r13, as well as all the other copies, reads "mas de sesenta yndios."

51. A "vara" is an old Spanish measure of length that corresponds to approximately thirty-three inches. A pole of four varas would measure about eleven feet.

were five nations together (according to the account given by the Frenchman) named Hapes, Jumenes, Xiabu, Mescale, and another. We counted eighty-five huts. We distributed among them some cotton tunics, small blankets, beads, rosaries, knives, and flour,[52] which pleased them very much, and we killed five head of cattle for them to eat. Counting all the people of all ages, we arrived at four hundred and ninety. [**folio 39v**] We stopped at a nearby arroyo for evening prayers.

Thursday, March 31, it was necessary to stop at this place because the horses had suffered a lot due to lack of water.

April, Friday, April 1st, we set out in search of the Río Bravo. We traveled five leagues, crossing some small hills; there was no lack of watering places in this distance; most of the direction of these five leagues was to the north. We halted with the company in front of the ford on this south bank; the river was sounded and found to be in good condition to cross the next day. The crossing is as wide as a musket shot.[53] We already had in our company a faithful Indian as a guide, who assured us that he knew all the land, and that he would take us to where there were men like us, settled with six or seven houses; and that they had women and children and were at a distance of about six days' journey from said Río Bravo. This Indian does not speak Spanish, but through another Indian, a poor interpreter, we were able to shed some light on what he was saying.

Saturday, April 2, we crossed the river and traveled about a league to the north to go around some ravines and small hills. Then we went in a northeasterly direction [**folio 40r**] for the most part until we arrived at some pools that were at five leagues' distance from the river; we named it Paraje de los Cuervos because at nightfall more than three thousand [crows] appeared. The road was flat and without brush.

Palm Sunday, April 3, we set out in a northeasterly direction through flat land for a distance of three leagues, and then there were two more through a few mesquite thickets. We crossed a few small dry arroyos and then we came upon one with water, on whose banks we stopped; so, this day we traveled five long leagues. We named this creek Arroyo de Ramos because we found it on this day. Here we observed the altitude of the sun with an astrolabe (albeit defective), and we found ourselves at 26°31' polar elevation. It should be noted that the tables of this observation were made before the so-called Gregorian Correction, which was in the year of 1582, in which the equi-

52. Relying on 89-D 52v3, West translates "arms" instead of "flour," as stated in the introduction.
53. West (1905, 205) omits this sentence because it does not appear in manuscript 89-D.

nox was on March 10. And following the *Ephemerides* of Andrea Argoli,[54] a Roman who places the equinox this year on March 20, we found, by these tables, that today, April 3, corresponds to March 24 of this year, which is the first one [**folio 40v**] after the leap year. And these tables, the author states, he took from *El arte de navegar* by Maestro Medina.[55] It has been necessary to provide these explanations lest it appear that there is some error because we found ourselves without modern tables.

Holy Monday, April 4, we traveled in a northeasterly direction most of the day, and at times northeast by north[56] for a distance of eight leagues. At the beginning the land was flat, and later there was a thicket of small mesquite trees; and having come out of it, we got into a larger one for three leagues. We came upon a river, which, although it carried little water, was recognized to flood its banks for almost half a league in times of rain. We named it Río de las Nueces because there were many walnut trees. It is somewhat rocky, and all its rocks are flint and very fine.

Holy Tuesday, April 5, we crossed said river. It was necessary to march half a league along its bank, and we entered through a glade and encountered a very dense thicket, which had to be cut through at its entrance with cutlasses and axes for almost a league because of the many prickly pear cactuses and mesquite that impeded our march. We continued [**folio 41r**] in an easterly direction, entered a mesquite thicket later, which, for stretches, forced us to cut a passage, and we traveled a distance of seven leagues. We came upon a river that we named Río Zarco because its water was blue. We marched, as I said, seven leagues with many detours.

Holy Wednesday, April 6, we marched about three leagues in a northeasterly direction and two to the east, through flat land with excellent pastures and through some very pleasant ravines, and for stretches, small forests of live

54. Andrea Argoli (1570–1657) was an Italian scholar. He studied medicine, mathematics, and astronomy and taught mathematics at La Sapienza University in Rome and later at the University of Padova. He was a prolific writer of works on mathematics, astronomy, and astrology. He wrote the three *Ephemerides*, which are diaries containing astronomical observations according to the Copernican system, in 1623, 1629, and 1652 (Mascella and Pelusi 2006).

55. Pedro de Medina (1493–1567) was a Spanish cosmographer, astronomer, chronicler, and moralist. He wrote several books, among them *El arte de navegar* (1545), a groundbreaking compendium about compass navigation. The book was widely read and translated into several languages (Bleiberg, Ihrie, and Pérez 1993, 1057).

56. Relying on manuscript 89-D 53v15–16, West (1905, 207) misstates the direction as "east-by-north" (78.75°). Manuscript 89-B 40v7–8 gives the direction as "quarta al norte," which corresponds to 33.75°. This difference of 45.00° is significant in any attempt to re-create the expedition route.

oaks.[57] We arrived at a river which we named Río Hondo[58] because on each side its descent is more than six or seven *estados*.[59] There are near the river, on one side as well as the other, some small hills, wooded some of them. The water was excellent and the horses drank with ease. When we went down to the river, we found some large white rocks, and on some of them we saw some crosses carved and other figures made by hand with much perfection, and it appears they are from a long time ago.

Holy Thursday, April 7, we marched in an easterly direction down said river, without having crossed it, for about four leagues, sometimes in an easterly direction and other times to the southeast; and we stopped on its bank, on this side [of the river], which is of the same quality [**folio 41v**] as at the previous stopping place. The land is mostly flat, although there were also some mesquite thickets. And although on our daily journeys, since we passed the habitation of the five Indian nations, which was on the 30th of the previous month, we came upon some Indian foot trails which were from a long time ago, we encountered no [Indians]. The land was mostly flat.[60]

Holy Friday, April 8, we crossed from the other bank of the Río Hondo and continued east by north[61] during most of the day. Near the river we came upon two ravines, one near the other, and it appears that during the times of rain, they swell so much, that the water rises more than one *estado*. We followed a little arroyo in a thicket, through which we had to cut a passage for a stretch to be able to pass the loaded mules, which was with much work, some of them getting stuck. After crossing this arroyo, we came upon very level land and then a thicket with tall mesquite trees and with some large pools of water in the middle, where we stopped, having marched this day eight long leagues to the east, as stated.

Holy Saturday, April 9, we set out in a northeasterly direction,[62] and because we encountered some thickets, [**folio 42r**] it was necessary to make

57. David C. Turpin (1987) identifies "encino" as 'live oak,' a small-leaved, evergreen species (*Quercus ilex*), and "roble" as 'oak,' a larger-leaved, deciduous species (*Quercus robur*). Both species are found together natively in the US Southwest.

58. The Spanish adjective *hondo* means 'deep.'

59. In his notes, Foster states that according to the *Documentary Relations of the Southwest*, an *estado* equals approximately seven feet when used as a measure of depth (Chapa 1997, 206). Accordingly, the descent to the Río Hondo would have been between forty-two and forty-nine feet.

60. West omits this last sentence (1905, 208).

61. West gives the direction as "east-northeast," which corresponds to 67.50° (1905, 208). The correct translation is "east by north" (78.75°).

62. Following 89-D 55r12, West states "we set out to the north" (1905, 209).

some detours, sometimes north by east, other times northeast by east.[63] The terrain was very comfortable. This day we crossed a dry arroyo and at a distance of one league we found another with very good water and much pasture. From it we pulled many bass.[64] We named it Arroyo del Vino because on this day, we opened a barrel and distributed [the wine] among all the men. We traveled five leagues this day. We found nuts under the trees, very well grown, as large as the ones from Spain, although very difficult to open. We saw many wild grapevines, which, as the Indians who traveled with us confirmed, bear, when in season, very large and tasty fruit. At this stopping place, around nine at night, the horses stampeded; although there were fifteen soldiers on guard, they could not recover all of them. A group of one hundred and two horses got away, as we recognized through the count made the following day.

Easter Sunday, April 10, the soldiers left in different directions to search for the horses, which were found in different trails. This detained them until evening prayer and for this reason the main company halted this day; and we observed the altitude of the pole and found it to be at 25°55'.[65]

Easter Monday, April 11, we set out in an easterly direction, crossing, at a short distance from the stopping place, two arroyos with good water, and then we encountered a [**folio 42v**] large forest of walnut trees and live oaks of more than five leagues; all pleasant and fertile land. It was necessary to march this day twelve leagues to have water. We came upon a very large river, although not with much water, and with a good ford to cross it. We gave it the name Río de Medina; its descent is some nine to ten *estados*. The course on this day was half to the east and half to the northeast. Along most of the way, there were live oaks and nut trees.

Easter Tuesday, April 12, we crossed the river, and the crossing was very convenient. We continued in an easterly direction for five leagues of low small hills without thicket. We crossed some ravines of red and yellow soil. We entered a mesquite thicket and found water in an arroyo, which, although at the beginning it was dry and we distrusted our guide, thinking that he had missed the watering place, at a distance of about one mile, it was flowing

63. West (1905, 209) translates "quarta al leste" (89-B 42r2) as "north-northeast (22.50°) instead of "northeast by east" (56.25°).

64. West confuses the word "robalos," which is 'bass' (a type of fish), with "robles" 'oak trees' (1905, 209). On the 1690 expedition de León stops at this arroyo and notes that it is the Arroyo de los Róbalos (90-C 7r23).

65. Manuscript 89-A 431v23–24 and its copies (89-C, 89-D, and 89-E) show a different latitude: 27°55'.

quite well. The land was very fertile with pastures and because we found near this arroyo a large dead lion, we named it Arroyo del León.

Wednesday, April 13, we set out in an easterly direction and sometimes east-northeast a distance of six leagues; about half a league from the stopping place, we passed by the tip of a small hill which ends in a cluster of live oaks, which was on our right. There were in it some small piles of rocks placed by hand. We followed some low small hills. There were about two leagues [**folio 43r**] of live oak woods, and at stretches it was necessary to cut through them; and later, until we arrived at a small creek, all the land was level.

Thursday, April 14, we set out in an east by northerly direction[66] in search of a large river, which the guide told us we would find. We arrived at two in the afternoon. We traveled six leagues, three of them over some hills and then over other hills with thickets and with some ravines, which made it necessary to clear through at times to be able to pass. The land was the most pleasant we had traveled. The river does not carry much water; it had a good ford, and its banks are full of trees. On the way, six buffalo were killed; they were the first ones we saw over a distance of more than one hundred leagues. We named this river Nuestra Señora de Guadalupe, whom we had brought from Coahuila as our protector and defender, and she was painted on our royal standard.

Friday, April 15, the day dawned rainy; nevertheless, we set out with the main company to the river crossing, which was about a league away, and we crossed it. And with the rain getting worse, we stopped at a little arroyo that was nearby. We advanced no more than two leagues this day. On this day we held war council because the guide said that we were already near the settlement, and it was determined that on the next day, sixty [**folio 43v**] soldiers should set out to reconnoiter it, and that the main company should remain at another stopping place farther ahead with sufficient guard.

Saturday, April 16, in accordance with what had been discussed the day before, the governor set out with the sixty soldiers, well equipped, after a mass to Our Lady of Guadalupe had been chanted with all solemnity. Likewise, the main company set out at the same time, and having traveled about three leagues with the sixty men, the rearguard sighted an Indian in the brush; and when taken to the governor and questioned, although with a poor interpreter,

66. West gives the translation "we moved forward, east-northeast" (1905, 210) for "Salimos para el rumbo / del leste quarta al nordeste" (89-B 43r4–5). The direction stated by West corresponds to 67.50°, whereas the direction given in the Spanish manuscript is the equivalent of 78.75°.

he declared that his *ranchería* was nearby and that four Frenchmen were there. We intensified our pace, guided by said Indian, after having sent [word] to the main company to stay at the place where they had brought the Indian because there was water.[67] Before we reached the *ranchería*, all the people left; we saw them as they were entering a thicket, and behind them were eight or ten dogs loaded with buffalo hides.[68] We sent the same Indian who had guided us to call them, and he accomplished that most of them came. It was ascertained that the four Frenchmen were not there, but that four days earlier, they had gone on to the Tejas. At this *ranchería* we found two Indians [**folio 44r**] who told us that at a two-day journey from there we would find the individuals in a *ranchería*. We gave these Indians gifts of tobacco, knives, and other things, so they would guide us, as they did, straightening our course to the north until sunset. And in a thicket, we found a village of more than two hundred and fifty persons. Here we tried to find out about said Frenchmen, our French prisoner[69] always serving as interpreter. And they responded that four days before, they [the Frenchmen] had gone to the Tejas Indians and that the others, who were settled by the little sea (which is the bay), all died at the hands of the coastal Indians; that said Frenchmen had six houses where they lived, and that it was three moons (that is, three months) since the event occurred; and that before this, they had gotten an illness of smallpox, and most had died of it. This day the main company marched three leagues east[70] and stopped where indicated by the governor, who with the sixty men went eight leagues to the north.

Sunday, April 17, having stayed to camp overnight next to the settlement of the Indians, we again set out in a northerly direction. And having [**folio 44v**] traveled five leagues we found some ranchos of Indians known to our French prisoner. From them we ascertained quite well the route of the four Frenchmen who were going to the Tejas, and that four days earlier they had passed by on horseback. Here we entered in consultation about what could be determined since the main company was very far away and on unknown territory, and it was determined to write a letter to the Frenchmen and to send it with an Indian. It was executed accordingly, the royal *Alférez* Francisco Martínez wrote it in French, and in substance it said that having been informed that the coastal Indians had killed some Christians, and that they had escaped, they

67. West omits the statement that the presence of water was the reason for selecting the stopping place (1905, 212).

68. This is one of the first documented sightings of an Indian travois pulled by dogs in Texas.

69. West translates "our French guide" (1905, 213).

70. West omits the miles traveled (1905, 213), as they are not included in manuscript 89-D 58r12.

could come with us, and that we would wait for them three or four days at the houses of the village from which they had left. This letter was signed by the governor, and Father Fray Damián Massanet, a religious of our Father Saint Francis, our chaplain, added at the bottom of the letter a few lines in Latin, in case any of the four should be a religious, exhorting them to come. And we dispatched the letter with an Indian courier and placed some paper in it for a response, and he assured us that he would catch up with them. Near evening prayer, an Indian came from [**folio 45r**] the north to see the Frenchman, of whom he must have had news. And when we asked him if there was much distance from there to the Tejas, he answered that it was many days' journey,[71] and he said that three days earlier, the four Frenchmen had passed through his *ranchería*.

Monday, April 18, considering the harm that the main camp could suffer (even though it had remained well garrisoned), we set out looking for it. On the way, the governor received a letter that on the night before the horses had stampeded and that more than a hundred horses had been lost; some had been found, but thirty-six were still missing. So we intensified our pace to the main camp, where we also received the news that a soldier had been lost while looking for the horses; with this news, different squadrons of soldiers were formed to search for him, but he did not appear this day.

Tuesday, April 19, since neither the soldier nor the horses had appeared, two squadrons of soldiers set out to search for them in different directions, and the governor personally went, and although many efforts were made, they did not appear this day, and they [the search parties] slept out in the open, to continue their search. This day Indians from different *rancherías* came to the main camp, to whom we gave gifts of tobacco and other things, [**folio 45v**] and they were asked to scour the land in search of the soldier and horses that were missing, promising them the corresponding.

Wednesday, April 20, the main company did not set out because neither the soldier nor the horses had appeared. The efforts were repeated this day with other squadrons of soldiers. And as soon as they left, the lost one arrived, guided by some Indians, and he said that he had slept that night in a *ranchería* of Indians, where he turned up. And fearing that they were going to kill him, he was uncertain if he should stay there, and that he received much welcome, and that it was quite lucky that he escaped from danger because these people

71. West translates "that it was not many days' journey" (1905, 214), following 89-D 59r6–7. Manuscript 89-C 138v3 provides the same information. However, both 89-A 434r26–27 and 89-B 45r4 state the opposite: "que hauia muchas / jornadas."

are so barbarous. This day, although the astrolabe was broken, we straightened it as best we could, and we observed the sun, and we found ourselves at 28°41' of pole elevation.

Thursday, April 21, we set out with the main company in an easterly direction, and at times east by north and northeast by north, traveling through some large plains, without trees for a long distance. We marched eight leagues as far as an arroyo with good water, and here the guide told us that the settlement of the French was on the bank of this arroyo and in the vicinity. The land was all very pleasant, and we came across many buffalo.

Friday, April 22, although the day had dawned rainy, and because we found ourselves near [**folio 46r**] the settlement, we set out with the entire company, and at a distance of three leagues down the arroyo we found it. And having stopped with the main body at about one harquebus shot from it, we went to see it. And we found all the houses sacked, all the chests and bottle-cases and all the other furniture that the settlers had [were] broken; more than two hundred books (as it appeared) torn and their leaves already rotten and scattered across the yards, all in French. From this we concluded that the perpetrators of these deaths had pulled everything they [the colonists] owned from the houses[72] and divided it among themselves, and what was of no use to them, they ripped apart, making a horrible sack of all they had. For besides the evidence of the act, having found everything in this form, we saw proof in the *rancherías* through which we passed before reaching the settlement; we had found some books the Indians had in the French language, in very good condition, with other small items of very little value. These books were recovered and their titles kept for memory. And not only did the Indians wreak havoc with the furnishings but also with the weapons, for we found more than one hundred stocks of flintlock harquebuses without locks or barrels, which they must have taken, which was confirmed by a barrel that was found at some distance from the houses. We found three dead bodies lying in the field; one of them seemed to have been that of a woman, from the dress that was still clinging to the bones. They were all picked up [**folio 46v**] and we gave them a burial with a mass chanted and the bodies present.[73] The main house of this settlement is of ship's timber made in the form of a fort, and the

72. Relying on 89-D 60v7–8, West gives the translation "chests" for "ca- / xas" (1905, 216), instead of "houses" from "cassas," as it appears in Manuscript 89-B 46r10.

73. Here West inserts a sentence from another location in the manuscript (89-D 61r6–9), explaining that she transferred it "because this is its logical place" (1905, 217). This change distorts the message of the original document.

roof is made of planks and another roof[74] with a slant for protection from the water. And also made of planks and next to it, without separation, is another room, although not as strong, which must have served as a chapel, in which they celebrated mass. The other five houses are made of palisade and covered with mud inside and out, and the roofs are of buffalo hides, all quite unfit for any defense. There were next to the fort and the houses eight pieces of artillery of iron, of medium size, for balls of four and six pounds,[75] three very old stone-throwing guns[76] whose chambers were missing. We found some large iron bars, ship's nails, all of which was estimated to be around twenty *arrobas*.[77] Some of the pieces of artillery were thrown on the ground and others on their carriages, although the carriages were broken. There were some barrels with broken heads, and because everything was thrown out, there was nothing worth anything. We also found some damaged tackle around the houses. We searched for the other bodies, and they could not be discovered, so we concluded that they had been thrown into the arroyo and eaten by alligators, because there were many.[78] The settlement was on an excellent and level location to be able to defend itself sufficiently from any attack. On the frame of the main door of the fort was the year when they settled, which was the year of 1684, with other details which were included [**folio 47r**] in a separate description of the place. This day, the main company traveled three leagues to the east. Therefore, as it appears from the total, the distance from the presidio of Coahuila to this settlement is one hundred thirty-six leagues.

Discovery of the Bahía del Espíritu Santo and its harbor.

Saturday, April 23, we set out with thirty men to reconnoiter the bay on the south side, trying to follow the arroyo down from the settlement. We took the French prisoner as our guide because he told us that he knew it and had traveled it all by boat. With this assurance, we let him guide us, but he did not do it down the arroyo, because he said that there was no crossing. We traveled five leagues to the southwest, and going around two arroyos, we marched east

74. West renders this as "with a second story" (1905, 217).

75. West translates "de quatro y seis libras de bala" (89-B 46v12 and 89-D 61r19) as "four or five pounders" (1905, 217).

76. "Pedre- / ros" (89-B 46v12–13) are 'stone-throwing guns.' West translates the word as "swivels" (1905, 217).

77. An *arroba* equals twenty-five pounds. Twenty *arrobas* would be the equivalent of five hundred pounds.

78. This is the sentence that West moved to another location in the text. See note 73 above.

another three leagues until we reached the shore of the bay, where we slept, for we arrived at sunset.

Sunday, April 24, we set out very early in the morning along the shore of the bay, which at that time[79] was at low tide. There are in its proximity many saltwater lagoons, which, at times, impeded our going on horseback because of the many marshes, so we went on foot for long stretches, leading the horses. One arm of the sea, which appeared to be the largest, points toward the north, another smaller one to the south and the smallest toward the settlement mentioned in this diary. [**folio 47v**] We traveled eight long leagues along the shore until it pleased God that we discover the mouth through which one enters the bay, which was about two leagues from the location we were able to reach on horseback. We received much joy from this and, as a sign, we fired a salvo with our harquebuses. The French prisoner affirmed that this was the mouth and harbor, and that he had entered through it when he came to these parts with Monsieur Felipe de Ta. The mouth of the harbor, from what could be gathered, is two short leagues long. There is a bar of low land in it, which is closer to the coast of Veracruz than the coast of Florida. And the vessels enter through the smallest, according to the Frenchman. The river which we named Nuestra Señora de Guadalupe enters into this bay through the south; although we did not see it because it was impossible to get through, but we concluded this because we saw that it was close by when we passed through and because the Frenchman affirmed it. The arm of the sea which stretches to the north of the bay is so wide that we could not see the land on the other side. On the shore of the bay which we tramped for eight leagues, we saw a topmast of a large ship, another small topgallant mast, a capstan, and some wooden staves of barrels and casks and other timber, all of which must have belonged to some ship that was lost in the bay or on the coast [**folio 48r**] and whose hull we did not see.[80] Having seen and explored the mouth of the bay, we returned the same way we had come, and we slept on the banks of an arroyo next to a small forest, where there had been an Indian village that had been abandoned some time ago. We found a book in the French language, a broken bottle-case, and other things which gave us indication that the Indians

---

79. West translates "a la sason" (89-B 47r18) as "that season" (1905, 218). The more appropriate meaning is 'then' or 'at that time.'

80. West renders the faulty transcription in manuscript 89-D 63r6 of "cuyo puerto divisamos" as "whose harbor we had sighted" (1905, 220). Manuscripts 89-A 437v13 and 89-B 48r1 show the correct phrase, "cuyo cerco no divuisamos," which means that they did not see the hull of the sunken ship. What de León saw was the wreckage of *La Belle*, one of La Salle's lost vessels.

of this village had been involved in the deaths of the French. In this little creek, whose water was somewhat brackish, we found four canoes.[81]

On April 25, we left from here and came to the main camp, where we found an answer to the letter that had been written to the Frenchmen who were going to the nation of the Tejas, which, read by the royal *alférez*, contained, in substance, that within two days they would arrive to where we were, that they were already tired of being among barbarians. The letter was signed by only one, whose signature read Jean L'Archevêque[82] from Bayonne; it was written with red ochre. Thirty-two leagues were traveled, going and returning, on the reconnaissance of the bay.[83] This day, Monday, April 25, the main company halted.

Discovery of the Río de San Marcos

Tuesday, April 26, it was decided [**folio 48v**] that the main company should set out along the same route by which we had come, because the water from the arroyo is brackish, as has been stated before, and the horses which drank from it got sick. In accordance, we marched three leagues up the arroyo. We stopped at the same place where we had halted on the way there, and with twenty men we set out to reconnoiter a very large river, which the French prisoner said was toward the north and entered the bay. And at a distance of about three leagues, we found it; we followed its bank until there was an obstruction from some lagoons. This river is very large, and it seemed larger than the Río Bravo, so large that it seems it can be navigated with a small vessel. We determined to see its entrance into the bay, even if it should prove difficult, which we finally did from a small hill, at a distance of about three-quarters of a league from the mouth of the river. And it appeared to us that it was about the same distance from it to the mouth of the arroyo where the French lived and from said mouth to the settlement, about a league and a half. We traveled fifteen leagues on this day. We observed the altitude of the pole on the shore of the bay this day, and we found ourselves (except for errors caused by the defective astrolabe) at 29°3',[84] more or less. We named

81. Although all three manuscripts (89-A 437v34, 89-B 48r11, and 89-D 63r17) show "quatro canoas," West renders it as "we found two canoes" (1905, 220).

82. See note 36, sec. 1.

83. West translates the distance as "fifty-two leagues" (1905, 221) because she relies on the faulty manuscript 89-D 63r5–6. However, 89-A 438r6, 89-B 48r22, and 89-C 140v15 all show "thirty-two leagues."

84. Manuscript 89-A 438v7 and its copies (89-C, 89-D, 89-E) indicate 26°3'.

this river San Marcos because we discovered it one day after [the saint's] feast day.

[**folio 49r**] The diary of our return continues with the new *entrada* made toward the north in search of the Frenchmen.

Wednesday, April 27, we set out with the main company and we made halt at some pools by a small forest, which is next to the trail.

Thursday, April 28, we set out following our course, and at the same time the governor left with thirty men toward the north bank to search for the Frenchmen who had written. The main company stopped on the Río de Nuestra Señora de Guadalupe, on the other bank.

Friday, April 29, the main company halted.

Saturday, April 30, again, the main company halted.

Sunday, May 1, close to evening prayer, the governor arrived with the men and brought two Frenchmen, streaked with paint as per Indian custom. He had found them at a distance of twenty-five leagues or more from where we had set out with the main company. One of them, the one who had written the letter, was called Juan;[85] the other was named Jacome,[86] a native of La Rochelle. They gave an account of the death of their people, saying first that from an illness of smallpox more than one hundred people died; and that those who remained, having a friendly relationship with the Indians of that entire region, never feared them. And that a little more than a month ago, five Indians arrived at the settlement [**folio 49v**] with the pretext of selling[87] them something, and they stopped at the most remote house of the settlement. And then, others kept arriving with the same pretext, and because the French did not suspect anything, they all went to see them at the house without weapons. When they were inside, other Indians kept coming and hugging them; and at the same time, a party of Indians, who had been hiding in the arroyo, came out and killed them all, stabbing and beating them; and among them, they killed two religious and a priest, and they sacked all the houses. And that they [the two Frenchmen] were not present because they had gone to the Tejas, but that when they heard the news of what had transpired, four of them came; and having found their companions dead, they buried up to fourteen bodies they found; and that they burned almost one hundred barrels of powder,

---

85. This is Jean L'Archevêque. See note 36, sec. 1.

86. This is Jacques Grôlet. See note 37, sec. 1.

87. West indicates that the Indians had arrived at the French settlement "under the pretext of telling them something" (1905, 223). However, all the extant manuscripts state "con pretex- / to de venderles algunas cossas" (89A 49r11–12).

Alonso de León and a rendition of the map of the 1689 expedition
(drawing by Raul E. Elizondo)

so that the Indians would not take it. And that the settlement was very well
equipped with all kinds of firearms, swords, and cutlasses, ornaments,[88] three
chalices and many books with very exquisite bindings. The two Frenchmen
are streaked in the fashion of the Indians, covered with antelope and buffalo
hides. We found them in a *ranchería* of the chief of the Tejas, who was sus-
taining them with much care. We brought him to camp [**folio 50r**] and we
gave him gifts. Although he does not speak Castilian, he is an Indian in whom
we recognized ability; and he had a shrine with some images. He was regaled
generously by the governor from the remnants of the cotton tunics, small
blankets, knives, beads, and other goods, and also the other Indians that came
with him. And he left very pleased, promising to come with some Indians

88. West omits the word "ornaments" (1905, 223).

from his nation to the Province of Coahuila. The governor took the statements of the two Frenchmen separately, about everything that was important and necessary in order to send them to His Excellency. And we continued our journey to the Río de las Nueces; and on Tuesday, May 10, the governor went ahead with a few men to send a dispatch to His Excellency, giving an account of this discovery. And we arrived at the presidio of Coahuila today, the 13th of said month of May, at nightfall. Herewith the diary ends, and for the record, it is signed by the governor. Alonso de León.

3.6 English Translation of Manuscript 90-B

[**folio 4v**] Diary, route, and demarcation of the land of the journey which, by order of the Most Excellent Señor Conde de Galve, viceroy and captain general of New Spain, was made by General Alonso de León, governor of the Province of [**folio 5r**] Coahuila and captain of the presidio, which, on behalf of His Majesty, was put there, and commander-in-chief of the soldiers who went on it [the journey] in a reconnaissance of the French who might be at the Bahía del Espíritu Santo and the Province of the Tejas; it is as follows:

Sunday, day 26 of the month of March of 1690. The pack animals and baggage set out from the Villa de Santiago de la Monclova to one league outside the Indian village, a league and a half from said town, in a northerly direction.[89]

Monday, March 27, the full royal company set out, and we went to halt below the small hills on the bank of the Río de Coahuila, the course was northeast by north,[90] we traveled three leagues.

Tuesday, March 28, we set out in a northeasterly direction downriver, and passing by the Puerto de Baluartes, we made a turn in a northerly direction; we stopped on the bank of the river, having marched eight leagues.[91]

Wednesday, March 29, the company set out downriver in an east by northerly direction,[92] and having passed the cottonwood, the company stopped

89. From the precise compass readings in the 1690 expedition diary, it is inferred that de León used the thirty-two-point compass. It consists of eight major winds, eight half winds, and sixteen quarter winds. The English equivalents of the Spanish quarter winds are frequently translated incorrectly in the extant English renditions (Bolton [1908] 1916; Chapa 1997).

90. Manuscript 90-B 5r13 states "nordeste quarta al norte," which is 'northeast by north' and equals 33.75°. However, manuscripts 90-D 1r13, 90-E 1v15–16, and 90-F 2r8–9 state "nordeste quarta al este." Bolton, relying on 90-D, translates the direction as "northeast-by-east," which corresponds to 56.25° ([1908] 1916, 405).

91. Bolton's translation here is based on 90-D.

92. Manuscript 90-B 5r21 reads "el rumbo de el leste quarta al nordeste." In English this is 'east by north' and corresponds to 78.75°. Bolton translates it as "east-by-northeast" ([1908] 1916, 405); however, this direction does not exist on the compass.

on the bank of the river, marching this day five leagues. All the land is flat, although there are some shrub oak *chaparros*[93] and *lechuguilla*[94] agaves.

Thursday, March 30, we set out in an east [**folio 5v**] by northerly[95] direction downriver as far as the junction of the Río de las Sabinas, having marched this day four leagues and a half. And that evening we were joined by the company from the Reino de León and the missionary padres that came with it.

Friday, March 31, we marched downriver and, traversing a hill in an easterly direction, crossed the Río de las Sabinas. The company stopped on the banks of the river; we marched two leagues.

Saturday, April 1, we marched in a northeasterly direction; we stopped at a pool of rainwater; the company traveled this day six leagues.

Sunday, April 2, after mass, we set out in a northeast by northerly direction, arriving at some pools of rainwater, where the company stopped, having marched five leagues. All is level land although there are some scrub oak *chaparros*.

Monday, April 3, we set out in a northerly direction through flat land along the bank of an arroyo. We found the Indians of the Frenchman,[96] to whom we gave tobacco and clothing; we traveled this day four leagues.

Tuesday, April 4, we set out in a northerly direction in search of the Río Grande; the company halted on its bank, and we found some [**folio 6r**] buffalo, having marched this day five leagues.

Wednesday, April 5, we stayed in place so that everyone might confess and comply with the church before crossing the river.

Thursday, April 6, we crossed the river and marched in a north by easterly[97] direction and stopped on the bank of a dry arroyo, having marched eight leagues. We slept this night without water.

---

93. *Chaparro* means 'short' in Spanish and is often used to describe "thick, low, and usually thorny scrub, much as chaparral is used in Texas today" (Foster 1995, 258).

94. *Lechuguilla* is a low-growing agave whose Spanish name means 'little lettuce.' It forms a circle of spiked leaves (Foster 1995, 253).

95. Bolton translates "we set out east-by-northeast" ([1908] 1916, 406), and Brierley, "the party set out along an east by northeast route" (Chapa 1997, 155). East by northeast corresponds to 67.50°; however, the correct translation is 'east by north,' which is the equivalent of 78.75°.

96. Here de León is referring to Jean Henri and the five Indian nations they had encountered the year before.

97. Bolton ([1908] 1916, 406) and Brierley (Chapa 1997, 156) translate this direction as "north-by-northeast." However, north by northeast is not an actual compass point. They possibly meant to say "north-northeast" (22.50°). This would be incorrect too, as "norte quarta al nordeste" (90-B 6r6) corresponds to 'north by east,' or 11.25°.

Friday, April 7, we marched in a northeasterly direction through flat land, where the company stopped at the Arroyo de Ramos, having traveled this day three leagues.

Saturday, April 8, the company set out in a northeast by northerly direction through level land, although in parts there are some mesquite trees, and we stopped on the bank of an arroyo which we named Caramanchel, and because the ford was bad, we spent most of the day crossing the pack animals. We marched this day three leagues.

Sunday, April 9, after mass, we set out in a northeast by northerly direction through flat land; and passing two ravines with trees, we entered a mesquite wood and came upon the ford of the Río de las Nueces; and we stopped in a [**folio 6v**] meadow along the river, having marched five leagues.

Monday, April 10, having crossed the river, we set out in an easterly direction through a tree-lined trail for about two leagues and then we continued in a northerly direction for another two; and making a turn to the east through flat land, although with some mesquite trees, we crossed the Río Zarco and the company halted, having marched this day seven leagues.

Tuesday, April 11, we set out in a northerly direction across some plains, crossing some small hills. We stopped at the Río Hondo, having marched six leagues.

Wednesday, April 12, we stayed in place with the company in order to search for two men who got lost in a rainstorm the day before while marching.[98]

Thursday, April 13 at noon the two men arrived, and at this time we had news from some Indians that six leagues from this stopping place, there was a gathering of Indians to where a Frenchman had come. I set out this day with twenty soldiers in a westerly direction along the river on the northern bank for about five leagues; I stopped for the night.

Friday, April 14 at sunrise I continued the route, and making a turn to the north, [**folio 7r**] across a plain, I arrived at the bank of a river, where the Indian *ranchería* was. A great quantity of them, small and large, came to meet us; and after giving them tobacco and biscuit, they gave us information that the Frenchmen were on the other side of the Río de Guadalupe; and one Indian had a French musket. And having received this news, we returned to the main body, a large number of Indians accompanying us to the camp, where we gave them gifts of clothing, flour, tobacco, and other trinkets, having traveled seven leagues.

---

98. Bolton ([1908] 1916) omits that the soldiers were lost while marching.

Saturday, April 15, the full company set out in an easterly direction, downriver, until reaching the ford, having marched six leagues.

Sunday, April 16, after mass, we crossed the river in an east by northerly direction through flat land; we reached the Arroyo de Chapa, where we made a bridge to cross it; and continuing until we reached some pools, the main company stopped next to them, having marched eight leagues.

Monday, April 17, we set out in a northeasterly direction and, because of some woods we encountered, we made some turns to the north-northeast and east until we arrived at the Arroyo de los Róbalos,[99] where the company stopped, having marched this day five leagues.

Tuesday, April 18, we set out in different [**folio 7v**] directions to look for one hundred twenty-six horses[100] which had stampeded, and when they appeared this day after noon,[101] the full company set out, and at a short distance, the guide lost his way, and we were forced to continue in a northerly direction in search of the Río de Medina. And because it was already late, the company stopped at a small hill, and we named it *real* del Rosario.[102] Although there was little water, it was enough for the company. We traveled this day four leagues.

Wednesday, April 19, we set out in a northerly direction, having arrived at the Río de Medina, above the ford, we stopped in some bottomlands,[103] having traveled seven leagues.

Thursday, April 20, we marched in an easterly direction, and at a distance of two leagues, we arrived at the ford of the river,[104] where the company stopped because it was necessary to prepare the crossing.

99. This creek had been named Arroyo del Vino on the prior expedition. Bolton notes this ([1908] 1916, 408); Foster identifies this river as the modern-day Atascosa River (Chapa 1997, 215).

100. Brierley misstates the number of horses: "to search for 120 horses that had stampeded" (Chapa 1997, 158).

101. Bolton omits the fact that the horses were recovered after noon ([1908] 1916, 408).

102. On the 1689 expedition, de León had recorded only the names of the rivers, not the stopping places. This is the first instance where the naming of a *real*, a royal camp, appears in his diary.

103. Misreading "paramos" 'we stopped' for "pasamos" 'we crossed,' Bolton gives the translation "having arrived at the Medina River above the ford, we crossed at a shoal" ([1908] 1916, 408). However, manuscript 90-D 3v12 shows "donde paro el real" 'where the company stopped,' and 90-B 7v12 states "paramos en un baxio" 'we stopped at a lowland.' The next day's entry helps solve the conundrum. Since they have to prepare the crossing, it is unlikely that they had crossed the river before.

104. The river crossing occurs on this day.

Friday, April 21, we marched in an easterly direction and arrived at the Arroyo del León; we marched this day five leagues.

Saturday, April 22, we marched in an easterly direction and at times to the northeast, and we stopped at an arroyo with brackish water; we marched six leagues.

Sunday, April 23, after mass, the royal company set out in an east by [**folio 8r**] northerly[105] direction through some live-oak woods, and we stopped by the Río de Guadalupe, where it forms an arroyo close to the river; we marched five leagues.

Monday, April 24, the company set out downriver, and, having crossed the river with some effort because it carried much water, we stopped on the other side, having marched two leagues.

Tuesday, April 25, I left with twenty soldiers, leaving the main body at said stopping place, and I went to reconnoiter the Bahía del Espíritu Santo in an easterly direction. We traveled this day fourteen leagues, and we stopped[106] on the margin of some small pools of water.

Wednesday, April 26, we arrived at the French settlement we saw last year, and having recognized that it was in the shape it was before and where the artillery was buried, we burned the wooden fort; and marching two leagues farther, we recognized in the bay what appeared to be two buoys, one at the tip of the mouth of the Río de San Marcos and the other one on one side, signaling the same channel. The sun was not observed because the day was cloudy. From there we turned around and went up the arroyo of the French settlement to see if we would run into some Indians to get information, and having found none, we stopped on the bank of said arroyo, having [**folio 8v**] marched this day, going and coming, fourteen leagues.

Thursday, April 27, we returned to the main company, having marched up the arroyo of the Frenchmen in search of some Indians to get some information; making some turns, we reached the camp; we traveled this day twenty leagues.

Friday, April 28, I left with eight soldiers up the Río de Guadalupe, making some smoke signals to see if we would run into some Indians who could give

105. Once more, the direction has been translated incorrectly. Bolton ([1908] 1916, 409) states that "the company set out east by northeast," but "rumbo de el leste quarta a el nordeste" (90-B 7v25–8r1) corresponds to 'east by north' (78.75°).

106. This is most likely a scribal error in 90-B. Manuscripts 90-A 419v1 and 90-C 127v7–8 show "paramos orillas de unos charquitos de agua," whereas 90-C 8r11–12 states "passa- / mos a orillas de vnos charquitos de agua." Because Manuscript 90-A is older than 90-B, it has been decided that "we stopped on the margin of some small pools of water" is correct.

us information; and having traveled six leagues, we returned to the main body, having marched on this day twelve leagues, going and coming.

Saturday, April 29, the full company set out in an easterly direction for about three leagues, and then we continued toward the northeast about another three leagues through flat land, and arriving at some pools of rainwater, we named it San Pedro Mártir. We marched this day six leagues.

Sunday, April 30 after mass, two soldiers arrived from the presidios of La Vizcaya, and they informed us that their companions were coming behind them to catch up with me by order of the Most Excellent Señor Conde de Galve, viceroy and captain general of New Spain, to join this expedition. I sent them to meet up with the pack animals and supplies,[107] and I left the main company at this stopping place to wait for them.[108] [**folio 9r**] I left with sixteen soldiers to clear some foot trails and to look for some Indians who might guide us and give us information about whether there were any Frenchmen in these places. I stopped this night by some pools of rainwater, having marched nine leagues.

Monday, May 1, I continued my journey passing some arroyos and uninhabited *rancherías* without finding any Indians. We slept on a small hill, having traveled twelve leagues.

Tuesday, May 2, I continued my journey, and I came to a meadow near the Río de San Marcos, where we slept, having traveled this day and taken some detours, having traveled this day fourteen leagues.

Wednesday, May 3, having put a cross on a tree, I reached the Río de San Marcos, and having crossed it, I continued my journey, and about five leagues from the river, at the edge of a small wood, we sighted an Indian woman and a boy; and calling them with a handkerchief, they did not want to come out, but instead they went into the thicket. We stopped this night on a hill, flat to one view,[109] leaving them in their *ranchería* a handkerchief, biscuit, tobacco, pocket knives, and knives. We traveled this day seven leagues.

Thursday, May 4, an Indian came to see us, and having spoken to him by signs, he told us that he was of the Tejas, and that this day we would arrive at

107. Bolton renders the Spanish "los embie a topar con bestias y vasti- / mento" (90-B 8v25–26) as "I sent to meet them with clothing and supplies" ([1908] 1916, 410). It appears that he misread "vestidos" 'clothing' for "vestias" 'beasts' or 'pack animals.'

108. De León sends the two soldiers into camp to get food and supplies at the location where the pack animals are kept. He orders the main company to wait for the other soldiers who are on their way from La Vizcaya, while he sets out with a small party to look for Indian guides.

109. Bolton gives the translation "level as a villa" ([1908] 1916, 411), misreading "vista" (90-B 9r21) as "villa."

a *ranchería*, [**folio 9v**] and that he would guide us with his wife and a young brother-in-law of his, who lived there. I gave him a horse on which to load his belongings, and at a distance of three leagues, we decided to send him on; and as we were returning to the stopping place where we had slept, he told us[110] to wait for him there that he would go to call the governor of the Tejas, among whom were some Frenchmen. We traveled this day six leagues.

Friday, May 5 in the morning, I dispatched Captain Francisco de Benavides with three soldiers to the main body to [have them] come marching. And around five in the afternoon, the Indian I had dispatched to the captain of the Tejas returned, [and said] that because the horse had run away, he was coming to notify me.

Saturday, May 6, I sent four soldiers to follow his trail to ascertain whether he had met with any other Indians, and having found another Indian, they brought him to the camp, to whom we offered clothing so that he would go to the Tejas to notify the governor to come to see us. Then, the first Indian,[111] envious of the offer, told me that I should give him another horse, that he would go to call the governor of the Tejas, and that he would leave his wife and a young brother-in-law of his to guide us until we met up with each other. So, I sent him on this day.

Sunday, May 7, and Monday May 8, we [**folio 10r**] halted where the Indian told us to wait for him, and also to see if we could see any smoke in order to set out and meet up with the main body, as this was the sign we had given them.

Tuesday, May 9, having sighted smoke, I set out with four soldiers to find the main company, and having crossed the Río de San Marcos, about noon, I encountered two Indians, and at a short distance, Captain Francisco Benavides with three soldiers and one Indian who spoke the Mexican language,[112] from whom I learned that a young Frenchman was at a *ranchería* about two days' march to the west and another one in another *ranchería* to the east. I dispatched said Captain Benavides with two soldiers to where I had left my men, [to tell them] that they should wait for me, and I went on to the main body, which I found by an arroyo, where they had just halted. And giving them the orders to continue marching for another day and to wait for me where the other men were, and having taken three horses, eight soldiers, and

110. Bolton states, "We told him" ([1908] 1916, 411).
111. Bolton omits "first," leading to confusion as to which of the two Indians is jealous or greedy ([1908] 1916, 411).
112. He spoke Nahuatl

supplies, and guided by the Indian who spoke the Mexican language, we traveled twelve leagues on this day.

Wednesday, May 10, continuing to the west about nine leagues, we followed the course through a wood of oaks and grapevines for another five leagues or so, and when we came out of the wood, we encountered some Indians and a young Frenchman named Pedro Talon.[113] And after he informed us there was no other in that area, we returned to sleep near the stopping place [**folio 10v**] of the night before, having traveled that day twenty-seven leagues, going and coming.

Thursday, May 11, we continued our journey in a northeasterly direction about twelve leagues as far as a tall hill that has a motte of very tall trees, where we found some Indians camped, who gave us news of another Frenchman, who was near there in a *ranchería*. I sent an Indian to call him, and another Indian later informed us that some other Frenchmen had arrived at the mouth of the Bahía del Espíritu Santo. And at the same time I dispatched two soldiers to the main company for four [men] to come with supplies and a change of horses so that, if the Frenchman did not come, to go search for him. This afternoon we crossed the Río de San Marcos because it had rained much, and we did not want it to swell and some of us get stuck on one side and others on the other side. We marched this day sixteen leagues.

Friday, May 12 in the morning, the Frenchman arrived with three Indians and said his name was Pedro Muñi,[114] and at the same time the soldiers I had sent for from the main body [arrived]. So we continued our journey until we reached it in a northeasterly direction; we traveled six leagues.

Saturday, May 13, the full company set out from the Paraje de San José on an easterly course about three [**folio 11r**] leagues and another three to the northeast, through some ravines and arroyos with little water; and stopping on the bank of an arroyo, we gave it the name of San Francisco de Asís. We marched six leagues.

Sunday, May 14, the company set out, crossing some ravines, in a northeasterly direction in search of the Río Colorado, and stopping on its bank we gave it the name of Río del Espíritu Santo, having marched six leagues.

Monday, May 15, the company set out downriver and at a distance of half a league, the river was crossed; and traversing a very dense thicket in a northeasterly direction, with some turns to the north, we stopped at an arroyo which we named San Juan. We traveled this day five leagues.

113. Pierre Talon. See note 42, sec. 1.
114. Pierre Meunier. See note 43, sec. 1.

Tuesday, May 16, the company set out in a northeasterly direction for about two leagues, crossing two arroyos on the same course, and the main body stopped by some pools, having marched four leagues, and we gave it the name of Beato Salvador de Horta.

Wednesday, May 17, the company set out in a northeast by northerly direction, and we stopped at an arroyo which we named San Diego de Alcalá. We traveled this day six leagues. [**folio 11v**]

Thursday, May 18, the company set out in a northeast by easterly direction, crossing several arroyos. At one of them, we encountered the Indian whom we had sent, with the governor of the Tejas, accompanied by fourteen of their principal Indians, to whom I distributed clothing and other valuables, from the ones I brought; said governor and his people showing much joy at having seen us, and that all his people were expecting us with much happiness. We turned to a very pleasant valley, where the company halted at an arroyo, and we named it Valle de Santa Elvira, having marched this day eight leagues.

Friday, May 19, we marched in a north by easterly[115] direction, and at a short distance we entered another very large and pleasant valley which we named [Valle] de Galve, and along its edge flows a large river which we named La Santísima Trinidad.[116] And although we prepared to cross, we spent most of the day taking the supplies across; and having crossed the river, we found another very pleasant valley which we named [Valle] de la Monclova, having traveled this day one league and a half.

Saturday, May 20, we marched in a northeast by easterly direction through some live-oak groves [**folio 12r**] and arroyos a distance of four leagues, and upon leaving the wood, we found a large valley which was named San Sebastián; and at one side of said valley, we found four dwellings of Indians, who had corn and beans planted, their houses very neat, and high beds on which to sleep. We gave them gifts and continued in a northeasterly direction through several groves of live oak and arroyos until some pools of rainwater, to which we gave the name of San Bernardino; having marched seven leagues.

Sunday, May 21 after mass we set out in a northeast by easterly direction through some groves of live oak and pine, crossing four arroyos without water. And having arrived at one arroyo with water, the company stopped in a clearing, to which we gave the name of San Carlos; having marched six leagues.

---

115. Bolton states the direction as "north by northeast" ([1908] 1916, 414).

116. Bolton's rendition conflates the Valle de Galve with the Río de la Santísima Trinidad: "we entered another very large and pleasant valley to which we gave the name of La Santísima Trinidad" ([1908] 1916, 414). His footnote mentions discrepancies between the manuscripts.

Monday, May 22, we set out in a northeast by easterly direction through some groves of live oak, traversing five dry arroyos and several small hills, where there are some veins of black and red stone, until we arrived at a valley settled with many houses of Tejas Indians, and around them many planted fields of corn, beans, squash, and watermelons;[117] and we gave it the name of San Francisco Xavier; [**folio 12v**] and making a turn to the north, along a hill with live oak about a quarter of a league, we came upon another valley with Tejas Indians and their houses. And the governor telling us that his house was very near, we stopped the company on the bank of an arroyo, and to this settlement we gave the name of San Francisco de los Tejas; having marched this day five leagues. And this evening, I went with the governor of said Tejas to leave him at his house, where his mother, his wife, and a daughter of his, and many people who were waiting for him came out to receive me, bringing out a bench for me to sit on and giving me corn tamales and *atole*[118] as an afternoon meal, with much cleanliness.

Tuesday, May 23, I set out with the religious missionary fathers a distance of about half a league, which is [the distance] from our camp to the house of the governor, in procession with officials and soldiers, who were followed by a large quantity of Indians with said Indian governor, and arriving at his house, the missionaries sang *Te Deum Laudamus*.[119] And having stayed at his house for a while, seated on some benches which said governor had ordered to bring outside, they brought some pots and bowls with cooked beans [**folio 13r**], corn *atole* and pinole,[120] which was eaten as an afternoon meal by said padres and soldiers, and we returned to the company's camp.

Wednesday, May 24, a chapel was set up in which to celebrate the feast of Corpus Christi; on this day, gifts had been given to the Indians such as clothing and other goods. And this day, I notified the governor to summon all his people to come to the feast of Corpus Christi.

Thursday, May 25, the feast of the Most Holy Sacrament was celebrated with all solemnity and procession; all the officers and soldiers, and the Indian governor, and many of his people accompanied the procession and attended the chanted mass. And after the mass finished, the ceremony of raising the

117. See note 44, sec. 1.
118. *Atole* is a hot drink made from cornmeal dough.
119. A Christian hymn of praise, sung in Latin. It is used during the liturgy to give thanks for special blessings.
120. Pinole is made from parched ground corn to which roasted herbs and water may be added.

standard was performed in the name of His Majesty (may God keep him). And I, said General Alonso de León, as the superior officer of all the companies which, by order of the Most Excellent Señor Conde de Galve, viceroy of this New Spain, had come on this journey, in the name of His Majesty, accepted said obedience which they give to His Majesty. And in his royal name, I promised to favor and help them, and I presented a staff with a cross to the governor, giving him the title of governor of all his villages, for him to rule and govern, and I explained to him, through an interpreter, [**folio 13v**] what he ought to observe and follow, and the respect and obedience that he and all his people ought to have for the priests, and that he should make all his families attend the religious teachings, so that they might be instructed in the matters of our holy Catholic faith, so that they might later be baptized and become Christians. He accepted said staff with much pleasure, promising to do all he had been told, and a royal salvo was fired three times. Likewise, the reverend *padre comisario* Fray Damián Massanet, who is in charge of these conversions in this mission, was given possession so that he might instruct them in the mysteries of our holy Catholic faith. And said governor and his people, having asked us to leave religious with them to teach them the Christian doctrine, in faith of their friendship, we asked said governor to give us three Indians from among the principal ones of this province, among them a brother, a nephew, and another cousin of said governor, who promised, with much pleasure, to come with us to meet the Most Excellent Señor Conde de Galve, viceroy and captain general of New Spain. This day the sun was observed, and we found ourselves at 34°7'.

Friday, May 26, I set out with the missionary padres and a few soldiers and officers with [**folio 14r**] said Indian governor in a northeasterly direction to see the most suitable place to put the mission. And we saw three small valleys where they told us two Frenchmen had died, where they had wanted to settle, and there we saw their graves and put a cross on a tree. And arriving at a river, to which we found no ford, but a tree which the Indians have placed across and a rope onto which they hold, we named this river San Miguel Arcángel, and from there we returned to the main company, having marched six leagues.

Saturday, May 27; Sunday, 28; Monday, 29; Tuesday, 30; and Wednesday, 31, we worked on building the church and the dwelling of the apostolic fathers in the middle of the principal settlement of the Tejas.

Thursday, June 1, I gave possession of said mission, with the reverend *padre comisario* Fray Damián Massanet having chanted mass in said church, with the Indian governor and his people attending the mass and the blessing of the church. This day, in the afternoon, I sent the main company in pursuit of the return trip to the Province of Coahuila along the same road we had come here. They stopped this night at the *real* de San Carlos, having marched five leagues. [**folio 14v**]

Friday, June 2, I set out with the reverend *padre comisario* Fray Damián Massanet and six soldiers from the village of San Francisco de los Tejas, following the main body. In our company came a brother of the governor, a nephew, and a cousin of his with another Indian of said village, and arriving at the main body, we continued to the *real* de San Bernardino, a little over half a league, the company marching this day six and a half leagues.

Saturday, June 3, we continued our march, traversing the valley of San Sebastián and that of La Monclova. We arrived at the Río de la Santísima Trinidad and because it was too swollen, we were unable to cross it. We stopped by the river, having marched this day six leagues and a half.

Sunday, June 4; Monday, 5; Tuesday, 6; Wednesday, 7; Thursday, 8; Friday, 9; Saturday, 10. This day a raft was made, and we began to cross the river.

Sunday, June 11, we finished crossing the river. At about two in the afternoon, the main body set out through the Valle de Galve as far as that of Santa Elvira, where they stopped by some pools of rainwater, having marched three leagues.

Monday, June 12, the company set out from said [**folio 15r**] quarters and passing through that of San Diego de Alcalá about two leagues, the company stopped by some rainwater pools, having marched nine leagues.

Tuesday, June 13, the company set out from said stopping place and passing by that of El Beato Salvador de Horta, we arrived at the Arroyo de San Juan, having traveled this day eight leagues.

Wednesday, June 14, the company set out from said stopping place and crossing the Río del Espíritu Santo, we arrived at a stretch of small hills, where it forms an arroyo with water, where the company halted, having traveled this day eight leagues.

Thursday, June 15, the company set out from said stopping place and passing through the *real* de San Francisco de Asís, we arrived at some arroyos with water, from where I had dispatched the Indian to call the governor of the Tejas, having traveled this day seven leagues.

Friday, June 16, the company set out from said stopping place and passing through the *real* de San Joseph, we arrived at an arroyo with water, where the company stopped; having traveled this day six leagues.

Saturday, June 17, the company set out from [**folio 15v**] said stopping place, and crossing the Río de San Marcos, we arrived at an arroyo with water, where the company stopped, having traveled this day five leagues, and we gave it the name of Jesús, María y Joseph de Buena Vista.

Sunday, June 18, the main body set out to continue its journey, and I, General Alonso de León, with sixteen soldiers, left in a northeasterly direction in search of two French boys and one French girl because some Indians gave me information that they were camped at said place. [We traveled] across some plains about four leagues until we reached a small wood, which we traversed, and then we continued in an easterly direction for about three leagues over another plain, where we came upon a small wood with a *ranchería* of Indians. From there we continued through other very large plains, with a great number of buffalo, to the bank of a little river which, at the beginning, forms at a cluster of trees; there we halted because it was already very dark, having marched this day seventeen leagues.

Monday, June 19, we continued our journey along the bank of said little river, [**folio 16r**] which has trees on both sides, and having crossed it and marched about two leagues, we came upon a *ranchería* of Indians to whom I gave gifts and who remained very much our friends. From there we continued our journey in a southerly direction over some plains, and after about one league, we came upon another *ranchería* of Indians, to whom we also gave gifts. From there we continued over said plains in the same direction about four leagues until we entered a small wood, which we crossed, and we continued our journey in a westerly direction. And crossing a large arroyo in a wood, we came upon a very large nation of Indians, to whom I gave gifts and who remained very much our friends, and they gave us Indians who guided us to another *ranchería*. From there we set out across some plains, and already very late at night, we stopped on the bank of an arroyo, having marched this day fifteen leagues.

Tuesday, June 20, we continued our journey in an easterly direction where we came upon a *ranchería* of Indians, to whom I gave gifts, and they gave us four Indians [**folio 16v**] to guide us to where the French children were. From there we went out over some plains that were covered with buffalo, in the same direction, to cross the Arroyo de los Franceses, and having crossed it, we continued to their old settlement, and from there we proceeded in a southerly direction until we reached the arroyo which the Indians call de las Canoas, and having crossed it, we came upon another small arroyo where we stopped, having traveled this day fourteen leagues.

Wednesday, June 21, we set out in a southeasterly direction and after about one league we came across two Indians who were coming on horseback from the nation that had the French children; they took us to their *ranchería*, which was at a tip of an inlet, where Roberto[121] and Madalena Talon[122] were. I discussed their ransom, and having given gifts to them [the Indians] and the ransom which they asked for, they came to us with a thousand shameless demands, asking for all the horses and even for the clothes we were wearing on our backs, while they went to bring the other French boy,[123] who was two leagues from there within the same nation. And having brought him, they continued [**folio 17r**] even more with their shamelessness, bringing bows and arrows, and a large number of Indians coming with shields asking for exorbitant things, and that if we did not give them to them, they would shoot us with arrows and kill us all. And saying this and shooting arrows was all at once, so we fell upon them, and having killed four of them and wounded others, they retreated, having wounded two of our horses. We started leaving in a very orderly manner and went to camp about four leagues from there, where we had slept the night before, having traveled this day twelve leagues.

Thursday, June 22, we set out at dawn in the same northerly direction across some very large plains along the bank of the Río de Guadalupe, and around ten o'clock at night we stopped near a small wood, having marched this day fourteen leagues.

Friday, June 23, we set out in a northerly direction for about two leagues, where we came across the trail of the main body which had passed, and after about three leagues we caught up with them at the ford of the Río de Guadalupe, where we stopped, having traveled five leagues. [**folio 17v**]

Saturday, June 24, Day of San Juan, the full company set out from said stopping place, and, crossing the Río de Guadalupe, we continued our journey to an arroyo which is before the Real de Agua Salada, where we halted, having marched this day seven leagues.

Sunday, June 25, the company set out from said stopping place and passing by the Real de la Salada, we arrived at the Arroyo del León, where the company stopped, having marched this day seven leagues.

Monday, June 26, the company set out from said stopping place, and we reached the Río de Medina, where the company stopped, having marched this day five leagues.

Tuesday, June 27, the company set out from said stopping place, and we arrived at an arroyo with water, where the company stopped, having marched this day eight leagues.

121. Robert Talon. See note 48, sec. 1.
122. Marie-Madeleine Talon. See note 46, sec. 1.
123. Lucien Talon. See note 47, sec. 1.

Wednesday, June 28, the company set out from said stopping place, and because the guide had lost his way, we halted at an arroyo with water above the ford of the Arroyo de los Róbalos, having marched this day five leagues.

Thursday, June 29, the company set out from said stopping place and passing by the Real del Aire, we arrived at some pools of water, where the company halted, having marched five leagues.

Friday, June 30, the company set out from said stopping place, and crossing the Río Hondo, we arrived at Las Cruces, about three leagues above the ford of the [**folio 18r**] Río Hondo, having marched this day eight leagues.

Saturday, July 1, the company set out from said stopping place and we arrived at the Río Zarco, having marched this day five leagues.

Sunday, July 2, the company set out from said stopping place, and crossing the Río de las Nueces, we arrived at some pools of water, where the company halted, having marched this day eight leagues.

Monday, July 3, the company set out from said stopping place, and crossing the Arroyo de Ramos, we arrived at some pools of water, where the company stopped, having marched this day ten leagues.

Tuesday, July 4, the company set out from said stopping place and we arrived at the Río Grande, and because it was very swollen, it could not be crossed, where the company stopped, having marched this day eight leagues.

Wednesday, July 5; Thursday, 6; Friday, 7; Saturday, 8; Sunday, 9, Monday, 10; and Tuesday, 11, we stayed in place on the bank of the Río Grande because we could not cross it, as it was still very swollen; from there I dispatched a courier to His Excellency, sending along a Frenchman named Pedro Muñi, the *autos*, map, and this course log, giving His Excellency an account of the entire journey. Alonso de León.

3.7 English Translation of Manuscript 90-D[124]

[**folio 1r**] Journey made by Governor Alonso de León by order of the Most Excellent Señor Conde de Galve, viceroy of this New Spain, in the company of

---

124. According to McLain, only four of the ninety-eight entries in manuscript 90-D contain historical content that is expressed in exactly the same words as in 90-B, with minor "variation in diction and orthography" (2005, 90). These entries correspond to April 5 (90-B 6r2–4 and 90-D 2r3–5), April 20 (90-B 7v14–17 and 90-D 3v14–16), June 23 (90-B 17r19–24 and 90-D 11r29–11v3), and June 25 (90-B 17v6–9 and 90-D 11v9–12). Consequently, the remaining ninety-four entries are different: a few have minor variation (vocabulary, syntax, spelling, etc.), and a great many of them have substantive changes (historical data, names of geographical features and participants). For a detailed list of the different entries see McLain (2005). A complete comparative analysis of every single linguistic deviation within those ninety-four entries would prove too exhaustive. Therefore, only the most significant differences between 90-B and 90-D will be addressed in these notes.

Captain Don Gregorio de Salinas Varona,[125] from the Province of Coahuila to the Bahía del Espíritu Santo and the Province of the Tejas on March 26, 1690.

Sunday, on said [March] 26, the pack animals and the baggage left the town of Santiago de la Monclova to stop one league outside the Indian village, from said town it was one league and a half in a northerly direction.

Monday, March 27, the full royal company set out, and we went to halt below the hills on the bank of the Río de Coahuila, the course was northeast by east,[126] 3 leagues.

Tuesday, March 28, we left said stopping place to the east-northeast,[127] downriver, and leaving the river, we entered through the Puerto de Baluartes, and from said pass, we took a turn of one league to stop on the bank of the river, where the company halted, having marched this day 8 leagues.

Wednesday, March 29, the company set out downriver, in an east by northerly[128] direction, and passing by the cottonwood a little more than one mile, the company stopped on the bank of the river, through flat terrain with some shrub oak *chaparros*[129] and *lechuguilla*[130] agaves, having marched this day 5 [leagues].

Thursday, March 30, the company set out in an east by northerly[131] direction downriver to the junction of the Río de las Sabinas, and it stopped on its bank, having marched this day through flat land with [**folio 1v**] some mesquite groves and *lechuguilla* agaves,[132] where we were joined by the company from the Reino de León and the missionary padres. This day we traveled 4 leagues.[133]

Friday, March 31, the company set out downriver, and traversing a hill that is in front in an easterly direction, we arrived at the Río de las Sabinas; having traveled about two leagues, we crossed the river, where the company stopped.

Saturday, April 1, we marched in a northeasterly direction a distance of six leagues, traversing some plains without water, quite difficult terrain because

125. Gregorio de Salinas Varona's name does not appear in the header of Manuscript 90-B. See note 62, sec. 1.

126. See note 90 above.

127. In Manuscript 90-B the course appears as "rumbo de el nordeste" 'northeast'; in 90-D, however, it is "al lesnordeste" 'east-northeast.'

128. Brierley gives the direction as "east by northeast" (Chapa 1997, 155). However, the Spanish "leste quarta al nordeste" (90-D 1r20) corresponds to 'east by north.'

129. See note 93 above.

130. See note 94 above.

131. See note 95 above.

132. The mesquite groves and *lechuguilla* agaves are not mentioned in 90-B.

133. In manuscript 90-B the distance traveled is "quatro leguas y media," that is, 'four and a half leagues.'

of the many mesquite trees, although flat,[134] where we came across a pool of fresh water,[135] where the company stopped.

Sunday, April 2, we set out in a northeast by northerly direction, passing some small hills of shrub oak *chaparros* and flat land. We arrived at some pools of rainwater, where the company stopped, having marched 5 leagues on that day.

Monday, April 3, we set out in a northerly direction through flat land with very few shrub oak as far as the bank of an arroyo, where we found the Indians of the Frenchman,[136] to whom we gave tobacco and clothing, where the company stopped, having marched 4 [leagues].

Tuesday, April 4, we set out in a northerly direction in search of the Río Grande through flat land with some mesquite trees, and having come upon the crossing, the company stopped on the bank of the river, where [**folio 2r**] we found some buffalo, having marched this day 5 leagues.

Wednesday, April 5, we stayed in place so that everyone might confess and comply with the church before crossing the river.

Thursday, April 6, we crossed the river and marched in a north by easterly[137] direction and stopped on the bank of a dry arroyo, having marched this day eight leagues. The company slept without water, having crossed some hills and scrub mesquite *chaparros*, 8 [leagues].[138]

Friday, April 7, the company set out in a northeasterly direction through flat land, where the company stopped on the Arroyo de Ramos, where there is a large live oak and some scrub mesquite,[139] having marched this day 3 leagues.

Saturday, April 8, the company set out in a northeast by northerly direction through flat land, at times with many mesquite trees, where we arrived at an arroyo and because it had a bad ford, most of the day was spent preparing and crossing the pack animals, where the company halted, having marched three leagues, and it was given the name of Caramanchel.

Sunday, April 9,[140] the company set out in a northeast by northerly direction across some plains, and passing two ravines with trees, we entered a

134. Manuscript 90-B does not make mention of the difficult terrain, the trees, or the flat land.

135. In manuscript 90-D the pools are "agua dulce" 'sweet water'; in 90-B they are "agua llovediza" 'rainwater.'

136. Refers to Jean Henri.

137. Brierley gives the direction as "north by northeast" instead of "north by east" (Chapa 1997, 156).

138. There is no reference to hills and mesquite *chaparros* in 90-B.

139. The reference to live oak and scrub mesquite is missing in 90-B.

140. Reference to Sunday mass is missing in 90-D.

mesquite grove and at about half a league, [**folio 2v**] we came upon the Río de las Nueces, where there are many flint stones[141] on the bank of the river. The company stopped at a large meadow which forms, having marched this day 5 [leagues].

Monday, April 10, we forded the river and marched in an easterly direction through a ravine which has many very dense thickets of nut and mesquite trees until we arrived at a hill after about 2 leagues, and then we continued in a northerly direction about 2 more leagues, and then we made another turn to the east through flat land full of mesquite trees, where we came upon the Río Zarco, and having crossed it, the company stopped on the other side, having marched this day 7 [leagues].[142]

Tuesday, April 11, the company set out in a northerly direction over some plains, in parts mesquite trees, small hills and ravines, where we came upon the Río Hondo, where the company halted, having marched 6 leagues.

Wednesday, April 12, the company was detained at said stopping place to search for two men who were lost on the march the day before.[143]

Thursday, April 13, we had news that six leagues from the company's camp there was a gathering of Indians to where a Frenchman had come. I set out this day in the afternoon with 20 men, including Captain Don Gregorio de Salinas Varona,[144] in a westerly direction, along the bank of the river on the other side for about 5 leagues, where I stopped for the night.

Friday, April 14, at sunrise I continued my journey in the same direction about half a league, and then I continued in a northerly direction across a plain which has many oak trees, to the bank of a river, [**folio 3r**] where we came upon the *ranchería* at about half a league, and where many Indian men, women, and children came out to receive us; we gave them gifts of tobacco, and they gave us information that the two Frenchmen were on the other side of the Río de Guadalupe; and one Indian had a French musket. From there we returned straight to the main body, many Indians accompanying us to the camp, where we gave them gifts of clothing, flour and tobacco. This day the two soldiers arrived at camp, us having marched this day 7 leagues.[145]

141. There is no reference to flint stones in 90-B.

142. The wording and some of the details are different in 90-B. There is no mention of nut trees.

143. Manuscript 90-B mentions that the two men were lost in a rainstorm. Manuscript 90-D does not mention the storm.

144. Manuscripts 90-A, 90-B, and 90-C do not mention any members of the detachment by name. Salinas Varona's name appears only in 90-D.

145. Although most of the general information is essentially the same in 90-B and 90-D, there are discrepancies in the wording and some details of this day's entry.

Saturday, April 15, the full company set out in an easterly direction, downriver, through some ravines with a few mesquite trees, where we came upon the ford of the river, where the company stopped to prepare for the river crossing, having marched this day 6 [leagues].[146]

Sunday, April 16, we crossed to the other side of the Río Hondo, continuing in an east by northerly[147] direction over flat land, where we came upon an arroyo, and it was necessary to prepare the crossing and clear [the brush] around it. From there we continued our journey until some pools of rainwater, where the company stopped, having marched this day 8 [leagues].[148]

Monday, April 17, the company set out in a northeasterly direction, and because of some woods that we encountered, it was necessary to make some detours, at times north by east[149] and east, where we came upon the Arroyo de los Róbalos,[150] where the company stopped, having marched this day 5 leagues.

[**folio 3v**] Tuesday, April 18, the soldiers set out in different directions to search for 126[151] horses that stampeded until they reappeared. This day in the afternoon, the full company set out and at a short distance, the guide lost his way and we were forced to continue in a northerly direction in search of the Río de Medina, and because it was already late, the company stopped by a small hill, which was named Real del Rosario,[152] having marched 4 leagues through flat land, in parts oak and mesquite trees.[153]

Wednesday, April 19, the company set out in a northerly direction in search of said Río de Medina, through woods of oaks, live oaks, and mesquite groves until we arrived at the gorge of the river, where the company stopped at the upper part of the river, having marched 7 leagues this day.

---

146. Manuscript 90-B provides no information on ravines, trees, or preparations for the river crossing.

147. Brierley translates the direction as "east by northeast" (Chapa 1997, 158) instead of "east by north."

148. In manuscript 90-D, the references to Sunday mass, the name of the arroyo (Arroyo de Chapa), and the bridge are missing. It is surprising that de León does not mention the arroyo named after Juan Bautista Chapa, his loyal secretary.

149. This is another instance of divergent directions: in 90-B it appears as "norte nordeste" 'north-northeast'; in 90-D as "norte quarta al nordeste" 'north by east.' Brierley translates it erroneously as "north by northeast" (Chapa 1997, 158).

150. See note 99 above.

151. See note 100 above.

152. McLain erroneously states the name as "Real del Traxio" (2005, 65).

153. Most of the information is identical in 90-B and 90-D; however, 90-B does not mention the flat land and the oak and mesquite trees, and 90-D does not mention that there was little water available.

Thursday, April 20, we set out in an easterly direction and at a distance of 2 leagues we came upon the ford of the river, where the company stopped because it was necessary to prepare the crossing.

Friday, April 21, we crossed the river, and we marched in an easterly direction over flat land with some oak trees, live oaks, mesquite groves, willows,[154] where we came upon the Arroyo del León, where the company stopped, having marched this day 5 leagues.

Saturday, April 22, the company moved out in an easterly and at times northeasterly direction through flat land with live oaks and oaks, until we came upon an arroyo of salty water,[155] where the company stopped, having marched 6 [leagues].

Sunday, April 23,[156] the company set out in an east by northerly[157] direction over flat land and hills with clumps of live oaks and oaks, where we arrived close to the Río de Guadalupe, where the company stopped by an arroyo, having marched 5 [leagues].

[**folio 4r**] Monday, April 24, the company set out downriver until reaching the ford which could be sounded, and most of the day was spent crossing the river, where the company stopped on the other side, having marched this day 2 leagues.

Tuesday, April 25, I set out with Captain Don Gregorio de Salinas Varona[158] and 20 soldiers on the way to the southeast[159] to reconnoiter the Bahía del Espíritu Santo. We traveled about 14 leagues this day through flat and fertile land, in parts some live oaks and oaks, and having arrived at a pool of rainwater, we stopped.

Wednesday, April 26, we continued our journey to the old settlement of the French, and at about 5 leagues we found it, said course toward the southeast,[160] where we stopped to burn the fort, and after it was burned, we went

154. No mention of the different tree species is made in 90-B.

155. In manuscript 90-B the expression is given as "agua salobre" 'brackish water,' but in 90-D it is "agua salada" 'salty water.'

156. The reference to Sunday mass that appears in 90-B is missing in 90-D.

157. Brierley renders the direction as "east by northeast" instead of "east by north" (Chapa 1997, 159).

158. Salinas Varona's name is not mentioned in 90-B.

159. Manuscript 90-D 4r6–7 reads "camino del hues- / te," but both 90-E and 90-F omit the direction. Strangely, "hueste" is a variant of "oeste," that is, 'west.' However, it does not make sense for the detachment to travel west. I suspect that this is a transcription error, where the scribe misread the original "sueste" as "hueste." Therefore, it is translated here as "southeast."

160. See note 159 above.

on to reconnoiter the bay for about 2 leagues, where we recognized there were two buoys, one at the mouth of the Río de San Marcos and the other on one side looking at the Río de Guadalupe, signaling a channel.[161] The sun was not observed because it was cloudy. From there we turned around upriver along the [Río] de los Franceses to see if we could find some Indians in their old *rancherías*, and we could not come across any, and because it was already late, we stopped on the bank of the river, having marched this day, going and coming, 14 leagues.[162]

Thursday, April 27, we returned to the main company, having marched this day 20 leagues upriver[163] to see if we could come across any Indians, and we found none.

[**folio 4v**] Friday, April 28, I set out with 8 soldiers up the Río de Guadalupe, making smoke signals to see if I would run into some Indians, for about 6 leagues, and because there was no response, I returned to the main body, having marched this day, going and coming, 12 [leagues].

Saturday, April 29, the full company set out in an easterly direction for about 3 leagues, and then we continued to the northeast about another [3] leagues through flat land, [with] some ravines and clumps of live oaks and oaks, and having arrived at some pools of rainwater, the company stopped at the foot of a hill, which was given the name of San Pedro Mártir, 6 [leagues].

Sunday, April 30 after mass, two soldiers having arrived from the presidios of El Parral,[164] who were following their companions,[165] I set out with 16 soldiers to clear some stretches of thickets and to see if I came across some Indians who could guide us to the Province of the Tejas; and arriving at some old *rancherías*, I stopped this night, having marched this day 9 leagues.[166]

Monday, May 1, I continued my journey and arrived at a tall hill, where I stopped because it was already late; we traveled 12 leagues on this day.

---

161. In manuscript 90-B, the Río de Guadalupe is not mentioned.

162. Manuscript 90-B mentions the eight French cannons that were buried the year before, "adonde esta la artillería enterrada' (90-B 8r16), but 90-D does not.

163. In 90-B the creek of the Frenchmen is mentioned.

164. In manuscript 90-B the soldiers arrived from the presidios of "La Vizcaya" (90-B 8v21); in 90-D they come from "El Parral' (90-D 5r10).

165. The phrase "que venian si- / guiendo sus compañeros" (90-D 4v 12–13) is erroneously rendered as "who were their companions" in Chapa (1997, 160), instead of "who were following their companions."

166. The entry in 90-B is much richer in information; it provides details on the soldiers arriving from the presidio and makes reference to the search for the Frenchmen, both of which are missing in 90-D.

Tuesday, May 2, I continued my journey and arrived at a meadow on the bank of the Río de San Marcos, which, because the river was deep, I was unable to cross to the other side; we traveled this day 14 leagues.

Wednesday, May 3, I continued my journey upriver as far as the ford, which I found to be very good, where I crossed it and continued my journey. And about 5 leagues beyond the river on the side of a wood, we saw two Indians, and calling them, they refused to come, instead they went into the woods, where I stopped this night to see if they might return, having marched this day 7 leagues.[167]

[**folio 5r**] Thursday, May 4, in the morning, the Indian came to see us, and having spoken to him by signs, he told us that he was of the Tejas, and that this day we would arrive at a *ranchería*, and continuing to guide us for about 3 leagues, he told us that it was very far, and that I should give him a horse, and that he would go call the captain of the Tejas. So I dispatched him and returned to the stopping place of the night before because he had told me to wait for him there; having marched this day 6 leagues, going and coming. This day, the 20 soldiers from the presidios of El Parral came to join the main company at the quarters of San Pedro Mártir.[168]

Friday, May 5, in the morning I dispatched 4 soldiers[169] to the main body to [tell them to] come marching. And at about 5 in the afternoon, the Indian I had dispatched to the captain of the Tejas returned, that because his horse had run away, he was not continuing, he was coming to notify me.

Saturday, May 6, I sent 4 men to follow the trail to see if he [the Indian] had met with any of the Indians,[170] and they ran into another Indian, whom they brought to me. And having offered to give him clothing, so he would go

167. The information provided in 90-B and 90-D is quite different. Manuscript 90-B is more specific. It mentions a cross being carved in a tree and the Indians they encountered as being a woman and a boy. These details as well as the fact that they left gifts for the Indians in a handkerchief are missing in 90-D.

168. Only 90-D mentions that twenty soldiers from El Parral arrived at the camp. This is not included in 90-B.

169. In 90-B Captain Francisco de Benavides is dispatched together with three soldiers to relay orders to the main company that was left behind. In 90-D no names are mentioned, only "four soldiers."

170. Brierley renders the sentence "enuie a 4 compañeros por el rras- / tro para que bieran si se auia juntado con algunos de los / jndios" (90-D 5r16–18) incorrectly as "I sent four members of the company out on the trail to see if anyone had met some of the Indians" (Chapa 1997, 161). From the manuscript it is clear that they followed the trail of the first Indian, whom they had dispatched with the horse, to see whether he had met other Indians, possibly because they did not believe that he had lost his horse.

to the Tejas to notify the governor that we were there, the first Indian, envious of the offer, told me that I should give him another horse, and that he would go to the Tejas, so I dispatched him at once. This day the 4 soldiers arrived at the main body.[171]

Sunday, May 7, the main company moved out from said quarters named San Pedro Mártir, following the route for about 3 leagues east by north[172] through dense woods of live oaks and oaks, where in parts it was necessary to [**folio 5v**] clear, with some narrow plains with meadows enclosed by live oaks and oaks and two dry arroyos. Then we continued in a westerly direction and sometimes to the north, encountering the same woods and scrub oak *chaparros* that needed to be cleared, and some plains, and 4 dry arroyos that carried very little water, where the company stopped on the bank of one of them, and it was given the name of La Aparición de San Miguel Arcángel, having marched on this day 9 [leagues].[173]

Monday, May 8, the main company moved out from said quarters in a northerly direction over some hills and ravines, passing 8 dry arroyos and some patches of live oaks and oaks, where the main company reached an arroyo that carries very little water, where we stopped in a clearing that forms a half moon and is in a northeasterly direction. It was named the quarters of San Gregorio Nazianzeno, having marched this day 9 leagues.[174]

Tuesday, May 9, the main body set out from said quarters named San Gregorio Nazianzeno in a northerly direction over hills and ravines and some patches of wood, live oaks, oaks, mulberry trees, and grapevines, where it was necessary to clear the way about 1 league; and having passed six dry arroyos and arrived at another arroyo, the company stopped at a hill which was given the name of Jesús, María y Joseph de Buena Vista, having marched this day 7 leagues.[175]

171. Manuscript 90-B states that the Indian left his wife and brother-in-law to guide de León's company.

172. In manuscript 90-D 5r27, "[??] quarta al nordeste" is missing a portion of the traveling direction. It could refer to "norte cuarta al nordeste" 'north by east' (11.25°), or to "leste quarta al nordeste" 'east by north' (78.75°). Since they travel in a northerly direction on the following day, it has been inferred that the logical choice would be 'north by east.' Brierley gives the direction as "[ ] by northeast" (Chapa 1997, 162) which I believe is incorrect.

173. The entries for May 7 and 8 in 90-D are very different from those in 90-B. According to 90-B, they remained in place waiting for the Indian and looking for smoke signals, the agreed-upon signal, to meet up with the main company. These 90-B entries record the steps of the small detachment of four soldiers, whereas 90-D registers the progress of the main company.

174. See note 173 above.

175. Manuscript 90-D has two entries for May 9. One is given from the vantage point of the main body, and the other from the smaller party that left in search of the French boy. Captain

Said day, May 9, in the evening,[176] I arrived at said main body, from where I set out with eight men, among them Captain Don Gregorio Salinas Varona, in search of a French boy[177] who was at a *ranchería* of Indians in a southwesterly direction, and having marched about 12 leagues, because it was night already, I stopped on the side of a [**folio 6r**] hill.

Wednesday, May 10, we set out before dawn, continuing the same course to the southwest about 9 leagues to a tall hill that forms before entering the wood. From there we continued in a westerly direction through a very dense wood of oaks, live oaks, many grapevines, and mulberry trees, and some clearings as we left [the woods], about 5 leagues, and at said exit from the woods, we came across the French boy called Pedro Talon,[178] who was marching with a *ranchería* of Indians. From there we turned around, following the same road, to near the same hill where I slept the night before, having marched this day 27 leagues, going and coming.[179]

Thursday, May 11, we proceeded to continue our journey before dawn in a northeasterly direction for about 12 leagues to a tall hill that forms a clump of very tall nut trees, where I came upon a *ranchería* of Indians who gave us news of another Frenchman who was near there with another Indian *ranchería*. I sent an Indian to look for him, and at the same time, I dispatched 2 soldiers to the main body to have 4 [men] come with supplies, so that, in case the Frenchman did not come, to go look for him. At this time, we went to cross the Río de San Marcos because it had rained much this afternoon, and for the river not to swell on us, having marched this day 16 leagues.[180]

On the next day, Friday morning, [May] 12, the Frenchman arrived with 3 Indians and the soldiers from the company, so we continued our journey

---

Gregorio de Salinas Varona is mentioned in 90-D. Both entries are vastly different from those in 90-B, which offers a longer and more detailed account, explaining the circumstances of the two young Frenchmen living among the Indians. Captain Francisco Benavides, but not Salinas Varona, is mentioned in 90-B.

176. Brierley mistranslates "Dicho dia 9 a la tarde" (90-D 5v15), which should be "Said day, the 9th, in the evening," as "On the same day at 9 in the evening" (Chapa 1997, 162).

177. The French boy is Pierre Talon.

178. See note 42, sec. 1.

179. The entries for May 10 are vastly different in 90-B and 90-D. Even though they both describe the capture of Pierre Talon, the details provided are not exactly the same. There is another entry for May 10 in 90-D following May 12. It is part of an insertion of three days (May 10, 11, and 12) that record the movement of the main company.

180. The content for this entry is quite similar in 90-B and 90-D; however, it is formulated very differently.

until we reached it [the main body], which I reached 6 leagues from the river in a northerly direction.[181]

*[**folio 6v**] Wednesday, [May] 10,[182] Captain Francisco Martínez continued with the main company in a northerly direction, across hills and ravines, to ford the Río de San Marcos, which they crossed, and they continued their journey in the same direction as far as a hill, where they had encountered the soldiers I had left, where they stopped, having traveled this day 8 leagues, and it was named San Elifonso.[183]

*Thursday, [May] 11, the quarters were moved to a better more advantageous stopping place about 3 miles in a northeasterly direction, where they stopped on a hill, to which they gave the name of San Joseph.

*Friday, [May] 12, the main company stopped to wait for us to arrive with the Frenchmen.

Saturday, May 13, the main company moved out from said quarters named San Joseph in an easterly direction about 3 leagues, and after about another 3 leagues to the northeast, across hills, ravines, and 3 arroyos that carry a little water, where the main company stopped on the bank of another brook, at the foot of a small wood that was named San Francisco de Asís, 6 [leagues].

Sunday, May 14, the main company moved out from the quarters named San Francisco de Asís over some hills and ravines in a northeasterly direction in search of the Río Colorado, with many woods on its banks, where the main company stopped and it was given the name of Río del Espíritu Santo, having marched this day 6 leagues.

Monday, May 15, the main company moved out from said quarters of the Río del Espíritu Santo in an easterly direction about 3 leagues through a very dense wood that was cleared in order for the pack animals to pass, and then in a [**folio 7r**] northeasterly direction about 1 league, through some small clearings and small woods, at stretches, and then in a northerly direction about another league, where the main company stopped by an arroyo we found, and which we named San Juan, 5 [leagues].

181. The information provided in 90-B and 90-D is almost identical. However, 90-D does not mention the name of the second Frenchman, Pierre Meunier, which appears as "Pedro Muñi" in 90-B.

182. These entries for May 10, 11, and 12 are marked with an asterisk because they are parallel entries to the three prior ones. Separate entries were made to provide the itinerary of the main company, led by Captain Francisco Martínez. De León separated from the company with a smaller detachment to search for the second Frenchman. These parallel entries do not appear in 90-B.

183. The name appears as San Ildefonso in 90-B.

Tuesday, May 16, the main company set out from said quarters named San Juan in a northeasterly direction about 2 leagues to a boggy arroyo, and then we followed another brook with a good crossing, where we continued in a northeast by northerly direction another 2 leagues, where we found some pools of water; the main body stopped, and we gave it the name of El Beato Salvador de Horta, having marched 4 [leagues].

Wednesday, May 17, the main company moved out from the quarters named El Beato Salvador de Horta in a northeast by northerly direction though flat land, where the main company stopped at an arroyo which was named San Diego de Alcalá, having marched this day 6 leagues.[184]

Thursday, May 18, the main body set out from the above-mentioned quarters in a northeast by easterly direction through flat land, although in parts it was necessary to prepare the crossing of some arroyos and clear some logs that hampered the crossing. This day we came upon the captain of the Tejas on the bank of a brook with 14 Indians who accompanied him, to whom I gave clothing and other goods. From there we continued the journey until we entered a very pleasant valley which we named Santa Elvira, where we came upon an arroyo and the main company stopped on its bank, and we named the quarters that of Santa Elvira, having marched this day 8 leagues.[185]

[**folio 7v**] Friday, May 19, the main company set out from said quarters of Santa Elvira in a north-northeasterly[186] direction, through a small wood, where we came upon another very large and pleasant valley, to which we gave the name of Galve. And at its exit, we came upon a large coppice of trees, where we came upon a large and deep river, which we named Río de la Santísima Trinidad. It was necessary to prepare for the fording, and we spent most of the day crossing the pack animals. And on the other side, we found another very pleasant valley, to which the name of Monclova was given, where the company stopped on the bank of the river, and the quarters were given the name of San Sebastián, having marched about a league and a half on this day.[187]

Saturday, May 20, the company set out from said Valle de la Monclova and the quarters of San Sebastián in a northeast by easterly direction through a wood of oaks, nut trees, and grapevines a distance of 4 leagues, and as we left

184. While the entries for May 15, 16, and 18 provide the same information, they are worded differently in 90-B and 90-D, with 90-D providing more details.

185. The wording is very different in 90-B and 90-D. For example, in 90-B the Caddo chief is referred to as "gouernador de los Texas" (90-B 11v4) and in 90-D as "capitan de los Tejas" (90-D 7r22).

186. Brierley gives this as "north by northeast" instead of "north-northeast" (Chapa 1997, 165).

187. The content of the entry for this day is very similar in 90-B and 90-D, but it is worded differently. The "quartel de San Sebastián" is not mentioned in 90-B.

the woods, we came upon another valley, which we named San Sebastián. And in a wood, which is in an easterly direction facing the road, we came upon 4 houses of Indians, to which we gave the name of San Bernardino. They have corn planted and much neatness in their houses; to these we gave them gifts, and from there we continued our journey in a northeasterly direction through another wood of oak trees. The trees [are] very light and tall, and 2 arroyos which carry very little water, and some clearings, where we came upon some pools of fresh water, where the company stopped on their shores, and we gave it the name the quarters of San Bernardino; having marched this day 7 [leagues].[188]

[**folio 8r**] Sunday, May 21, the company moved out from said quarters of San Bernardino in a northeast by easterly direction across a wood of oaks, live oaks, and some pines and vines with bunches of grapes on both sides of the road, where we crossed 4 deep arroyos with bad crossings and without water and some small hills with dead soil full of oak trees, all the wood is very sparse, and having arrived at an arroyo with water, the main body stopped in the same wood, where it forms a clearing, and it was named the quarters of San Carlos, having marched this day 6 [leagues].[189]

Monday, May 22, the company set out from said quarters of San Carlos in a northeast by easterly direction through the aforementioned wood of oaks and some pine trees, and, in parts, grapevines along the road, on both sides; and having passed five dry arroyos and two small hills, both of them with veins of metal, scrub oak *chaparros* and tall oak trees; and then we came upon a valley with many houses of the Tejas Indians and around them their planted fields of corn and beans and squash and watermelons. From there we took another turn to the north over a tall hill with the same scrub oak *chaparros*, and we fell into another valley with the same houses of Indians and planted fields, where the governor of the Indians said that it was very close to his house, that we should stop at the edge of the valley, near a brook, where the royal company stopped, and it was given the name of valley and quarters of La Madre de Jesús María de Ágreda,[190] having marched this day 5 leagues.[191]

188. The May 20 entries are vastly different in 90-B and 90-D.
189. Manuscript 90-D provides more geographical details than 90-B.
190. The stopping place is called San Francisco Xavier in 90-B.
191 Manuscripts 90-B and 90-D have vastly different entries for May 22. For example, there is no reference in 90-D to the mother, wife, and daughter of the governor of the Tejas, and no mention is made of the corn tamales and *atole* they are offered as an afternoon meal. Some information is missing between this entry and the next. Folio 8v of 90-D is blank and it appears that the writer left space for entries that were never completed.

[**folio 8v is blank**]

[**folio 9r**] The first was named San Antonio de Padua, the second Santa Juana, the third Santa Margarita, the fourth San Carlos; of the four valleys, these are the names.[192]

On [May] 25 the altitude of the settlement of the Tejas was observed, which is at 34°7'.[193]

On [May] 27, 28, 29, 30, and 31, they worked on making the church and the dwelling of the apostolic missionaries, and they took possession of house and church on said [May] 31.[194]

Thursday, June 1, the church was blessed, and the reverend *padre comisario* Fray Damián Massanet sang the mass, and after the blessing of the church which was done with a procession, this day in the afternoon, the main company moved out from said quarters of San Francisco de los Tejas in pursuit of the return to the Province of Coahuila, along the same road we had taken. It stopped this night at the quarters of San Carlos, having marched 5 leagues.

Friday, June 2, Governor Alonso de León and the captains Don Gregorio de Salinas Varona and Francisco Martínez[195] and the reverend *padre comisario* Fray Damián Massanet and 4 soldiers set out in pursuit of the main body from said quarters of San Francisco de los Tejas, and we met them in the aforementioned quarters, and from there we continued our journey with the main body until the valley which is on this side of the quarters of San Bernardino, about half a league, where the [**folio 9v**] main company stopped, having marched this day 6 [leagues].

Saturday, June 3, the company set out from the quarters of San Bernardino and, passing through the Valle de San Sebastián and the Valle de la Monclova, we arrived at the Río de la Santísima Trinidad, and because it was too swollen and could not be forded, we made halt on its bank in said Valle de la Monclova, having marched this day 7 [leagues].[196]

---

192. The entries for May 23, 24, and 26 are missing. Manuscript 90-B contains extensive entries for these days and also for May 25, which is missing in 90-D. Manuscripts 90-E and 90-F show entries for May 23, 24, 25, and 26, but they end with the May 26 entry.

193. Manuscript 90-B offers a very detailed, extensive entry providing a careful description of the celebration of the feast of Corpus Christi, the presentation of the staff to the governor of the Tejas, and the religious instructions given to the Indians. It also mentions arrangements being made for three members of the Tejas to return to New Spain with the expedition party to meet the Conde de Galve. None of this information is present in 90-D.

194. Manuscript 90-B has a very similar short entry for these days.

195. Don Gregorio de Salinas Varona and Francisco Martínez are not mentioned in 90-B. Otherwise, the entry is almost identical in both manuscripts.

196. Manuscript 90-B gives the distance marched as six and a half leagues, 90-D as seven leagues.

Sunday, June 4; Monday, 5; Tuesday, 6; Wednesday, 7; Thursday, 8; Friday, 9; Saturday, 10; this day a raft was built to cross the river, and we began the crossing.

Sunday, June 11, we finished crossing at about two in the afternoon, and the main company set out through the Valle de Galves until reaching that of Santa Elvira, where we stopped near some pools of fresh water, having marched 3 [leagues].

Monday, June 12, the main company set out from said quarters and having passed the quarters named San Diego de Alcalá about 2 leagues, the company stopped near some pools of rainwater, having marched this day 9 [leagues].

Tuesday, June 13, the company set out from said quarters, and having passed the quarters of El Beato Salvador de Horta and arrived at that of San Juan, the company stopped; having marched this day eight leagues.

Wednesday, June 14, the company set out from the aforementioned quarters and crossing the Río del Espíritu Santo, we arrived at a small hill near a live oak from which four grow from the one. Here the company stopped by a pool of rainwater, having marched on this day 9 [leagues].[197]

Thursday, June 15, the company set out from the aforementioned quarters and, passing by that of San Francisco de Asís, we arrived at an arroyo with water at the foot of a hill where we stopped by a small clump of trees, having marched this day 7 [leagues].[198]

[**folio 10r**] Friday, June 16, the company set out from the aforementioned quarters and, passing by that of San Joseph and San Ildefonso, it arrived near an arroyo with rainwater at the foot of a hillock which has some oaks and small live oaks on the eastern side and the creek to the west, where we stopped, having marched this day 7 [leagues].[199]

Saturday, June 17, the company set out from the above-mentioned stopping place to cross the Río de San Marcos until reaching the stopping place and encampment of Jesús, María y Joseph de Buena Vista, where it stopped, having marched this day 5 [leagues].

At this camp there were many nations of Indians, such as the Cantona, the Thoaga, the Chana, and Cabas.[200]

197. The distance marched on this day is given as eight leagues in 90-B and nine leagues in 90-D.

198. Manuscript 90-B identifies this stopping place as the one from which the Indian was dispatched to summon the governor of the Tejas.

199. San Ildefonso is not mentioned in 90-B. The distance marched is also different: six leagues in 90-B and seven leagues in 90-D.

200. Manuscript 90-B does not provide the names of the Indian groups they encountered.

Sunday, June 18, the company moved out continuing its journey and Governor Alonso de León and Captain Don Gregorio de Salinas Varona[201] and 16 soldiers left in a northeasterly direction in search of 2 French boys and a French girl, across some plains for about 4 leagues until we reached a small wooded area which we passed and then we continued in an easterly direction for about another 3 leagues, where we came upon another Indian *rancheria* in a small forest; they call themselves the Tho-o.[202] From there we continued until eight at night in a southeasterly direction across some plains, where there was an infinite number of buffalo, to the bank of a brook, which at the beginning forms a patch of trees where we stopped, having marched on this day about 16 leagues.

Monday, June 19, at dawn we continued our journey along the bank of the brook, which has trees on both sides, and after crossing it and having traveled about 2 [**folio 10v**] leagues we came upon another nation of Indians called the Co-oc,[203] to whom we gave gifts and they remained our friends. From there we continued our journey in a southerly direction across some plains, and after about one league we came upon another nation of Indians called the Tho-o. From there we continued in a southerly direction across a plain with countless buffalo, for about 4 leagues until we entered a small wooded area. And continuing our journey toward the west and crossing a large arroyo, in a wooded area we came upon a very large nation of Indians, which had more than three thousand people,[204] which call themselves the Ta-na-aman,[205] to whom we gave gifts and they remained our friends; and they gave us Indians to guide us to another *rancheria*, and from there we set out across some plains, and it was already very dark when we stopped on the bank of an arroyo, having marched on this day about fifteen leagues.

Tuesday, June 20, we continued our journey in an easterly direction, where we came upon a nation of Indians called Caisquetebana,[206] to whom we gave gifts and they gave us 4 Indians to guide us to where the French children were. From there we set out in the same direction to cross the Arroyo de los Franceses, and having crossed it we continued to the Frenchmen's settlement and from there we continued in a southerly direction to the Arroyo de las Canoas and having crossed it we came upon a brook, where we stopped, having marched on this day 14 [leagues].

201. Salinas Varona is not mentioned in 90-B.
202. The name of this Indian nation is not mentioned in 90-B.
203. The name of this Indian nation is not mentioned in 90-B.
204. The number of Indians is not mentioned in 90-B
205. The name of this Indian nation is not mentioned in 90-B.
206. This name is not mentioned in 90-B.

Wednesday, June 21, we set out in a southeasterly direction, and after about 1 league, we came upon two Indians on horseback from the nation that had the French children, who [**folio 11r**] guided us to their *ranchería*, which was at the tip of an inlet, they are called the nation of the Cascossi, where the two French children, Roberto and Madalena Talon, were. We discussed their ransom, and after having given them gifts and the ransom for both, they came with a thousand shameless demands, asking us to give them all our horses and even the clothes we wore on our backs, while they went looking for the other French boy, who was 2 leagues from there within the same nation. And having brought him, they continued further with their shameless demands, bringing bows and arrows; and a large number of Indians came, prepared with leather shields, demanding exorbitant things, and that if we did not give them to them, they were going to shoot their arrows at us and kill us all. And saying this and starting to shoot arrows happened at the same time. Therefore, we fell upon them, and having killed four and injured two of them, they withdrew after injuring 2 of our horses. We moved out to sleep about 4 leagues from there, where we had slept the night before, having marched on this day 12 leagues in a northerly direction, where we stopped in a plain on the bank of an arroyo[207]

Thursday, June 22, at dawn we set out north across some plains along the Río de Guadalupe, where we found some patches of Brazil wood and at about 10 at night, we stopped near a small wooded area, having marched this day 14 [leagues].[208]

Friday, June 23, we set out in a northerly direction for about two leagues, where we came upon the tracks [**folio 11v**] of the main body that had passed through there, and after about 3 leagues we came upon the ford of the Guadalupe, where we stopped, having marched this day 5 [leagues].[209]

Saturday, June 24, the full company moved out from said ford to cross the Río de Guadalupe, and having crossed it, we continued our journey to an arroyo which is before the quarters of Agua Salada, where we stopped, having marched this day 7 [leagues].

Sunday, June 25, the company moved out continuing its journey, and passing by the quarters of Agua Salada, we reached the Arroyo del León, having marched 7 leagues this day, the royal company stopped.

207. This long entry is almost identical in 90-B and 90-D, except that in 90-D the name of the Indian nation, the "Cascossi," is mentioned.

208. This is essentially the same entry as in 90-B, except for some syntactical changes and the mention of Brazil wood in 90-D.

209. The entry for June 23 is identical in 90-B and 90-D.

Monday, June 26, the company moved out continuing its journey until it crossed the Río de Medina, where it stopped, having marched this day 6 [leagues].[210]

Tuesday, June 27, the company moved out from said stopping place on the river through woods of oak trees and mesquite brush in a southeasterly and southerly direction until it reached an arroyo, where the company stopped, having marched this day 7 [leagues].[211]

Wednesday, June 28, the company moved out from the above-mentioned stopping place to the west through woods of oaks and plains, for about 4 leagues, and then we continued in a southerly direction for about one league, where we came upon some pools of rainwater, surrounded by mesquite brush and prickly pear cactuses, where there was a *ranchería* of Indians called the Tho-o-e, where the company stopped, having marched this day 5 [leagues].[212]

[**folio 12r**] Thursday, June 29, Day of the Apostle Saint Peter, the company moved out from said stopping place, and passing by the pools of El Aire, in a ravine, the company stopped by some pools of rainwater. On this day, the tired horses were separated, of which there were 207, with 25 men, so that they could bring them little by little. This day, we marched about 4 leagues.[213]

Friday, June 30, the company set out from the above-mentioned stopping place to cross the Río Hondo, and having crossed it, it [the company] stopped. We marched about 3 leagues as far as the ford of Las Cruces, where we stopped on the banks of the river, having marched this day 9 [leagues].[214]

Saturday, July 1, the company moved out from said ford of Las Cruces to cross the Río Frío, and having arrived at it, the company stopped, having marched this day 5 [leagues].[215]

Sunday, July 2, we crossed the river, and the company continued its journey to cross the Río de las Nueces, where it stopped; and having reached the river,

210. Manuscript 90-B gives the distance marched as five leagues.

211. Manuscript 90-B fails to mention the trees and the direction in which the company marched. The daily distance is also different: eight leagues in 90-B, seven leagues in 90-D.

212. The two entries for this day are very different. Manuscript 90-B mentions that the guide lost his way and that they stopped above the Arroyo de los Róbalos. It makes no mention of the trees and plants they saw, the direction in which they traveled, or the Indians they encountered.

213. The entries diverge considerably for this day. Manuscript 90-B omits the information about the horses and gives the distance marched as five leagues.

214. The ford is called "ford of the Río Hondo" in 90-B and the daily distance traveled is given as eight leagues. Brierley misinterprets "paró" (90-D 12r10) 'it stopped,' to mean that the river stopped or went belowground (Chapa 1997, 219). However, the grammatical subject of "paró" is "el real"; that is, the company stopped.

215. Manuscript 90-B mentions the Río Zarco instead of the Río Frío in the entry of July 1.

we crossed it and continued our journey as far as some pools of water, which are before arriving at the Arroyo de Caramanchel, where we stopped, having marched this day 8 [leagues].[216]

[**folio 12v**] Monday, July 3, the company moved out from said quarters and after crossing the arroyo and quarters of Caramanchel, we arrived at the pools of Ramos, where we continued our journey as far as the quarters where we had slept without water, where the company stopped, [and] the pools had water, having marched this day 8 [leagues].[217]

Tuesday, July 4,[218] the company moved out from the aforementioned stopping place to cross the Río Grande and having reached it, because it was very swollen, it was necessary to stop on the other side, on the bank, having marched this day 8 [leagues].

From [July] 4 to Wednesday, [July] 12, I was detained, and this said day in the afternoon, although it [the river] was very swollen and nobody dared to ford it, I jumped in to cross it,[219] the horse swimming. And with the water reaching below my chest, I crossed it to give the news to His Excellency of our journey, and then the *padre comisario* Fray Damián Massanet followed me and four soldiers and a young Frenchman named Pedro Moñe.[220]

Thursday, July 13, I marched as far as the green water pools that are from said river 14 [leagues].[221]

Friday, July 14, before dawn we set out and continued our journey to cross the Río de las Sabinas, where we arrived upstream of the junction, where we stopped, having marched on this day 17 [leagues].

Saturday, July 15, we set out continuing our journey until the town of Santiago de la Monclova, having marched on this day 12 [leagues].

[**folio 13r**] Cantona, Toaga, Chana, Cabas, Tho-o, Cooc, Na-aman, Cazique, Tebana, Ca-co-ossi, Mojoman.[222]

---

216. The Arroyo de Caramanchel is not mentioned in 90-B.

217. The arroyo and quarters of Caramanchel are not mentioned in 90-B and the distance traveled is ten leagues.

218. Brierley omits this entire entry (Chapa 1997, 171).

219. This information does not appear in 90-B.

220. Manuscript 90-B differs considerably from 90-D here. The 90-B entry does not include July 4 or 12 as part of the days the company was detained at the swollen Río Grande. Neither does it provide a description of how de León and other members of the small party jumped into the river and crossed it with their horses. Fray Damián Massanet is not mentioned in 90-B.

221. Manuscript 90-D is the only document from the 1690 expedition to include entries for July 12, 13, 14, and 15. Manuscripts 90-A, 90-B, and 90-C conclude with the July 5–11 entry, while manuscripts 90-E and 90-F go only to May 26.

222. This list of Indian groups does not seem to be part of the diary proper.

Summary and Conclusions

Archival documents are the cornerstone of humanities scholarship because they provide textual platforms for multiple disciplines. Spanish colonial manuscripts are particularly suited for multidisciplinary research. As such, General Alonso de León's expedition diaries from 1686 to 1690 provide significant data on the early history of Texas and on the Spanish language spoken by the members of the first official military explorations into the region and can benefit historians, linguists, ethnographers, anthropologists, archaeologists, and other scholars alike. Information culled from the diaries has, for instance, been instrumental for Texas archaeology. In 1996, a close reading of the journals led to the excavation of the eight French cannons that de León buried within the premises of the destroyed French settlement in 1689. This, in turn, confirmed the location of Fort Saint Louis and helped uncover thousands of French and Spanish artifacts. The unearthing of the skeletal remains of three members of La Salle's expedition in 2000 can also be attributed to information found in the 1689 journal. Even the 1995 discovery of *La Belle*, La Salle's last ship, which sank in Matagorda Bay, was in part thanks to indications in de León's journals that confirmed prior sightings of wreckage recorded during the maritime expeditions. In the hope of stimulating further research, the general's diaries have been addressed in this work using an interdisciplinary approach that combines historical research, paleography, linguistic analysis, and translation.

The overall aspects of de León's five expeditions in search of La Salle are not new to historians. In fact, the very first accounts of these exploratory journeys were published over one hundred years ago in the form of Spanish transcriptions and English translations (e.g., Portillo 1886; West 1905; Bolton [1908] 1916; García 1909). To this day, de León and his expeditions continue to draw scholarly attention and attract popular interest as more recent print publications (Ashford 1971; Bannon 1970; Chapa 1997; Chipman 1992; Chipman and Joseph 1999, 2001; Dunn [1917] 1971; Foster 1995; Gómez Canedo 1988; Weddle 1991, 1999; Ximenes 1963) and numerous Internet websites attest. Erstwhile de León scholarship, however, has been fragmented, and some studies have relied on partially inexact and erroneous information. Hence, many of the existing historical accounts contain factual errors because they are based on deficient manuscripts or inaccurate English translations that include misreadings or misunderstandings of the Spanish primary texts. Some of these errors are substantial and have misinformed historical interpretation for more than a century. Other errors, seemingly minor, have contributed to an accumulation of misinterpretations that, taken as a whole, further distort our understanding of the past.

From its inception, the main purpose of this book has been to render a more accurate presentation of actual historical events through the identification of the most reliable primary sources and the application of rigorous philological practice. This was achieved by analyzing all known extant diaries linguistically, establishing the genetic relationship between them, and selecting one archetype from each manuscript family. Authoritative transcriptions of all the manuscripts, following best practices in the field of Spanish paleography, have produced reliable source documents that can offer more complete data and be used as textual platforms for scholars who interpret the past. The production of faithful, annotated English translations was the final step in the process of addressing misconceptions and rectifying factual errors. Because the new translations have been based on the archetype of each expedition diary but also take subsequent manuscript copies into consideration, prior errors resulting from misreading, misunderstanding, or mistranslating the source texts have been identified, noted, and corrected.

By comparing primary sources with the extant Spanish- and English-language publications and by providing a critical analysis of the secondary sources, this study begs the reinterpretation of certain historical aspects of de León's five expeditions. Despite the plentiful scholarship on the matter, the general's journals have never been published together in their unabridged versions, with both Spanish transcriptions and English translations. This fresh look at de León scholarship was inspired by the groundbreaking work in critically edited Spanish colonial documents of scholars such as Craddock (1996, 1998), De Marco (2000a, 2000b), Hendricks (1988, 1992), Imhoff (2002), Kania (2000), Kessell (1989), and others, as well as the publications of the Cíbola Project at the University of California–Berkeley, and the Vargas Project at the University of New Mexico.

Unmediated access to primary texts in their original language is always the ideal scenario for any type of research. Language barriers often make it impossible to satisfy this requirement, however, and translation becomes a necessary tool to unlock information held in the original documents. In spite of the potential for misreading and misunderstanding, translation has provided invaluable access to information for centuries, even millennia. Most foundational texts of Western civilization have come to us via translation. In fact, there would be very little scholarship without translation. Being cognizant of the potential pitfalls of translation and avoiding them is crucial in order to bring a translated text as close to the original as possible. One of the recurrent problems of Spanish colonial texts is the multiple copying, which, over time, has allowed scribal errors to seep in and distort information. Consequently, ascertaining archetypes and using them as source texts for translation is of utmost importance. The philological approach has been meticulously followed in the treatment of de León's diaries. Paleographic transcriptions of the archetypes have been used as the basis for the English translations. Great care has been taken to stay as close to the Spanish texts as possible in order to provide the most accurate translation. During this process, the archetypes were compared to existing publications in both Spanish and English, which in turn allowed for identification of discrepancies, errors, and mistranslations. The following is a summary of the most salient substantive differences detected.

Only one copy of the original 1686 diary and a narrative summary of the 1687 expedition exist (86-A, 87-A). Modernized Spanish transcriptions of the manuscripts by García (1909) and Cavazos Garza ([1961] 2005) served as the basis for Brierley's English translation in Foster's edition of Chapa (1997). This translation is very good and quite accurate. Nevertheless, there are a few discrepancies, which are documented in the notes. Three examples bear pointing out. One of the inaccuracies was due to misreading punctuation signs in the manuscript, which resulted in the wrong participant being identified as the Indian guide (Chapa 1997, 106). The correct rendition of "Alonso, yndio capitan de la rancheria zacatil, nues-/tro guia; Bernabe, yndio; Matheo, yndio" (86-A 48v16–17) is "Alonso, an Indian captain from the Zacatil *ranchería*, our guide; Bernabe, an Indian; Mateo, an Indian." The number of men who set out with de León to reconnoiter the land is also misstated as "two" (Chapa 1997, 107), but the original manuscript has it as "twelve": "Sali con efecto con doze compañeros" (86-A 49v9–10); twelve men accompanied the general, not two. Another mistranslation occurred because the translator did not consider a secondary meaning of the word *avenida*, which, according to the dictionary of the Spanish Royal Academy, can also refer to a violent flood of a river or current. The Spanish sentence "sobre que discurri que ay alguna poblazon zercana y que / alguna abenida les llebo alguna milpa" is rendered by Brierley (Chapa 1997, 112) as "I concluded that there was some settlement nearby and that corn had been brought to it by some means," instead of "from which I inferred that there was some settlement nearby and that flooding had carried away some of their corn fields." The new English translations rectify these inaccuracies.

By contrast, the *autos* and diary of the 1688 expedition have been published only in a partial Spanish transcription by Gómez Canedo (1988) and in English narrative summaries by Ximenes (1963) and Weddle (1999). None of the publications are based on the archetype manuscript. Consequently, the transcription and translation errors that were detected are chiefly, although not exclusively, caused by reliance on a manuscript copy marred by scribal errors. Although the mistakes may appear to be minor, they do misinform historical interpretation. For example, Weddle (1999, 136), relying on the faulty manuscript 88-C, states that all the Indians gathered in the French chief's dwelling served as interpreters for Agustín, the Tlaxcaltecan. The archetype, however, confirms that Agustín was aided by only one Indian, who was present in the lodge and happened to be an acquaintance: "Por lo cual se balio de vno de los yndios que estaban / con el contenido y conocido suio que le siruio de ynterprete" (88-A 17v17–18). On the other hand, Ximenes (1963) seriously misinterprets the source text. His English translation "a Spaniard was hunting with the Indians and through his services de León learned that the *ranchería* was nearby and that the Frenchman was their leader" is incorrect (1963, 86). De León uses the term "hombre español" as a synonym for white man or European when questioning the Indians about the Frenchman: "y llegando a hablarles mediante ynterprete, les pregunte que donde / estaba vn hombre español, y me dieron por razon que estaba en distancia / de cinco o seis leguas de alli" (88-A 18r33–35). It is utterly improbable that a Spaniard would have been hunting and living with a band of Indians devoted to a French chief. Had this been the case, de León would certainly have had much more to say about his countryman and the entire situation. He surely would have questioned the man, mentioned his name, arrested him, and returned him to New Spain. Two additional examples of mistranslation worth pointing out can be found in the description of the buffalo hunt. Ximenes (1963) gives the number of Indian hunters they encountered as fifteen hundred, while all three Spanish manuscripts state that there were about five hundred hunters. Conversely, Weddle (1999, 137) reports that the Indians helped the Spaniards kill *cíbolas*, but in fact the opposite was the case. The Spaniards with their firearms were the ones who aided the Indians in the hunt, as can be elucidated from the archetype: "Les aiudamos a matar algunas de las / dichas ciuolas" (88-A 22r16–17). In several other instances there are misinterpretations of important details about the discovery and capture of Yan Jarri, the Frenchman who lived among the natives.

In fact, an important adjustment needs to be made apropos the Frenchman's name. Manuscripts 88-A, 88-B, and 88-C give the name as "Yan Jarri." Some historians have kept the name exactly as it appears in de León's diary or changed it to "Jean Jarri," while others have transformed it to "Jean Géry" (e.g., Chapa 1997; Dunn [1917] 1971; Foster 1995; Weddle 1991, 1999). Only Ximenes (1963) reports the name as "Jean Henri," which seems to be the correct form. A linguistic analysis of Spanish primary sources supports this claim. It is evident that "Yan Jarri" was the approximate phonetic rendition of the name pronounced in French and written down by Spaniards who were not versed in French. Nobody in de León's detachment spoke the language, and the Frenchman himself was illiterate and did not know how to read or write. He was therefore unable to write his own name. Thus, when he told de León his name, the general or his scribe wrote it down as it was heard by the ears of a Spanish speaker: "Yan Jarri." This Spanish rendition of the name reflected the French pronunciation of *Jean* as "Yan" and *Henri* as "Jarri." In seventeenth-century French, *Henri* was pronounced with an aspirated /h/ for the letter *h*, an alveolar nasal /ã/ for *en*, a uvular approximant /ʁ/ for *r*, and an /i/ for *i*. The first three sounds do not exist in Spanish. Thus, "Jarri," with the Spanish velar fricative /x/ represented by the letter *j*, /a/ for the nasalized *en*, and an alveolar trill /r/ represented by the double *r*, was a very close approximation to French pronunciation. In fact, "Jarri" was how "Henri" sounded to the members of de León's expedition. Later, after the Frenchman was apprehended and sent to Mexico City for questioning by Spaniards who were fluent in French, his name invariably appears as "Juan Enrique" in the reports. Naturally, "Juan Enrique" is the Spanish translation of "Jean Henri." Based on this analysis, it appears that the Frenchman's name was likely Jean Henri. Therefore, it is recommended that this name be used or, as an alternative, de León's original rendition: Yan Jarri. Conversely, "Jean Géry" does not seem to be a viable option. Had the Frenchman pronounced his name "Jean Géry" in French, de León would have spelled it "Yan Yeri" or even "Yan Cheri," since French *g* before *e* or *i* is pronounced /ʒ/, also referred to as soft *g*.

The most numerous and egregious transcription and translation errors can be found in publications dealing with de León's 1689 expedition. Ironically, this is the most important of de León's five expeditions. The 1689 exploratory journey has garnered considerable interest among scholars because it was the most successful one: it finally led to the discovery of La Salle's colony on the Texas coast. The diary maps the route across Texas and reports finding the abandoned French fort, learning of La Salle's fate, recovering two Frenchmen, and making first-time contact with the Caddo

Indians. Unfortunately, the textual transmission of this key information has been tainted by scribal errors committed during the copying process, which in turn resulted in faulty English renditions. In fact, the oldest and best-known English translation, by West (1905), was based on the least reliable manuscript (89-D) and includes a great deal of mistakes and inaccuracies. Besides the errors forced by the faulty manuscript, West's work also includes frequent misinterpretations, omissions, and mistranslations. Unfortunately, for over a century, this flawed text has been regarded as the official secondary source for scholarship related to de León's most momentous journey. The new English translation contained in this book is the first retranslation of the 1689 manuscript since 1905. It is actually the first unabridged translation of the archetype, manuscript 89-B. It is high time that the substantive errors be corrected and the historical canon updated regarding the general's most successful expedition.

The errors are too numerous to address individually in this summary, but they are pointed out in the annotated translation in section 3. Besides West's frequent misunderstanding of individual words, expressions, and context, two categories of recurrent translation errors stand out: numbers and compass directions. West misstates numbers on several occasions. For example, the number of Indians in the group who welcomed the military company before crossing the Río Grande at the beginning of the journey is stated as "seventy" (West 1905, 204) instead of "sixty," as per manuscript 89-B 29rB, which says "sessenta." The weight of the cannonballs found in the French fort is reported to be "four or five pounders" (West 1905, 217) instead of "four and six pounders," based on the Spanish "de a quatro y seis libras" (89-B 46v12). The distance from the French fort to the bay is given as "fifty-two leagues" (West 1905, 221) rather than "thirty-two leagues," as the translation of "treintta y dos leguas" found in the archetype (89-B 48r22) would indicate. When four Indian canoes are found in a creek, "hallamos cuatro canoas" according to the manuscript (89-B 48r10–11), West renders it as "two canoes" (1905, 220). De León's daily stated compass directions are often mistranslated too. The errors do not occur when rendering cardinal points (north, east, south, west) or ordinal points (northeast, southeast, southwest, northwest), but with the quarter points between them. Consequently, the directions that include the Spanish term "quarta" listed in the diary are the ones often stated incorrectly. For example, according to *South America Pilot* (1916), the correct equivalent for "leste quarta al nordeste" (89B 43r4–5) is "east by north," but West renders it as "east-northeast" (1905, 208); "nordeste quarta al norte" (89B 38v21) is translated as "northeast" (1905, 204), when the correct translation would be "northeast by north." These translation errors cause de León's route to be off by several degrees each time the direction is misstated. These compounded errors are detrimental for researchers trying to reconstruct the expedition route.

Similar, albeit fewer, errors can be found in the English publications regarding the 1690 expedition. Bolton's translation of manuscript 90-B and Brierley's rendition of manuscript 90-D contain the same type of compass direction errors. Aside from these, the English versions are quite accurate and well done and present only a handful of minor misinterpretations and mistranslations. For instance, at one point Bolton misreads "vestias" (90-B 8v25) 'pack animals' as "vestidos" 'dresses or clothing' ([1908] 1916, 410) and translates the sentences as "I sent to meet them with clothing and supplies" in lieu of "I sent them to meet up with the pack animals and supplies." Brierley, on the other hand, misstates the number of horses that stampede one day as 120 (Chapa 1997, 158) instead of 126 (90-D 3v2).

While these translation errors may not appear of much consequence to the larger picture of the five expeditions, they nevertheless misstate facts and eliminate information for English readers. Scholars who have depended solely on the English translations have invariably been misinformed about pertinent details. The new English translations correct all the errors found in all the previous translations and offer a more accurate account of de León's important exploratory journeys. The copious notes provided also establish connections between the five individual expeditions, explain the discrepancies between the manuscripts and published historical accounts, and supply additional information about the participants. Thus, existing misconceptions about the journeys may be dispelled and errors rectified.

Further research is still needed on the six manuscripts pertaining to the 1690 expedition. Foster (1997) first identified manuscript 90-D as a revised diary, and McLain (2005) discovered two additional manuscript copies (90-E and 90-F) that she also classified as revised. However, these three diaries have very little in common with the three official ones (90-A, 90-B, and 90-C) that were sent to the authorities in Mexico City and Spain. The majority of the entries are markedly different. Can the manuscripts still be considered revised copies? Why would de León even want to completely revise an official document after it had already been read by his superiors? Who else was involved in the rewriting process and what other sources were used, since most entries are so unlike those of the official diary? While some conjectures have been formed as to the possible reason for and purpose of the "revised" manuscripts, many questions still remain.

References

Primary Sources

86-A Yale Collection of Western Americana, Beinecke Rare Book and Manuscript Library, MSS S-327, folios 46r–53r.

87-A Yale Collection of Western Americana, Beinecke Rare Book and Manuscript Library, MSS S-327, folios 53r–53v.

88-A Benson Latin American Collection, University of Texas–Austin, WBS 2053, folios 17r–22v.

88-B Archivo General de Indias (AGI), Audiencia de México, legajo 616, expediente 62, folios 3v–12r.

88-C Archivo General de Indias (AGI), Audiencia de México, legajo 616, expediente 65, folios 4r–16r.

89-A Archivo General de la Nación (AGN), Ramo de Provincias Internas, volumen 182, folios 428r–440v.

89-B Archivo General de Indias (AGI), Audiencia de México, legajo 616, expediente 65, folios 37v–50r.

89-C Biblioteca Nacional de México (BNMx), Archivo Franciscano, caja 1, expedientes 13 y 14, folios 133v–141v.

89-D Archivo General de la Nación (AGN), Ramo de Historia, volumen 27, folios 51r–66r.

89-E University of California–Berkeley, Bancroft Library, M-M 278–281, document 24, folios 305r–318r.

90-A Archivo General de la Nación (AGN), Ramo de Provincias Internas, volumen 182, expediente 6, folios 418r–426v.

90-B Archivo General de Indias (AGI), Audiencia de México, legajo 617, folios 4v–18r.

90-C Biblioteca Nacional de México (BNMx), Archivo Franciscano, caja 1, expedientes 12 y 13, folios126v–133v.

90-D Yale Collection of Western Americana, Beinecke Rare Book and Manuscript Library, MSS S-327, folios 1r–13r.

90-E Gilcrease Museum, Tulsa, Oklahoma, Hispanic Documents Section, item 67.1, folios 1r–9r.

90-F Gilcrease Museum, Tulsa, Oklahoma, Hispanic Documents Section, item 67.2, folios 1v–11r.

Secondary Sources

Alessio Robles, Vito. (1938) 1978. *Coahuila y Texas en la época colonial.* Mexico City: Editorial Porrúa.

Arizona State Museum. Documentary Relations of the Southwest, University of Arizona. http://www.statemuseum.arizona.edu/oer/.

Ashford, Gerald. 1971. *Spanish Texas: Yesterday and Today.* Austin, TX: Jenkins.

Bannon, John Francis. 1970. *The Spanish Borderlands Frontier, 1513–1821.* New York: Holt, Reinhart and Winston.

Baranowski, Edward. 2011. "Documents from the 1602–1603 Sebastían Vizcaíno Expedition up the California Coast." Berkeley: Cíbola Project, Research Center for Romance Studies, University of California.

Barnes, Thomas C., Thomas H. Naylor, and Charles W. Polzer. 1981. *Northern New Spain: A Research Guide.* Tucson: University of Arizona Press.

Barr, Juliana. 2007. *Peace Came in the Form of a Woman.* Chapel Hill: University of North Carolina Press.

Blackman, Ann. 2005. *Wild Rose: Rose O'Neale Greenhow, Civil War Spy.* New York: Random House.

Blake, Robert Bruce. 2010. "L'Archeveque, Jean." *Handbook of Texas Online.* Texas State Historical Association. Accessed September 1, 2015. http://www.tshaonline.org/handbook/online/articles/flabc.

Bleiberg, Germán, Maureen Ihrie, and Janet Pérez, eds. 1993. *Dictionary of the Literature of the Spanish Peninsula.* Vol. 2. Westport, CT: Greenwood Press.

Bolton, Herbert Eugene. (1908) 1916. *Spanish Exploration in the Southwest, 1542–1706.* New York: Charles Scribner's Sons.

———. (1913) 1977. *Guide to Materials for the History of the United States in the Principal Archives of Mexico.* Millwood, NY: Kraus Reprint.

———. 1917. "The Mission as a Frontier Institution in the Spanish-American Colonies." *American Historical Review* 23:42–61.

Branum, Lawanda Carter. 1974. "A Transcription and Linguistic Analysis of a Diary of the 1690 Alonso de León Expedition." Master's thesis, University of Texas at Arlington.

Bruseth, James E., and Toni Turner. 2005. *From a Watery Grave: The Discovery and Excavation of La Salle's Shipwreck, La Belle.* College Station: Texas A&M University Press.

Cabeza de Vaca, Álvar Núñez. 1542. *Naufragios*. N. p.: El Aleph, 2000.

———. 1993. *The Account: Álvar Núñez Cabeza de Vaca's Relación*. Translated by Martín Favata and José Fernández. Houston: Arte Público Press.

Calvert, Robert A., Arnoldo de León, and Gregg Cantrell. 2002. *The History of Texas*. Wheeling, IL: Harlan Davidson.

Campbell, Thomas. 2010. "Tlaxcalan Indians." *Handbook of Texas Online*. Texas State Historical Association. Accessed March 20, 2015. http://www .tshaonline.org/handbook/online/articles/bmt58.

Carlin, Roberta A., Barbara De Marco, and Jerry R. Craddock. 2009. "The Desertion of the Colonists of New Mexico 1601: 1st Part." Berkeley: Cíbola Project, Research Center for Romance Studies, University of California.

Casis, Lilia M. 1899. "Carta de Don Damián Manzanet a Don Carlos de Sigüenza sobre el descubrimiento de la Bahía del Espíritu Santo." *The Quarterly* 2 (4): 253–312.

Castañeda, Carlos E. 1936. *Our Catholic Heritage in Texas, 1519–1936*. 7 vols. Austin, TX: Von Boekman-Jones.

Cavazos Garza, Israel. (1961) 2005. *Estudio preliminar y notas. Historia de Nuevo León con noticias sobre Coahuila, Tamaulipas, Texas y Nuevo México, por Alonso de León, Juan Bautista Chapa y Fernando Sánchez de Zamora*. Monterrey, México: Fondo Editorial Nuevo León.

———. 1993. *El general Alonso de León: Descubridor de Texas*. Monterrey, México: Real Ayuntamiento de Monterrey.

———. 1994. *Dos Alonso de León: El cronista y el descubridor*. Monterrey, México: Gobierno del Estado de Nuevo León.

Chapa, Juan Bautista. (1961) 2005. *Historia de Nuevo León con noticias sobre Coahuila, Tamaulipas, Texas y Nuevo México*. Monterrey, México: Fondo Editorial Nuevo León.

———. 1997. *Texas and Northeastern Mexico, 1630–1690*. Edited by William C. Foster. Translated by Ned F. Brierley. Austin: University of Texas Press.

Chipman, Donald E. 1992. *Spanish Texas, 1519–1821*. Austin: University of Texas Press.

Chipman, Donald E., and Harriet Denise Joseph. 1999. *Notable Men and Women of Spanish Texas* Austin: University of Texas Press.

———. 2001. *Explorers and Settlers of Spanish Texas*. Austin: University of Texas Press.

Coll, Magdalena, Heather Bamford, Heather McMichael, and John H. R. Polt. 2009. "Doña Teresa de Aguilera y Roche ante la Inquisición (1664), 1a parte." Berkeley: Cíbola Project, Research Center for Romance Studies, University of California.

Corominas, Joan, and José A. Pascual. 1980–1991. *Diccionario crítico etimológico castellano e hispánico.* 6 vols. Madrid: Gredos.

Cottrell, Debbie Mauldin. 2010. "Casis, Lilia Mary." *Handbook of Texas Online.* Texas State Historical Association. Accessed March 15, 2015. http://www .tshaonline.org/handbook/online/articles/fcace.

Covarrubias Horozco, Sebastián de. (1611) 2006. *Tesoro de la lengua castellana o española.* Edited by Ignacio Arellano and Rafael Zafra. Madrid: Iberoamericana.

Craddock, Jerry R. 1996. "Philological Notes on the Hammond and Rey Translation of the [Relación de la] entrada que hizo en el Nuevo Mexico Francisco Sanchez Chamuscado en junio de [15]81 by Hernán Gallegos, Notary of the Expedition." *Romance Philology* 49:351–63.

———. 1997. "Review of Documentos para la historia lingüística de Hispanoamérica siglos XVI a XVII by María Beatriz Fontanella de Weinberg and Documentos lingüísticos de la Nueva España: Altiplano-Central by Concepción Company." *Romance Philology* 51:144–49.

———. 1998. "Juan de Oñate in Quivira." *Journal of the Southwest* 40:481–540.

———. 2008. "Fray Marcos de Niza, Relación (1539): Edition and Commentary." *Romance Philology* 53:51–164. Berkeley: Cíbola Project, Research Center for Romance Studies, University of California.

Craddock, Jerry R., and John H. R. Polt. 1999. *Zaldívar and the Cattle of Cíbola.* Dallas: William P. Clements Center for Southwest Studies, Southern Methodist University.

———. 2010. "Letter of Luis Gascó de Velasco against Oñate." Berkeley: Cíbola Project, Research Center for Romance Studies, University of California.

———. 2014. "Trial of the Indians of Acoma, 1598–1599." Berkeley: Cíbola Project, Research Center for Romance Studies, University of California.

Crivelli, Camillus. 1909. "Francisco de la Rosa Figueroa." In *The Catholic Encyclopedia*, vol. 6, 71. New York: Robert Appleton.

Cunningham, Debbie S. 2004. "Domingo Ramon's 1716 Expedition into Texas: On Foik's Translation." *Southwest Journal of Linguistics* 23:35–43.

———. 2006. "The Domingo Ramón Diary of the 1716 Expedition into the Province of the Tejas Indians: An Annotated Translation." *Southwest Historical Quarterly* 110:38–67.

Curiel, Guadalupe. 1994. *La historia de Texas en la Biblioteca Nacional de México: 1528–1848.* Mexico City: Universidad Nacional Autónoma de México.

de León, Alonso, Juan Bautista Chapa, and Fernando Sánchez de Zamora. (1961)

2005. *Historia de Nuevo León con noticias sobre Coahuila, Tamaulipas, Texas y Nuevo México*. Monterrey, México: Fondo Editorial Nuevo León.

Del Hoyo, Eugenio. 1979. *Historia del Nuevo Reino de León (1577–1723)*. Mexico City: Editorial Libros de México.

Del Valle, José. 1998. "Andalucismo, poligénesis y koineización: Dialectología e ideología." *Hispanic Review* 66 (2): 131–49.

De Marco, Barbara. 2000a. "Voices from the Archives, Part 1: Testimony of Pueblo Indians in the 1689 Pueblo Revolt." *Romance Philology* 53:375–448.

———. 2000b. "Voices from the Archives, Part 2: Ayeta's 1693 Letter to the Viceroy." *Romance Philology* 53:449–508.

De Marco, Barbara, and Jerry R. Craddock, eds. 1999–2000. "Documenting the Colonial Experience, with Special Regards to Spanish in the American Southwest." Special issue, *Romance Philology* 53.

Dunn, William Edward. (1917) 1971. *Spanish and French Rivalry in the Gulf Region of the United States, 1678–1702: The Beginnings of Texas and Pensacola*. Freeport, NY: Books for Libraries Press.

Foster, William C. 1995. *Spanish Expeditions into Texas, 1689–1768*. Austin: University of Texas Press.

———. 1997. Introduction to *Texas and Northeastern Mexico, 1630–1690*, by Juan Bautista Chapa. Translated by Ned F. Brierley. Austin: University of Texas Press.

———. 1998. Introduction to *The La Salle Expedition to Texas*, by Henri Joutel. Austin: Texas State Historical Association.

Frago Gracia, Juan Antonio. 1999. "Criterio filológico y edición de textos indianos; sobre documentos de la Nueva España." *Romance Philology* 53:119–36.

García, Genaro, ed. 1909. *Colección de documentos inéditos o muy raros para la historia de México*. Tomo 25, *Historia de Nuevo León*. Mexico City: Librería de la Vda. de Ch. Bouret.

Gerhard, Peter. 1993. *The North Frontier of New Spain*. Norman: University of Oklahoma Press.

Gómez Canedo, Lino. 1988. *Primeras exploraciones y poblamiento de Texas, 1686–1694*. Monterrey, México: Instituto Tecnológico y de Estudios Superiores de Monterrey.

Hadley, Diana, Thomas H. Naylor, and Mardith K. Schuetz-Miller, eds. 1997. *The Presidio and Militia on the Northern Frontier of New Spain*. Vol. 2, part 2, *The Central Corridor and the Texas Corridor*. Tucson: University of Arizona Press.

Hamilton, Nancy. 2010. "Ysleta, TX." *Handbook of Texas Online.* Texas State Historical Association. Accessed March 20, 2015. http://www.tshaonline.org/*handbook/online/articles/hny06.*

Hendricks, Rick, ed. 1988. *The Text and Concordance of "Correspondence of Don Diego de Vargas, 1675–1706."* Vargas Project Microfiche Series 1. Albuquerque: University of New Mexico Press.

———. 1992. *The Text and Concordance of "By Force of Arms: The Journal of Don Diego de Vargas, New Mexico, 1691–93."* Vargas Project Microfiche Series 2. Albuquerque: University of New Mexico Press.

Hendricks, Rick, José Ignacio Avellaneda, and Meredith D. Dodge, eds. 1993. *The Text and Concordance of "To the Royal Crown Restored: The Journals of Don Diego de Vargas, New Mexico, 1692–1694."* Vargas Project Microfiche Series 3. Albuquerque: University of New Mexico Press.

Hickerson, Nancy P. 1994. *The Jumanos: Hunters and Traders of the South Plains.* Austin: University of Texas Press.

Hough-Snee, Dexter Z. 2013. "Campaign Journal of Diego de Vargas, Governor of New Mexico, Sept. 1–Oct. 14, 1694." Berkeley: Cíbola Project, Research Center for Romance Studies, University of California.

Hoyt, Cathryn A. 1992. "Riches, Religion, and Politics: Early Exploration in Texas." In *Hispanic Texas: A Historical Guide,* edited by Helen Simons and Cathryn A. Hoyt, 13–16. Austin: University of Texas Press.

Imhoff, Brian. 2002. *The Diary of Juan Domínguez de Mendoza's Expedition into Texas (1683–1684).* Dallas: William P. Clements Center for Southwest Studies, Southern Methodist University.

———. 2006. "Sobre un texto colonial del suroeste estadounidense: Una aportación filológica. *Lexis* 30 (2): 211–30.

Joutel, Henri. 1998. *The La Salle Expedition to Texas.* Edited by William C. Foster. Translated by Johanna S. Warren. Austin: Texas State Historical Association.

Kania, Sonia. 2000. "A Linguistic Analysis of Colonial Documents from New Galicia (1561–1647)." PhD diss., University of Wisconsin–Madison.

———. 2008. "Probanza de méritos of Vicente de Zaldivar: A Linguistic Analysis of Part 1 (1601–1602)." *Southwest Journal of Linguistics* 27 (1): 17–51.

Kessell, John L., ed. 1989. *Remote beyond Compare: Letters of Don Diego de Vargas, 1691–1693.* Albuquerque: University of New Mexico Press.

Kessell, John L., and Rick Hendricks, eds. 1992. *By Force of Arms: The Journals of Don Diego de Vargas, 1691–1693.* Albuquerque: University of New Mexico Press.

Kessell, John L., Rick Hendricks, and Meredith D. Dodge, eds. 1995. *To the Royal Crown Restored: The Journals of Don Diego de Vargas, New Mexico, 1692–1694.* Albuquerque: University of New Mexico Press.

Kessell, John L., Rick Hendricks, Meredith D. Dodge, and Larry D. Miller, eds. 1998. *Blood on the Boulder: The Journals of Don Diego de Vargas, New Mexico, 1694–1697.* 2 vols. Albuquerque: University of New Mexico Press.

———, eds. 2000. *That Disturbances Cease: The Journals of Don Diego de Vargas, New Mexico, 1697–1700.* Albuquerque: University of New Mexico Press.

———, eds. 2002. *A Settling of Accounts: The Journals of Don Diego de Vargas, New Mexico, 1700–1704.* Albuquerque: University of New Mexico Press.

Lerner, Isaías. 1974. *Arcaísmos léxicos del español de América.* Madrid: Ínsula.

Lipsky, John M. 2007. *El español de América.* 5th ed. Madrid: Cátedra.

Mackenzie, David. 1997. *A Manual of Manuscript Transcription for the Dictionary of the Old Spanish Language.* Madison, WI: Hispanic Seminary of Medieval Studies.

Mascella, Raffaele, and Danilo Pelusi. 2006. "Uno scienziato abruzzese: Andrea Argoli." *Ratio Mathematica: Rivista.* Accademia Piceno Aprutina dei Velati. Accessed January 31, 2015. http://www.apav.it/ratio_online/num1/Argoli2 .pdf.

McLain, Jana. 2005. "Alonso de León 1690 Expedition Diary into Texas: An Edition and Study of the Spanish Texts with Semi-Paleographic Transcriptions." Master's thesis, Texas A&M University.

Meyer, Michael, William Sherman, and Susan Deeds. 2010. *The Course of Mexican History.* 9th ed. Oxford: Oxford University Press.

Moliner, Maria. 2007. *Diccionario del uso del español.* 2 vols. Madrid: Gredos.

Naylor, Thomas H., and Charles W. Polzer, SJ. 1981. *Pedro de Rivera and the Military Regulations for Northern Spain, 1724–1729.* Tucson: University of Arizona Press.

———. 1986. *The Presidio and Militia on the Northern Frontier of New Spain.* Tucson: University of Arizona Press.

Newcomb, W. W. 1961. *The Indians of Texas.* Austin: University of Texas Press.

Nostas, Alissa, Magdalena Coll, and Brian Imhoff. 2013. "Accusation against Juan Domínguez de Mendoza for Blasphemy (1667)." Berkeley: Cíbola Project, Research Center for Romance Studies, University of California.

Perales, Monica, and Raúl A. Ramos. 2010. *Recovering the Hispanic History of Texas Project.* Houston: Arte Público Press.

Polzer, Charles W., SJ. 1999. "Documentary Relations of the Southwest: A Description." *Romance Philology* 53:153–63.

Polzer, Charles W., SJ, and Thomas E. Sheridan, eds. 1997. *The Presidio and Militia on the Northern Frontier of New Spain*. Vol. 2, part 1, *The Californias and Sinaloa-Sonora*. Tucson: University of Arizona Press.

Portillo, Esteban L. 1886. *Apuntes para la historia antigua de Coahuila y Texas*. Saltillo, México: Tipografía El Golfo de México de Severo Fernández.

Real Academia Española. 1963. *Diccionario de autoridades*. 3 vols. Madrid: Gredos.

———. 2001. *Diccionario de la lengua española*. 2 vols. Madrid: Espasa-Calpe.

Schiappapietra, Giovanni Battista (Juan Bautista Chapa). 2013. *Da Albisola al nuovo regno di Leon*. Neive, Italy: Fondaziona Schiappapietra.

Sheridan, Thomas E. 1999. *Empire of Sand: The Seri Indians and the Struggle for Spanish Sonora, 1653–1803*. Tucson: University of Arizona Press.

Sheridan, Thomas E., and Thomas H. Naylor, eds. 1971. *Rarámuri*. Flagstaff, AZ: Northland Press.

Simpson, Lesley Byrd. 1982. *The Encomienda in New Spain: The Beginning of Spanish Mexico*. Berkeley: University of California Press.

Smith, Todd F. 1995. *The Caddo Indians*. College Station: Texas A&M University Press.

South America Pilot. 1916. Vol. 1. United States Hydrographic Office under the Authority of the Secretary of the Navy. Washington, DC: Government Printing Office.

Turpin, David C. 1987. "Encino, Roble; Live Oak, Oak: Categorical Terms for Oak Trees in the New World." *SECOL Review* 11 (1): 43–65.

Weber, David J. 2005. *Bárbaros: Spaniards and Their Savages in the Age of Enlightenment*. New Haven, CT: Yale University Press.

Weddle, Robert S. 1991. *The French Thorn: Rival Explorers in the Spanish Sea, 1682–1762*. College Station: Texas A&M University Press.

———. 1992. "Cross and Crown: The Spanish Mission in Texas." In *Hispanic Texas: A Historical Guide*, edited by Helen Simons and Cathryn A. Hoyt, 25–35. Austin: University of Texas Press.

———. 1999. *Wilderness Manhunt: The Spanish Search for La Salle*. College Station: Texas A&M University Press.

———. 2010a. "Ecay Múzquiz, José Antonio de." *Handbook of Texas Online*. Texas State Historical Association. Accessed August 17, 2015. http://www.tshaonline.org/handbook/online/articles/fec05.

———. 2010b. "Grollet, Jacques." *Handbook of Texas Online*. Texas State Historical Association. Accessed August 17, 2015. http://www.tshaonline.org/handbook/online/articles/fgr74.

————. 2010c. "Meunier, Pierre." *Handbook of Texas Online.* Texas State Historical Association. Accessed August 18, 2015. http://www.tshaonline.org/handbook/online/articles/fme73.

————. 2010d. "Salinas Varona, Gregorio de." *Handbook of Texas Online.* Texas State Historical Association. Accessed September 15, 2015. http://www.tshaonline.org/handbook/online/articles/fsa10.

————. 2010e. "Talon Children." *Handbook of Texas Online.* Texas State Historical Association. Accessed August 18, 2015. http://www.tshaonline.org/handbook/online/articles/fta60.

West, Elizabeth Howard. 1905. "De León's Expedition of 1689." *Quarterly of the Texas State Historical Association* 8:199–224.

Winfrey, Dorman H. 2010. "West, Elizabeth Howard." *Handbook of Texas Online.* Texas State Historical Association. Accessed March 20, 2015. http://www.tshaonline.org/handbook/online/articles/fwe32.

Ximenes, Ben Cuellar. 1963. *Gallant Outcasts.* San Antonio, TX: Taylor.

Yengle, Patricia N. 2013. "El juicio de residencia de don Antonio de Otermín, gobernador de Nuevo México." Berkeley: Cíbola Project, Research Center for Romance Studies, University of California.

Index

Gregorian Correction, in manuscript
89-B, 156–57
Grolet, Jacques, 22–23, 169–70
Gumendio, Pascual de, 136
Gutiérrez, José, 32–33
Gutiérrez, Joseph, 136, 147, 150, 153, 156

harina, translation error, xiii–xiv,
158n52
Hasinai Confederacy. *See* Tejas Indians
Henri, Jean, 19–20, 150–53, 208–209. *See
also* French explorers and survivors
Herrera, Matías de, 136
Hispanic History of Texas Project
(HHTP), 3
*Historia de Nuevo León con noticias so-
bre... y México* (Cavazos Garza), 5–6,
14, 18, 20n27
horse stampedes, 21, 161, 164, 174, 189

Ignacio (Indian interpreter), 150
Indians: earliest explorer contacts, 9–12;
manuscript 86-A, 16–17, 137, 138,
139–41, 142, 143; manuscript 87-A,
144, 145; manuscript 88-A, 18–19,
145–47, 148–50, 154–55; manuscript
89-B, 20–23, 157–58, 160, 162–65,
167–68, 169–71; manuscript 90-
B, 25–26, 172, 173, 176–78, 179,
180–81, 183–84; manuscript 90-D,
187, 188, 192–93, 194, 196, 197–98,
199, 200–201, 202, 203; missionary
conflicts, 28–29; translation errors
summarized, xii–xiv

Jarri, Yan. *See* Henri, Jean
Jesús, María y Joseph de Buena Vista,
183, 193, 199
Jesús María, Francisco de, 24

José (servant boy/page), 136
Joutel, Henri, 13
Juan (servant boys/pages), 136
Jumano Indians, 10–11, 12

Kanellos, Nicolás, 3
Karankawa Indians, 26–27
Kessell, John L., 2

La Aparición de San Miguel Arcángel,
193
La Belle wreck, 18n21, 167n80, 205. *See
also* shipwreck artifacts
La Madre de Jesús María de Ágreda, 197
l'Archevêque, Jean, 22–23, 168, 169–70
La Salle, 12–13, 15–16, 22n36, *29*
Leal, Antonio, 135, 136
Lerma, Gaspar de, 135
Lira, Nicolás de, 136
livestock. *See* companies, personnel and
provisions
López, Francisco López, 10
Losa, Nicolás de, 136
Los Baluartes, 154, 156

manuscript 86-A, 1686 expedition:
overview, 30–31; English translation,
134–44; folio 52r of, *49*; in previous
scholarship, 5, 7; Spanish transcription, 50–61; transcription methodology, 47–48; translation methodology,
133–34
manuscript 87-A, 1687 expedition:
overview, 30–31; English translation,
144–45; folio 53r of, *62*; in previous
scholarship, 5, 7; Spanish transcription, 63; transcription methodology,
47–48; translation methodology,
133–34

manuscript 88-A, 1688 expedition: overview, 31–34; English translation, 145–56; folio 52r of, *64*; in previous scholarship, 6; Spanish transcription, 65–75; transcription methodology, 47–48; translation methodology, 133–34

manuscript 88-B, 1688 expedition, 31–34, 147n33

manuscript 88-C, 1688 expedition, 31–34, 36, 146n31, 147n33

manuscript 89-A, 1689 expedition: overview, 34–35; astrolab reading copy errors, 21n32, 22n35; and manuscript 90-A, 35, 36; previous errors in translation, xii–xv; shipwreck description, 167n80

manuscript 89-B, 1689 expedition: overview, 34–35, 36; English translation, 156–71; Spanish transcription, 77–93; transcription methodology, 47–48; translation methodology, 133–34

manuscript 89-C, 1689 expedition, 34–35, 36

manuscript 89-D, 1689 expedition, xii–xv, 6, 34–35, 36–37 171n90. *See also* manuscript 89-B, 1689 expedition

manuscript 89-E, 1689 expedition, 34–35, 37–38

manuscript 90-A, 1690 expedition: overview, 39–42; and manuscript 89-A, 35, 36, 40; and manuscript 90-B, 175n106; in previous scholarship, 6, 7

manuscript 90-B, 1690 expedition: overview, 39–42; English translation, 171–85; in previous scholarship, 6, 7, 8; Spanish transcription, 95–113; transcription methodology, 47–48; translation methodology, 133–34

manuscript 90-C, 1690 expedition, 36, 39, 41–42, 175n106

manuscript 90-D, 1690 expedition: overview, 39, 42—45, 211; English translation, 185–203; folio 5v of, *114*; in previous scholarship, 6, 7, 8; Spanish transcription, 115–32; transcription methodology, 47–48; translation methodology, 133–34

manuscript 90-E, 1690 expedition, 8, 39, 43–45, *76*, 211

manuscript 90-F, 1690 expedition, 39, 43, 44–45, *94*, 211

manuscript 90-O, 1690 expedition, 39

Martin, Diego, 135

Martínez, Francisco, 163, 195, 198

Massanet, Damián: conflicts with de León, 23–24, 27, 28; letter to Sigüenza y Góngora, xiv–xv, xviii, 6; manuscript 89-B, 20, 164; manuscript 90-B, 25–26, 181–82; manuscript 90-D, 198, 203

Matagorda Bay, 12–13, 18

Mateo (Indian), 136, 207

McLain, Jana, 8, 39, 40n58, 41n59, 42, 44, 185n124, 189n152

Medina, Nicolás de, 18, 136, 144, 153

Medina, Pedro de, 159

Mendiondo, Martín de, 18, 144, 148, 153

Mendoza expedition, 3

Mendoza-López expedition, 12

Meunier, Pierre, 13n10, 25, 27, 42, 44, 178, 185, 203

Miguel (servant boy/page), 136

military garrisons, 10, 23–24, 28–29

mining frontier, 10

missionaries: manuscript 86-A, 136; manuscript 89-B, 23, 164; manuscript 90-B, 25–26, 180–82; manu

Other Titles in the Elma Dill Russell Spencer Series in the West and Southwest

www.ingramcontent.com/pod-product-compliance
Lightning Source LLC
Chambersburg PA
CBHW070643150426
42811CB00050B/519